Religion in Crisis and Custom

Religion in Crisis and Custom

A SOCIOLOGICAL AND PSYCHOLOGICAL STUDY

by *Anton T. Boisen*

Harper & Brothers
Publishers . New York

TO THE MEMORY OF

ARTHUR ERASTUS HOLT

IN TOKEN OF

A GREAT INDEBTEDNESS

Library of Congress catalog card number: 55-8519

Contents

Preface

IN attempting to convey his affirmative appreciation of the work of Anton T. Boisen, the late Harry Stack Sullivan drew upon words used by Boisen to describe the founder of the Society of Friends, George Fox: ". . . We are struck by the power, the courage, the depth and tenderness of feeling, the clear insight and intelligence. . . ." About the qualities revealed by Anton T. Boisen in the present book, I can do no better than support Sullivan's judgment.

There is no brief way of describing what this book is about without making it sound impossible to write. Perhaps the best description is that given by Rockwell C. Smith, who has called it "the social psychology of religious experience." It deals with psychology and psychiatry, with sociology, and with theology. Its breadth is great, yet its focus is clear. Sullivan wrote of Boisen's "remarkable capacity for digesting and synthesizing data."

Boisen's primary concern is with crisis experiences. He holds that crises, whether personal or social, compel reorganization of person and group. They push us back to fundamentals, to what he calls the "universal and abiding," especially in social relatedness. There may of course be failure; the attempted reorganization may not succeed. Either person or group may quail before the crisis. He or it may go to pieces or slide back into pattern or custom more rigid than before. But crisis experiences may also be creative, leading to constructive reorganization and new purpose in life. In their interim stages they may be misunderstood. But a true understanding of such experiences is essential to a grasp of what religion means to the person and to the social group.

In his previous book, *The Exploration of the Inner World*, the author developed the thesis that there is an interrelationship between some forms of religious experience and some forms of mental disorder. He saw some mental disorders as reactions to crisis situations. These forms, to be sharply distinguished from the chronically malignant forms in which defeat and failure have been accepted, are closely akin to the dramatic and eruptive types of religious experience. In them religious concern is much in evidence and the creative forces are exceptionally active. So also are the forces that may lead to destruction. Boisen attempted to determine the conditions under which the creative or the destructive forces become victorious.

The present book covers a wider territory. It seeks to show that the same principle (of crisis) applies also to religious groups and movements and not alone to individual persons. Under the stress of such crises as economic dislocation or war, men are compelled to think and feel together in a new way regarding the ultimate realities of life. New values are brought to birth, and new depths of experience are sensed and felt. There may be new insights that come as revelations, that carry authority, and that must be shared with others. The content of the insights is often not new, but always the animating spirit gives new vitality even to old ideas. It is thus that religious faith is re-created.

Sometimes the churches of custom, Boisen believes, are able to absorb the new insights emerging from crisis experience, but at other times a new group is formed. In either case the new spirit has to be channeled into institutional forms, and in this process the spirit may be lost, at least in part. We have then a church of custom which in time is likely to be reabsorbed into the main body from which it sprang. Within organized religion we thus see a recurrent process—a movement from creative emergence to new custom, and somewhere along the line another eruption against the crystallized custom.

It is Boisen's contention that this process is especially evident in

America, where the absence of an established church makes it possible for the creative religious forces to run their course with a maximum of freedom. It was especially apparent in the rise of the Holy Roller sects during the depression of the 1930's. In both of its phases, it is seen in the strength of the movement for co-operation among American churches, along with the existence of scores of small religious denominations to an extent unknown elsewhere in the world.

Boisen has also a methodological thesis. He believes that rigorous but imaginative methods of science should be applied to religious phenomena, that no holds should be barred in our study of religion in persons and in groups. He believes that theology should be more concerned with study of this kind. Far from threatening the bases of our faith, he is convinced that truth of this order can be far more revealing than we have yet recognized. He has spent many years working with disturbed patients in mental hospitals where he has served, and not a little time in attending meetings of Holy Roller and other eruptive religious groups in many parts of the United States. In this volume he has attempted with remarkable success to bring the results of these studies together into an integrated theory.

Boisen brings to his task a varied equipment. Before entering the ministry he was a teacher of modern languages and a forester. Following his graduation from Union Theological Seminary, where he specialized in the psychology of religion under George A. Coe, he engaged in rural church work. During World War I he was an overseas Y.M.C.A. secretary. On his return he served as state supervisor of the North Dakota Rural Survey for the Interchurch World Movement. Then came the climactic experience of his own life—an acute mental disturbance that proved to have for him positive religious value. From it he emerged, in Sullivan's words, "with certain socially valuable insights and a new purpose in life."

This new purpose had both practical and theoretical dimensions. Boisen became a founder of the movement for clinical pastoral training. Modern pastoral counseling owes much to him. He was among the first to believe that the study of psychiatry and psychology could shed light on theology itself. His theoretical interests are brought together, in readable summary form, in the present book.

As a study in the psychological understanding of religion, this book continues and extends the author's contribution, so basic that Edmund S. Conklin called it "probably the most important contribution since the famous Varieties of William James." The psychological side of his thesis is here put more simply and succinctly than ever before.

The genuinely new ground of this book is in the sociology of religious movements and in the relation of the psychology of religion to the sociology of religion. This is why Rockwell C. Smith's phrase, "the social psychology of religious experience," is so apt. The sociologist, psychologist, and psychiatrist will find much that is provocative in its pages. The pastor, chaplain, and theologian have long since learned that beneath every Boisen theory there is a hard core of relevance to the most practical aspects of their ministry.

This book is wrought out of the "living human documents" to the study and help of whom Boisen has dedicated his life for forty years. The field that drew his interest four decades ago has now expanded in some respects beyond what he then dreamed of. Yet any thoughtful workers in any aspect of this vast area—especially those like myself who have had the privilege of being his students—continue to recognize that the years but show how we are beginning to catch up to the depth of Boisen's original insights. In this field, and in this book, he is still the master.

Seward Hiltner

Foreword

THIS book is a sociological and psychological study of religion with special reference to American Protestantism.

Its starting point is the observation that religious experience arises spontaneously when men are forced to think and feel intensely regarding the things that matter most. It assumes that religious experience is rooted in the social nature of man. It is the sense of fellowship raised to the level of the abiding and universal. It is the attempt at orientation with reference to that which is supreme in the system of loyalties. It is the response to that in the universe upon which men feel dependent for love and for protection. Most religions associate this abiding fellowship with some idea of God, and the idea of God represents something which is operative in the lives of all men whether they recognize it or not.

The sense of being in direct contact with God, a frequent experience in time of crisis, is momentous. It may have a creative function, producing values and insights which demand translation into habit and custom.

How are the powerful emotions and the new insights derived from mystical experiences communicated to others? How are they transmitted from one generation to another? How are they expressed in the interpersonal relationships of everyday life after the period of stress and crisis has passed? These are among the problems with which this book is concerned. It deals also with the interaction between the conservative and creative forces in organized religion, with the processes by which religious faith is organized and validated, and with the means by which it is perpetuated and re-created. The concluding sec-

xiii

tion is concerned with the future of the Christian religion in the present world crisis.

The field which this book attempts to cover is a vast one, and the complexity of the problems it presents is so great that scientific workers have been inclined to shy away from it. But the task of science is the co-operative testing and organizing of experience through the discovery of constant relationships among changes. The mere fact that a certain area of experience is difficult and baffling provides no release from the duty of attacking it. Hence this attempt to apply the methods of empirical observation and generalization to the realm of motives and values and the even rasher attempt to consider the significance of our findings in the domain of theology.

In taking on this task I have had the benefit of a fairly wide acquaintance with the social and religious conditions in widely separated sections of rural America in the capacity of field investigator and then of pastor. I have served for twenty-six years as chaplain and research worker in two important mental hospitals in the endeavor to discover the religious significance of the experiences encountered there. I have also given considerable attention to the religious adjustments in the ordinary parish and to the Holiness sects which grew so rapidly during the economic depression of the 1930's. Last, but not least, is the personal experience which sent me into the wilderness of the lost. Mental disorder it was, of the most profound and unmistakable variety, and yet at the same time problem-solving religious experience. To the insights derived from that experience this book owes whatever of distinction it may possess.

In centering attention upon American Protestantism I have been guided by the consideration that I have had unusual opportunities to observe Protestant churches in action and only meager opportunity to observe other forms of organized religion. I have not hesitated, however, to make use of the observations of other workers in order that my own findings may be viewed in a larger setting.

To those whose influence has made possible this inquiry I am happy to acknowledge my indebtedness. Among these I think particularly of William Lowe Bryan, who first started me on the adventure with which this book deals; of George Albert Coe, who was my guide in the study of the psychology of religion; of Warren Wilson, who sent me forth armed with a questionnaire to investigate the religious conditions in rural America, and Fred Eastman, my colleague in that early adventure and throughout the years that have followed; of Richard C. Cabot, Macfie Campbell, William A. Bryan, and Charles F. Read, who gave me the opportunity to explore the little-known country of the nether regions; of Arthur Cushman McGiffert, with whose help I have inquired into the theological significance of my findings; and of Arthur E. Holt, who was to have collaborated in the writing of this volume and whose influence is reflected in its every page.

For the bringing forth of this book I am also indebted to Professor E. A. Ross of the University of Wisconsin, who first suggested it, and with whose help the original outline was worked out. Professor Ernest W. Burgess of the University of Chicago and President McGiffert of the Chicago Theological Seminary have read the manuscript and have given valuable suggestions.

Chapters II, IV, V, and XI have been previously published in *Psychiatry*, either in whole or in part; Chapter II and part of Chapter IV in the *Journal of Religion*; Chapter V in *Social Action*; and Chapter VI in *Religion in Life*. They are here reproduced with the permission of these journals. The title of the book and some of its important sections were used for the first time at the Pacific School of Religion under the auspices of the Earle Lectureship. Grateful acknowledgment is made of the grants-in-aid from the Congregational Council for Social Action and from the Social Science Research Council, which made possible six profitable months spent in the field in the study of the Pentecostal sects; also of the support given by the Chicago Theological Seminary over a period of seventeen years to a project about which at first it had many doubts.

These acknowledgments would not be complete without recognition of the help received from Mrs. Marjorie Peters Bower in the rewriting of a refractory chapter and of the indebtedness to Seward Hiltner and Simon Doniger for their part in making the publication of this book a possibility.

ANTON T. BOISEN

I. Crisis and Custom:
Recurrent Process

T HE task which this book undertakes is to inquire into the nature and significance of crisis experiences, both personal and social, and their relation to the religious beliefs and practices of everyday living. It is particularly concerned with the ebb and flow of religious feeling which has characterized the experience of the great saints as well as of their humbler brethren.

Few serious-minded persons go through life without at some time feeling the stirring of higher possibilities and without grappling desperately with questions concerning their ultimate destiny and their relationship to that which is for them supreme. Such experiences are commonly associated with the making of important transitions and with the solution of problems of major importance. But these periods of vision and quickening are transitory. They are succeeded by long periods of engrossment with the duties and pleasures of routine existence, when habit and custom and sense of duty take the place of spontaneity and enthusiasm.

It is recorded in Martin Luther's *Table Talk* that Frau Kaethe once said to her husband, "Herr Doctor, how comes it that in popedom we prayed so earnestly, so diligently and so often, while now our prayer is quite cold? Indeed, we pray very seldom." [1]

This question must have been somewhat embarrassing to Dr.

[1] Walch, *Luther's Saemmtliche Schriften*, 24 vols. (Halle, 1740–53), XXII, 810.

1

Luther. It appears from the *Table Talk* that he was wont to discourse eloquently on the subject of prayer and what it accomplishes in the life of the Christian. Yet his wife's question seems to have had ample basis, as may be inferred from another passage, where he is reported as saying, "I have to compel myself every day to pray and let it suffice, when I go to bed, if I repeat the Commandments, the Lord's Prayer, and after that a saying, or two sayings from the Bible, think upon these, and so go to sleep." [2]

This coldness was in sharp contrast with the intensity of Luther's religious concern at the time of his struggle in the monastery and at the time of the trial at Worms.

Another striking example of the succession of enthusiasm and coldness is to be found in the case of John Bunyan when he was a young man. He describes it thus in his own inimitable style:

> By these things my mind was so turned that it lay like a horse leech at the vein. Yea, it was so fixed on eternity and on the things about the kingdom of God, that neither pleasures nor profits nor persuasions nor threats could loose it or make it let go its hold; and though I speak it with shame, yet it is indeed a certain truth; it would have been as difficult for me to have taken my mind from heaven to earth, as I have found it often since to get again from earth to heaven.[3]

In Bunyan's case the crisis experience reached an intensity which was definitely pathological. In that experience he thought he had committed the unpardonable sin and suffered great distress of mind. Professor Royce, in his study of John Bunyan, speaks of him as "a man of genius who bore with heroic perseverance a heavy and morbid load of nervous ill and in the end won the mastery over it." [4] John Bunyan himself took a different view. He wrote an account of his experience under the title *Grace Abounding to the Chief of Sinners*, and in the subtitle he explains that it was written "for the support

[2] *Ibid.*, XXII, 832.

[3] John Bunyan, *Grace Abounding to the Chief of Sinners*, paragraph 42.

[4] Josiah Royce, "The Case of John Bunyan," in *Studies in Good and Evil* (New York: Appleton, 1898), p. 30.

of the weak and tempted people of God." It seems clear that he regarded it as a religious experience of real value.

This book supports the view that John Bunyan was right in his own interpretation. Even though his condition was severely pathological, it did have for him creative value. It was a crisis in his struggle for self-realization, a crisis originating not in outward circumstances but in inner stresses. Through it he was sensitized to a realm of life to which otherwise he would have been deaf and blind. Through it he was transformed from a commonplace village tinker into the immortal author of *Pilgrim's Progress*. He became a man of genius not *in spite of* his "heavy and morbid load of nervous ill" but precisely *because of* it.

Herein we find a simple but far-reaching principle which I propose to apply to the study of religion in its various manifestations. My thesis is that religious experience is rooted in the social nature of man and arises spontaneously under the pressure of crisis situations. Whereas in normal states of mind we tend to think sluggishly in an accepted currency of ideas, there is likely to be in time of crisis a speeding up of the intellectual and emotional processes. As one stands face to face with the ultimate realities of life and death, religion and theology tend to come alive. Meaning tends to outstrip symbol and we have to seek for new words to express the new ideas which come surging in. Among these ideas we frequently find the sense of contact with that ultimate reality to which we give the name of "God."

Crisis experiences are thus associated with new insights. Such insights may come as sudden bursts of illumination following a period of narrowed attention and problem-solving activity. As such they are akin to insight and discovery in other fields, but they have as their distinctive features a sense of identification with a Greater-than-self and a new vision of the individual's role in life. This means a new awareness of the individual's continuity with society at its best. It means also redirection and reinforcement of his course of activity.

Crisis experiences carry with them a tremendous emotional impact. Sometimes the effect may be shattering, particularly where there is a great accumulation of unsolved problems and wide gaps between the ideal and the actual. But even though the emotional turmoil may reach the point of psychosis, it may nonetheless be regarded as creative. It may be an attempt at reorganization and a manifestation of nature's power to heal analogous to fever or inflammation in the body. And even a psychosis may eventuate in a socially valuable remaking of the personality.

Crisis experiences result in religious quickening; they are creative; but they may break as well as make. This is true of the individual, and it is true also of the group. I propose therefore to inquire to what extent and under what conditions crisis experiences are associated with religious quickening and under what circumstances with disaster. What forms does the religious quickening assume? What is its personal and social significance? What is its relationship to the organized habits and customs of the workaday world? What is the significance of the idea of God and of the sense of mystical identification which, at least in our culture, appear so frequently under the stress of crisis situations?

We begin with the religious behavior of ordinary people in a particular setting. We study the religious institutions of a Midwestern county, chosen not at random but because of its representative character out of twenty-four counties which I have surveyed in different parts of the country. Here we find evidence that the church is still a going concern and that it is still by far the most important of our voluntary institutions. Here also we see organized religion functioning in its beginning, in its mature and in its terminal stages, and we see that the new sects, so much in evidence in this county, are associated with economic distress.

We then turn to a consideration of personal religion in a community where an old-line church serves as custodian of the ancient faith and of the standards on which the personal and social organization is built. We find here an enormous amount of mental illness, explainable in large part by the inner conflicts which these same standards produce. We are thus faced with the problem of mental illness in its relation to religion.

For light upon this problem of mental illness and religious experience we turn next to a consideration of crises in personality development as seen in a mental hospital. Here we discover that a sharp distinction must be made between disturbances in which the battle is still on and those in which some adaptation to defeat and failure has been made and accepted. Among those who have thrown in the sponge and those who are seeking to maintain their self-respect by means of delusional misinterpretation there is little religious concern and little hope of recovery. But the patient who is trying honestly to face his real difficulties has a marked religious concern and a relatively good chance of recovery. Our conclusion is that cases of the latter type belong in the group of crisis experiences and that the emotional disturbance which characterizes them is not an evil but is incidental to a healing process. A further conclusion is that mental illness in general is the price we have to pay for being human and having the power of choice and the capacity for growth.

A study of the Pentecostal sects carries us to a consideration of social crisis. The rapid growth of these sects during the 1930's was associated with the economic difficulties of that period. Such an association is no isolated phenomenon. Other periods of economic tribulation have been marked by the development of mystical religion. At such times men are forced to think and feel together intensely about the things which matter most. With all their vagaries these Pentecostal sects are nevertheless manifestations of religion in its creative phase.

Religious concern is thus seen to be associated not only with personal but also with social crisis. War, however, which is a social crisis of the first magnitude, seems to be an exception to this principle. What important religious movements have grown out of a war situation? Our study of personal crisis in the mental hospital suggests an explanation. The prevailing reaction patterns in time of war are of the malignant rather than of the benign type, owing to the dominance of hatred and the replacement of civilian Christian standards by the military. One great exception supports this explanation: In the Hebrew prophetic religion the reaction to national disaster was self-blame rather than hating and blaming the enemy, and out of this benign reaction came a religious movement of the greatest importance.

The study of the origins of religion is concluded with the consideration of religious leadership in our representative Midwestern county. We find there an exemplification of the process by which an individual may become the nucleus of a new social formation.

Our general conclusion is that the emotion and vision of the creative crisis periods are not ends in themselves. They must be translated into personal and social organization if their purpose is to be accomplished. The rest of the book is therefore taken up with a consideration of the interplay of the conservative and creative forces in organized religion and of the social significance of American Protestantism, all in the light of the central thesis.

We examine the history of the Methodist Church as an outstanding example of the evolution of a mystical sect into a great church. We take a brief look at the conservative Asian religions through the eyes of a great sociologist in order to provide a background for a consideration of the more dynamic Hebrew-Christian religion. We then study in some detail the types of churches which have grown up in Protestant America, where the principle of religious freedom has given maximum scope to the creative forces. Following this study of the divergent tendencies within American Protestantism, we turn to the social significance of religious faith in general and to the means within the social process by which superior beliefs are sifted out from the inferior.

We then evaluate the common core of Christian faith, considering not so much the writings of theologians as the beliefs prevalent among the common people. Next, we examine the means employed by American churches for the perpetuation and re-creation of their faith. Here again we are concerned not with what ought to be but with what is and why. We do give some attention, however, to the means by which the creative forces in organized religion can be kept alive and vigorous.

The final chapter seeks to apply the principles derived from this study to a consideration of the tremendous social crisis through which the world is now passing. Our conclusion is that like an acute psychosis in an individual such a crisis is an attempt at reorganization which may either make or break, depending upon the honesty and fair-mindedness with which we face and eradicate the long-standing evils which have been responsible for the recent holocaust.

Throughout this study we shall assume with George H. Mead that the personality is dependent upon language to provide the solid structure by which judgments are guided and action in large measure determined.[5] We shall assume furthermore that beyond what can be put into words lies a domain of enormous importance: the field of intuition, of artistic feeling, of what the Freudians call the "unconscious." We shall follow John Dewey, however, in recognizing that this realm of dim awareness is not detached from consciousness but is in constant and active participation in all thought and action and feeling.[6]

[5] Mind, Self and Society (Chicago: University of Chicago Press, 1935), particularly Sections III and IV.

[6] Experience and Nature (Chicago: Open Court Publishing Co., 1925), pp. 298–311.

II. Holy Rollers
and Churches of Custom

THE central theme of this book, "religion in crisis and custom," may be exemplified in any part of the United States of America. We have no lack of churches, and wherever there are churches and people, there in varying degrees we can see the emergence of the creative forces of religion under the stress of personal and social crisis and their gradual transmutation into custom and tradition.

Such a development is to be seen in the rise of the Holy Roller churches of my own native town and of the county in which it is located. Most of these churches sprang up among the underprivileged classes during the 1930's, and their emotional fervor may be explained as a reaction to the social crisis induced by the economic distress of that period. The problem which they present to the "old-line" churches of custom and tradition may be taken as the starting point of this study.

1. "COME-OUTERS" AND REVIVALISTS IN MIDDLE COUNTY—1850

Blankton, as we shall call it, is a city of twenty-eight thousand inhabitants. It contains a college, and it is located in what is known as the Bible belt, in a county which we shall call Middle County.

Blankton was settled by people of English and Scotch-Irish ancestry. They came swarming over the mountains in the early part of the last century. Most of them had been driven out of their former

8

homes in Virginia and the Carolinas by a disastrous competition with slave labor which had left them impoverished.

Within the general stream of migration was a group of churches which are of interest to us as churches of tradition and custom in their more radical manifestations. They were represented in Blankton by four Psalm-singing Presbyterian churches, the Covenanters, as some of them were called. All of them were organized and led by men who came from the same neighborhood in South Carolina. They had left the South because their religious convictions did not permit them to own slaves. My great-grandfather, a Covenanter minister who visited that neighborhood in 1802 to confer with them regarding the sin of slaveholding, gives the following account of their attitude:

Previous to the dispensation of the sacrament of the Lord's Supper we stated the decision of the Presbytery respecting slave-holders, declaring that such must either emancipate their slaves or be refused admission to the Lord's Table. We were no less surprised than delighted to find with what alacrity those concerned came forward and complied with the decree of Presbytery. In one day, it is believed, in that small community of the Reformed Presbyterian Church not less than three thousand guineas were sacrificed on the altar of principle. The people promptly cleansed their hands from the pollution of the accursed thing. A nobler, more generous and magnanimous people than those South Carolinians are seldom met with.[1]

These Psalm singers were characterized by a strong loyalty to family and clan and by a firm belief in the literal inspiration and authority of the Scriptures, with a stress upon the Old Testament which was reflected in their given names.

The Old Testament influence among these people is shown in the church roll of Blankton's United Presbyterian Church as compiled for its hundredth anniversary. Out of a total of 1959 persons, 235 had given names drawn from the Old Testament. The name Sarah occurred 47 times; Samuel, 43 times; Joseph, 30; David, 28; Hannah,

[1] Samuel Brown Wylie, *Life of Alexander McLeod* (New York: Charles Scribner's Sons, 1855), p. 53.

12; Rachel, 10; Ruth, 6; Rebecca, 5. Other names were Moses, Daniel, Jacob, Abraham, Enoch, Aaron, Reuben, Jesse, Ebenezer, Ezra, Karenhapuk. The number of persons with New Testament names was 578.

Another characteristic was their religious austerity and their great respect for education. They demanded ministers with good professional training and they came to Blankton largely because of the presence of the college. Their services were long, and the character of their sermons may be inferred from the following entry in the diary of my grandfather, a member of the college faculty and a minister in the "New Side" Reformed Presbyterian Church:

Sabbath, August 12, 1838. This morning about ten o'clock I started in company with Dr. Hamill to go to the Seceder Church, where the sacrament was to be held; got there about eleven o'clock. The psalm had already been explained. Mr. Hall preached from the text, "And they crucified Jesus." The sermon was good, nothing extraordinary, however. After an intermission of a few minutes the exercises were continued by a Mr. G. He began by exhorting to the duty of self-examination. He debarred [excluded from the communion table] all who would sing any human composition in worship or who would learn to sing by using verses of hymns. His general observations and remarks on the particular sins to which they were to direct their attention occupied about two hours and a half. It was the most tedious piece of work I have ever listened to. After an abrupt termination the tables were filled, the blessing asked, the words of the institution read, but not explained, and the words to the communicants spun out about an hour and a half long, neither good nor bad. After that I left. I got home about six o'clock.

It need hardly be said that these people made little attempt to win converts from among their unchurched neighbors and that their membership was recruited almost entirely through birth and immigration.

The first church to be established in Middle County, however, was the Presbyterian Church, one of those that sang other hymns than the Psalms of David. These Presbyterians came from Virginia by way of Kentucky. Their leaders had been largely instrumental in the launching of the college and their membership was made up largely of college people and their kin. In the middle of the century this church was split into "New School" and "Old School" branches. Thus at a time when the town's population numbered scarcely twelve hundred, Blankton possessed six different Presbyterian churches: the New School Presbyterian, the Old School Presbyterian, the Associate Reformed Presbyterian, the Associate Presbyterian (or "Seceders"), and the Old Side and New Side Reformed Presbyterians, both laying claim to the name "Covenanter." In the county at large there were two Cumberland Presbyterian churches. (The issues involved in these differences will be considered in Chapter X.)

Three other church groups were much in evidence throughout the county: the Methodists, the Disciples of Christ, and the Baptists, the latter including three deviant groups in addition to the major body. These were the churches of the rank and file of the people. They had arisen in time of economic stress and had adapted themselves to pioneer conditions and to the needs of pioneer people. Instead of holding rigidly to the requirement of an educated ministry they ordained laymen, whose deficiency in professional training was counterbalanced by zeal in good works. They adopted the circuit-rider system and thus were able to give service to sparsely settled country districts. They brought people together in large numbers at camp meetings and revivals, and there, under the contagion of the singing and the impact of the testimonies and the zealous efforts of the workers, many converts were made. The Methodists and the Baptists preached salvation from sin and taught that, in order to be saved, one must have a clear-cut conversion experience of the mystical variety. They expanded through the missionary efforts of their converts, who were recruited in large measure from people of Presbyterian background.

Thus in this early period in Middle County there were three groups of churches, a more or less liberal group consisting chiefly of college people and their associates, a very conservative group characterized by loyalty to family and clan, and churches representing the revivalist movement which was at that time sweeping the Ohio Valley.

2. GROWING LIBERALISM IN THE 1890's

At the end of the last century, when I was growing up in Blankton and when the town had a population of five thousand and the college an enrollment of five hundred, the six Presbyterian churches had been reduced to three. The New School and the Old School had repaired their differences. The Associate and the Associate Reformed had concluded that the only difference between them was that one sang the *Psalms of David* and the other *David's Psalms*; they therefore combined to form a "United Presbyterian" congregation. Meanwhile, the New Siders had cast in their lot with their more liberal brethren; but the Old Siders stood stanchly by their "Reformation Principles," still clinging to the Psalms of David and still refusing to vote or to sit in juries until the Constitution of the United States should be amended to include a declaration of religious faith. We thus had left a Presbyterian church that was "united," one that was "reformed," and one that was neither "united" nor "reformed."

During this period the number of churches had been augmented by the addition of a small Roman Catholic church and a small Episcopal church. The Church of Christ had by this time "come out" from the Disciples of Christ because it could find no scriptural warrant for the use of organs in the service of worship.

The Negroes and their churches arrived in Blankton some time in the late fifties. Their coming was due somewhat to the Covenanters. Having left the South because of their opposition to slaveholding, they were sympathetic toward the Negroes. In this their attitude differed from that of most of their neighbors, whose reaction to their former unhappy experience with slavery was one of hatred for the Negroes and indifference toward the institution of slavery. The Covenanters therefore collaborated with the underground railroad in prewar days and following the war they encouraged Negroes to settle among them. They even received Negroes into their membership.

The churches of tradition and custom were thus strongly entrenched in Blankton toward the end of the last century; yet on the whole our people were fairly liberal and forward-looking. Aside from the older members, there were few, even of the Scotch-Irish, who laid much stress upon the distinctive doctrines. Those of the younger generation merely identified themselves with the church of their parents and grandparents and wanted it to prosper without being themselves required to make great sacrifice of time or money. They accepted the faith of their fathers as their faith without scrutinizing it closely. Of course they saw some differences. The Presbyterian Church from the early years had been identified with the college clientele and its services of worship were adjusted to the standards of the "cultured." In the Methodist Church, on the other hand, some of the older people still shouted their "Amens" whenever the spirit moved them without regard for the susceptibilities of the sophisticated. The Methodists, together with the Baptists and the Disciples, still held that one must be "converted" in order to become a Christian, and they had certain techniques for inducing that experience. Those of us who belonged to the more sedate communions went sometimes to the Methodist Church to see the fun. But all believed more or less in revivals, and when Wilbur Chapman came to town, all participated in his evangelistic services.

The general situation thus remained much the same as in the early days. The Methodists, the Disciples, and the Baptists were still revivalistic and still dominant among the rank and file of the people. The Presbyterians held their own in the college group, and the rearguard churches of tradition and custom were vigorous, even though the "U.P.'s" (United Presbyterians) were yielding somewhat to the onslaughts of liberalism and their broad-minded and scholarly minister often referred sadly to the "tragedy of loyalty" represented in their divisions.

3. The Present-Day Church Situation in Middle County

Going back to Blankton after half a century, I find striking changes. The town now has twenty-eight thousand inhabitants and the university twelve thousand students. The churches also have grown. An outstanding feature is a noteworthy change of type and the development of an ecumenical spirit among the leading churches. The Methodists today have taken their place alongside the Presbyterians in their ministry to college people. They worship in a large and costly building. The older people with their "Amens" have long since passed away. There is now a stately service, and efforts to induce the conversion experience have been discontinued. What is true of the First Methodist Church is true also of the Disciples of Christ, of the First Baptist Church, and of the fine new Methodist Church on the other side of the tracks. In all these one-time revivalistic churches conversion experiences of the old type are seldom encountered. There is little difference in the form of service or the message of the minister as one goes from one to the other. And the "sin of occasional hearing" is only an interesting memory.

But I find today a number of churches of which I had never heard in the 1890's. Among the thirty-three churches within Blankton's city limits are three Pentecostal Assemblies of Jesus Christ, two Churches of the Nazarene, an Assembly of God, a Church of God, a Church of Jesus Christ, a Free Methodist, and several others whose exact affiliations are hard to determine. The aggregate membership in these new sects is well over seventeen hundred. All of them have come to town within fifty years. Some of them did not exist anywhere before that time.

In these new churches I find somewhat the same type of service and somewhat the same message I used to hear in the Methodist Church years ago. These people are interested in saving souls and they believe that men need to be converted in order to be saved. They emphasize the reality of sin and guilt and they proclaim deliverance through the "wonder-working power of the Blood of the Lamb." Like the Methodists and the Baptists of years gone by, they have sprung from the spontaneous religious fervor of the common people who have been drawn in from the surrounding countryside to man the mills and quarries, and who during the depression were having tough going.

These Holy Rollers fill their churches not only on Sunday mornings but also on Sunday evenings and even during the week. They go, most of them, not from a sense of duty, but because of an interest which makes each believer a zealous missionary, eager to share with others the blessing he has found. The older churches look on wonderingly. Troubled by the crudities of these new forms of religion, they speculate on the secret of their appeal. What needs do they meet? What values do they represent? And how about their own task and that of Protestant Christianity in general? Out of what experiences do churches arise? What functions do they serve? What has produced the multiplication of churches in Blankton and in America at large?

With these and related questions this book attempts to deal. Let us begin by looking more closely at the present church situation in Middle County, taking this county as representative of those regions in the United States in which Protestantism holds sway.

Middle County, with an area of 420 square smiles and a population of 40,000, has now about 90 churches. Of these 33 are located in Blankton. The rest are in the county at large. The city churches are, some of them, large and prosperous. Three have a resident membership of more than 900 and five have an annual budget of more than $25,000. With only a few exceptions Blankton's churches employ a minister full time and have preaching every Sunday. Their aggregate annual budget is about $300,000. The country and village churches, as a rule, have the services of a minister only once or twice a month, but Sunday schools, conducted by laymen, are held every Sunday. Their total budget is about $50,000.

Of the county's 40,000 inhabitants, about 14,000 may be counted as church members. Since there are no Jewish synagogues in the county and the Catholic membership is small, this means that more than a third of the population, or more than half of those thirteen years of age and over, have made the voluntary confession of faith which the evangelical Protestant churches require as a condition of membership. On a given Sunday a visit to one of these churches will find about a third of its membership at the service of worship, which is the focal point of its many activities, or taking part in the church school as teachers or pupils.

Among Blankton's churches there is a certain degree of social stratification. Six of them are much influenced by the university. Their membership is composed in large part of persons connected with the university and of those who make some pretensions to "culture." In these churches the people are well dressed. The minister and the choir wear vestments and the services are dignified. Their chief feature is a sermon, some thirty minutes in length, dealing with some problem relating to the conduct of life and appealing to the intelligence and loyalty of the congregation. There is also a devotional service with, as a rule, three congregational hymns, one or two unison prayers, a responsive reading—usually an English rendering of some ancient Hebrew Psalm—a reading from the Bible, a prayer by the minister, and one or two special numbers by the choir.

Thirteen of Blankton's churches belong to the new group. Their congregations are made up largely of mill workers and their families, people who have not felt at home in the established churches. They have found little satisfaction in the formal type of service which there prevails and, rightly or wrongly, they have felt that they were not wanted. They have therefore organized churches of their own.

The new churches are for the most part small and unpretentious. Many of them are only one-room frame buildings, but their members are very much in earnest. Most of them tithe faithfully and refrain from "worldly amusements," such as card playing, dancing, and theatregoing. They meet more frequently and for longer periods than the older churches and their services are characterized by spontaneity and enthusiasm. In some of them the services are essentially musical and dramatic performances. All the new churches believe that one has to be "converted" in order to be "saved" and that this conversion must be followed by a "second blessing," or "sanctification." Five of them go further and teach that the believer must in addition be "baptized by the Holy Spirit" and give evidence thereof by "speaking with tongues," as the early Christians did on the Day of Pentecost.

There are also a number of churches which do not belong in either of these two groups. They are not churches of the disinherited. Neither do they make any special appeal to the university group. Some of them merely happen to be on the other side of the tracks and their membership is recruited from a respectable middle-class constituency of small tradesmen, artisans, and mill workers living in that section. Others are small conservative bodies of the "die-hard" type. There are also three Negro churches which serve a colony of about five hundred.

In the county at large the chief differences are between the older churches and the emotional sects. The latter have been engaged in a vigorous evangelistic campaign. Some of the older churches are located in the villages. Others are in the open country. The latter are composed almost entirely of farmers.

The churches of Middle County are served by about fifty ministers among whom there are wide differences in ability and training and point of view. Ten of them have had both college and seminary training. Four have had seminary but not college training. Seven have had college training but not the professional preparation which the seminary affords. The ministers who serve the college group in Blankton are able men with fine training and a liberal point of view. Some of the country and village churches are supplied by students and teachers in the university. For the most part the country ministers are poorly paid and not well trained. A number of them are lay preachers. Among the Holiness perachers are men of real ability and earnestness, but they are deficient in professional training.

All in all it may be said that the churches of this county are very much alive. Evidence of this may be found in the number of persons who belong to them, in the sacrifices they make to support them, and in the many activities in which they engage.

Next to the school the church is the most widely distributed of the county's institutions and it means most in the lives of its people. Church and school have a common task, that of transmitting the cultural heritage. They differ in that the school is concerned with funded knowledge of a factual nature, while the churches are entrusted with the transmission of the organized beliefs and attitudes regarding the end and meaning of life and the ways of living and working together. The schools in this county are without exception under the control of the community and of the state. The churches are voluntary organizations, dependent entirely upon the free co-operation and support of individuals. In contrast with most other voluntary organizations, the church is not restricted in its membership, nor are its meetings closed or secret. Anyone may attend, even though he may come to criticize. The church, moreover, is built upon the family as a unit, where other organizations are restricted according to age or sex or special interest.

Scrutiny of those who belong to the churches of Middle County indicates that they include a large proportion of the county's well-meaning and public-spirited citizens. They are far from being saints, but they take seriously the loyalty to the best they know. In the church they consider together the problems relating to their ultimate destiny, both individual and collective. In the church they bring themselves into an emotional relationship to the God whom they regard as the source of their life and the controller of their destiny and the one to whom they owe unreserved allegiance. In the church they seek not merely the improvement of their personal and family and community life but the welfare of the entire world. With only a few exceptions the churches of Middle County give of their time and strength to the missionary enterprise. In 1954 their aggregate contribution was approximately $45,000.

At its best the church calls forth in its people a deep emotional response. To those who are assembled it brings back tender memories of their loved ones at their best and of those to whom they have most looked up, and it directs their attention back across the centuries to a beautiful and majestic figure. In the historical life and teachings of the Church's Founder they see the finest expression of the human spirit and the ideal, or norm, by which they seek to direct their lives. They see this figure of Jesus glorified through his sacrificial death and exalted through the devotion of countless men and women who down through the centuries have responded to his appeal and given all they have to the cause he represents. All these memories and associations, aided by religious symbolism and music, can be used with telling effect by the able preacher to stir the emotions and wills of his hearers. Even those who are halfhearted in their devotion commonly turn to the church in the great crises of life, when they find themselves standing on the threshold of the unknown. In time of marriage, of birth of children, and of death they seek its blessing and its support.

The Holy Rollers, who have appeared on the scene only within the past forty years, are people who are taking their religion in earnest. They appeal to much the same class of people and rely upon somewhat the same methods as did the Methodists and Baptists and Disciples of a hundred years ago. They have arisen out of the common soil of human nature and are expressions of the religious fervor of the common people when under the pressure of frustration and hardship they are forced to think and feel together about the things that matter most. The various factors involved in their rapid development in Blankton and the part one man played in that development must await our consideration of religious experience in personal and social crisis.

RECONSIDERATION

Middle County was selected for the beginning of this study because it throws into clear relief the part played by custom and crisis in the development of organized religion. We see here the spontaneous origin of religious experience under the pressure of personal and social crisis and its expression in organized form. We see also the life cycle of organized religion as exemplified in the coexistence throughout the 135 years of Middle County's history of the beginning, the middle, and the terminal stages of organized religion, the types being constant as regards general characteristics but shifting as regards the identity of their constituent bodies.

Although not an average county, Middle County is nevertheless representative of American Protestantism as it operates in almost any part of the country. A survey of the county shows the role of the church in our American culture as the most important of our voluntary organizations.

III. *Personality Adjustments*
and Churches of Custom

THIS chapter will try to answer the questions, How does religion enter into the common life of our people? How does it affect their beliefs, their conduct, the organization of their personalities? In seeking the answers we shall examine the adjustments of the members of a representative American village in the same general region as Middle County, approaching this study with the assumption that the personality has its basis in social organization, and therefore in religion, and that "mental health" is equivalent to "moral" or "spiritual" health.

The community in question is centered in a village of five hundred inhabitants in an excellent farming section. Since there is but one church, community and parish are roughly identical. As compared with other villages in this region, Springville, as we shall call it, is considerably above the average in economic prosperity, educational level, community spirit, and homogeneity. It is a small face-to-face community of old American stock in which everybody knows everybody else. It is thus one of those primary groups in which, according to Cooley,[1] human nature asserts itself and the processes of social interaction can be studied to best advantage.

We base our inquiry upon a study made by a very able young minister who had had two years of clinical experience in a good mental hospital and was unusually well equipped to evaluate per-

[1] Charles Horton Cooley, *Social Organization* (New York: Charles Scribner's Sons, 1927), p. 30.

sonality adjustments. More than that, fine relationship with his people enabled him to draw upon that common fund of information about the individual members of the community on the basis of which business is done and social intercourse conducted. Sometimes, as in much of the village gossip, such information takes on a malicious tinge; but it approximates the truth. Certainly the success or failure of the merchant or the banker will depend largely upon the accuracy of the judgments as to whom he can and to whom he cannot give credit. And the executive, the leader, the teacher will stand or fall in accordance with his ability to judge character. In any case the community judgments are something to be reckoned with. This young minister therefore took account of them but sought to go beyond them in accuracy and kindliness.

1. Types of Adjustment

a. THE FAITHFUL

Going systematically through the village, he listed 322 persons over twelve years of age.[2] Of this number he placed 52, or 16 per cent, in the group which he called the faithful. These were persons who in his judgment had taken seriously the loyalty represented by their parents, by the church, by organized society, and were growing in the direction of socialization and unification on a basis conceived of as universal and abiding. They were persons whom he and other community leaders could count upon to support worthy causes by their presence, their interest, their financial support; those whose lives were devoted to the service of something beyond themselves. These people were not free from faults, of course, but they were ready to face them and try to correct them and they were able to maintain a reasonable degree of discipline. Here are thumbnail sketches of some of those in this group:

[2] Unfortunately, he did not extend the study to include the farm homes, nor even complete the village. Samplings of the uncompleted section of the village, which contained about a fifth of the total population, indicated that its inclusion would not have changed the picture.

Girl of 13, belongs to junior choir, regular in church school, liked by schoolmates. She is quiet, considerate, shows satisfactory development.

Girl of 15, in second year high school, attends church school 100 per cent. She is highly intelligent and industrious, accepts responsibility and sees it through. She is developing steadily into a fine type of womanhood.

Boy of 14, in first year high school, attends church school 100 per cent. He is Scout patrol leader, good athlete, highly intelligent. He shows some traces of "smart-aleckiness," but is honest, active and growing.

Girl of 21, graduate of teachers' college, plays the organ in church, teaches in church school, deeply interested in church and community affairs. She has shown steady and satisfactory development.

Man of 28, principal of high school, active in community affairs, attends church 40 per cent. His ideal of service is well-developed. He is honest, capable, meets problems intelligently and does something about them. He is doing an important job well.

Woman of 27, wife of high school principal, is well-adjusted, earnest, cheerful, very intelligent, a real educator's wife who understands what he is doing and helps him do it.

Man of 55, a farmer and truck driver, is generous, honest, hard-working, ready to help anyone in need, innocent of all theology but truly religious. Attends church 10 per cent, contributes liberally.

Woman of 27, wife of a mechanic, operates a beauty parlor. She is extroverted, self-confident, has a good sense of humor. She is active in the community, interested in the church and ready to take responsibility. Church attendance 90 per cent.

Woman of 55, wife of farmer and truck driver, works in a store. Church attendance 100 per cent, always on hand at church affairs; little other social participation. She is a pleasant, cheerful, motherly woman with a good mind and good judgment.

Woman of 28, works as stenographer in bank. She teaches a class in the church school and is always on hand at church and community affairs. She is steady and reliable—has severe moral code for herself and frowns on those who depart from it. She is ready to assume responsibility and see it through. She is unmarried but "dates."

Man of 22, a truck driver and farmer, a hard-working, honest fellow who gives everything he has to whatever he does. He came from a broken home and was handicapped at the start but is growing in the right direction. He serves faithfully as Cub Scout leader and attends church 10 per cent.

Woman of 28, graduate of a good college, has taught six years. She is tall and somewhat overweight but a highly intelligent person who works herself into exhaustion in a good cause.

Man of 50, a physician, does not attend church but practices what the church teaches. He is devoted to his work and is thoroughly honest with himself and with his patients.

Man of 75, a retired farmer, quite well-to-do, has a high index of civic interest. He had a considerable patrimony to begin with and has given a good account of his stewardship. He has been a hard worker and a good manager. He is friendly, cheerful and well-liked.

Woman of 70, wife of the retired farmer, a very well-balanced, outgoing, highly intelligent person with liberal views who has given freely of time and money in all good causes. Church attendance 10 per cent.

Man of 42, the largest farm operator in the county, has had one year in college. He is direct, honest, well-balanced, healthy in body and mind, public-spirited and efficient.

Woman of 39, wife of the farm operator. She is a college graduate and is very intelligent, dependable and forward-looking; the finest type of young matron, doing a "corking job" with her two sons.

Man of 68, runs a small store, a cheerful, honest, public-spirited person; a devout church member who is conservative in his views but broad in his spirit. He is meeting courageously and with quiet faith the problem of failing health.

Woman of 65, wife of the small storekeeper, is well-adjusted, friendly, interested in community affairs and well-liked. She is meeting the problem of failing health serene and unafraid.

b. THE COMPLACENT

More than half the persons included in this study belonged in the group which the young minister called the complacent. They were persons who were fairly comfortable in their vocational, sexual, and social adjustments but who apparently gave little thought to things that were beyond their immediate needs and duties and pleasures. Most of them would profess allegiance to the church and all of them would accept its standards. Their conduct would show no glaring inconsistencies, but they were not taking their religion very much in earnest. They were outwardly respectable persons whose best potentialities—in terms of their own ideals—were not in process of being realized. They were not of those who watch with their lights burning. Here are some of his characterizations:

Man of 44, a barber with high school education, thrifty, cautious, conservative in his views, honest in his business dealings. He gives passive support to worthy causes. Church attendance 5 per cent. He is a substantial citizen with many good qualities.

Woman of 44, wife of the barber, shares her husband's conservative views and is an affectionate, cheerful wife and mother of narrow outlook and limited interests.

Boy of 17, a high school student who is making a good record in athletics and is intelligent, well-liked and has no obvious maladjustments. He shows no interest in church and seems quite self-satisfied.

Man of 32, a mechanic with high school education, genial, self-centered, easygoing, capable of much better things; some social participation but no great interest. He attends church 15 per cent but gives no financial support.

Man of 55, elevator operator and mayor of village, is pleasant, steady, honest, a fair mayor but no civic leader. He is conventional in his outlook but has made the most of an average endowment.

Woman of 45, wife of carpenter, is complacent, obese, friendly, devoted to her children. She has no interest in the church but is devoted to the Legion Auxiliary.

Man of 55, a quiet, good-natured, easygoing person, but steady and dependable. He attends church regularly and is a conventional Christian but makes no especially significant effort for God or country.

Woman of 55, wife of this good-natured man, is a home-loving person, shy, companionable, likes to be sheltered, a clinging-vine type.

Man of 70, a day laborer whose life has been one of uninterrupted, unimaginative hard work. He has no special interests but is steady and well-disciplined.

Man of 55, a carpenter, is shrewd, quiet, friendly, but inclined to be smug and self-satisfied.

Man of 55, active in community affairs, morals above reproach except in politics. He is devoted to his children, contributes generously to church and attends 50 per cent.

Man of 55, a retired farmer, hard-working, shrewd, thrifty, utterly self-centered; no interest in church or community; the lord of his household.

Girl of 21, daughter of a domineering father, is a graduate of a teachers' college. She is ambitious, loud, unreflective but is aware that she has some problems. She is conventionally religious and attends church 75 per cent.

Young man of 22, a student in a state university, is very intelligent and wants to be an author. He likes to make people squirm and is anything but well-liked. He is still thinking and growing but is adjusting on a self-centered level.

Man of 38, a barber with high school education, no social participation, no interest in church. He is fairly pleasant to meet and is trustworthy and industrious.

Woman of 38, wife of this barber, belongs to church and attends occasionally. She is a plump, easygoing person with no interests beyond her family.

Woman of 25, a teachers' college graduate, is married but has no children. A "Main Street" type, interests secular, attitude self-satisfied; church attendance 10 per cent.

C. THE PAGAN

Twenty-nine persons, or about 9 per cent of the total number, were placed in a group which, for want of a better name, were called the pagans. This term was chosen to designate those who had either rebelled against, or had never learned to take seriously, the authority of their parents and the standards of the community in which they were reared and had sought refuge in groups of easy standards where they found social support for their antisocial and rebellious attitudes.

It was, however, difficult to find any who exactly fitted that definition. Delinquent gangs did not exist in Springville. There were indeed several young people who were inwardly rebellious against a tyrannical father or a domineering mother, several also who were not taking any too seriously the accepted standards of the community, but none that had found much in the way of social support. Springville's pagans were for the most part older persons of the "playboy" type who had gone their own way regardless of community opinion and seemed to be suffering no particular pangs of conscience. Although more or less ostracized by the respectable people of the community, they had found solace in the fellowship of the poolroom and the barbershop. Closer examination raised the question whether even they fitted the definition. It was observed that most of them did not want their children to follow in their footsteps but encouraged them to go to the church school. It seemed more in accordance with the facts to look upon them as persons who had failed to make good in terms of the community standards and who had finally acquiesced in the community judgments, accepting their assigned roles and deriving such comfort and social support as might be available. The somewhat caustic community judgments are epitomized as follows:

Boy of 17, dull, backward, always in trouble. He hangs around poolrooms and has a reputation for petty thieving.

Girl of 25, easygoing, happy-go-lucky, no interest in higher values.

Girl of 23, daughter of a dissolute father, a friendly, not unattractive young woman who runs with men of questionable character and is suspected of sexual irregularities. She does not seem to mind.

Man of 30, with high school education, a good mechanic who works when he feels like it. He is addicted to hunting trips and "wet parties." He has no sense of responsibility toward family or community.

Man of 45, an unintelligent person whose fellowships and interests are on a negative social plane. He gambles, drinks, patronizes slot machines and does not "give a hoot" whether school keeps or not. He is easygoing, cheerful, unambitious.

Man of 48, an aggressive, loud-mouthed salesman and small-town politician, successful in business but unconcerned about the rights of others.

Man of 48, inherited a fortune of $75,000 and has squandered most of it on gambling, drinking and women. He is a man of considerable native ability who might have been a leader but has affronted all decent community standards and is now a social outcast. As a boy he had been able to make his mother laugh when she started to punish him. He has been trying to get by on that basis ever since.

Man of 44, an easygoing, middle-aged playboy, violates community dicta without any sense of discomfort. He has rebelled against responsibility and routine.

Man of 45, a parasitic playboy, likes to get things with the least possible effort. He has spent much time "chasing" the girls. He has "kicked over the traces" and seems comfortable about it.

d. THE MENTALLY ILL

Eighty-one persons, or 25 per cent, were regarded as more or less
ill mentally. That is, they had more or less serious maladjustments,
and instead of defying the community judgments or socializing their
inferiorities among the poolroom and barber shop habitués, they
subjected themselves to self-blame and self-punishment, or resorted
to various concealment devices, or took refuge in drink or daydreaming. Among them three types may be distinguished:

i. *The Difficult*

There were forty-five persons who were problems to themselves
without admitting it and problems to others without losing caste.
They were those who under the stress of inner disharmony and sense
of failure refused to admit defeat or error and resorted to the various
devices of concealment in order to maintain self-respect and escape
self-condemnation. Among them were six who sought refuge in im-
aginary illness, three who indulged excessively in malicious gossip,
eight who were overparticular about legalistic trivialities, eight who
tyrannized over all who were so unfortunate as to be in their power,
seven who were chronically irritable, seven who were bitter and
suspicious. Here are some of the community judgments:

Man of 45, aggressive, domineering, self-centered. He has an ungovern-
able temper and tries to control every action of his children.
Woman of 52, an eccentric Christian, was ultraconservative, but has
now taken up vegetarianism. She is chronically uncomfortable both to
others and to herself.
Woman of 65, wife of a well-to-do farmer, mother of a large family.
She "rules the roost," nagging, crying, pleading, doing anything to have
her way.
Man of 45, headstrong, stubborn, aggressively ignorant, chronically
uncomfortable, holds grudges and "shoots off his face" at the slightest
provocation.
Woman of 70, with low intelligence and bad temper. She sits in her
rocking chair most of the day nursing grudges.
Man of 45, startlingly lazy, a "blowhard" and braggart and "alibi
artist" who is keenly interested in the ladies.

Woman of 28, the daughter of a neurotic mother, a divorcee who lives the life of a recluse and often goes to bed for weeks at a time.

Woman of 30, a widow who lives a "hermetically sealed" life; she talks constantly of a heart ailment and indulges in self-pity.

Woman of 27, daughter of a badly maladjusted mother, is of the clinging-vine type, ready to talk of her troubles by the hour to anyone who will listen. She is irresponsible, living in a world of phantasy and has frequent one-sided love affairs.

Woman of 44, a domineering person with low output of energy who spends much of her time reading the movie magazines and maintains her self-respect by slandering her neighbors.

Woman of 48, constantly complaining of her husband's infidelities, quarrelsome and irritable at home and abroad. She enjoys and purveys malicious gossip.

Woman of 50, who had an explosion three years ago, left home, slept in the railway station, ate at the restaurant and was wild enough to have been sent to a state hospital. She is "down" on everyone—a smoldering volcano.

Woman of 60, with good education, lives alone since death of her mother ten years ago. She believes that everyone is against her and that mysterious things are going on.

Woman of 35, definitely paranoid since the birth of her second child. She never leaves home, is unsocial, hypochondriacal, apathetic toward her children.

ii. The Defeated

There were sixteen persons who, in the face of accumulating difficulties and frustrations, had made little or no attempt to keep up the struggle, but had resorted to such devices as drink or daydreaming and seemed, in whatever way, to have "thrown in the sponge." The community judgments of a number of these are as follows:

Boy of 16, dreamy, irresponsible, plays a fair game of baseball, but otherwise participates little in social life. He is a potential schizophrenic.

Girl of 16, with borderline intelligence, has little drive and does much daydreaming.

Man of 36, son of a tyrannical, irascible father, is soft-spoken, subservient, without social interest. There seems to be much phantasy.

Man of 35, shiftless, irresponsible, sexually lax, a chronic alcoholic.

Man of 36, an ambitionless sneak thief, who is drunk much of the time.

Man of 38, a periodic drunkard and wife-beater, spends most of his time and money in saloons. He is looked down upon by the entire community and accepts it. He goes around with his tail between his legs.

Man of 40, a periodic drinker, now in a state hospital. He is not without social feeling and was at one time a leader in the community.

Man of 45, a W.P.A. worker, shiftless, irresponsible, dishonest, quarrelsome and alcoholic.

Man of 33, a vicious, shiftless, hostile alcoholic who blames the world for his misfortunes and "takes it out" on his wife.

Woman of 27, a "white rabbit" with borderline intelligence, a poorly organized person with two children of preschool age.

iii. The Distressed

There were twenty who were problems to themselves and knew it. They were characterized by severe intrapsychic conflict. Such conflict is not always an evil. It may be a precondition of reorganization, the outcome being dependent upon the nature and relative strength of the contending forces and upon the factors in the life situation.

In cases where the conflict is between the desire for self-expression on the one hand and the authority of the parents on the other, there will be repressed hostility which is likely to manifest itself in irregular or delinquent behavior. In cases where the subject has accepted for himself some socially valued role and is struggling against unruly tendencies within himself, or against environmental frustrations, the outcome is likely to be constructive. Eight persons seemed to belong in the first group, twelve in the second. Here are some instances:

Boy of 21, son of an aggressive, domineering father, is outwardly submissive and easygoing, but there is much repressed hostility.

Girl of 24, daughter of the same tyrannical father, outwardly phlegmatic but boiling within. Her rebellion is expressing itself in the form of sex escapades.

Woman of 34, with good education, married to the son of an overdominant and tyrannical father. She is chafing under the domination of her father-in-law and is birdlike, nervous and self-assertive. She recognizes her problems and is trying to master them.

Girl of 17, dreamy and irresponsible. She has a violent temper and is rebellious at home and in school.

Girl of 17, intelligent, but loud-mouthed, "smart-alecky," and independent. She is aware of her problems, but is handling them the wrong way.

Woman of 26, daughter of a dissolute father, has been sexually indiscreet but is not self-satisfied.

Boy of 17, a small-town "smart-aleck." He has a swaggering attitude but is moody. He is having growing pains.

Boy of 15, worships his father, is acutely conscious of his own small stature and is uncertain of himself.

Girl of 20, a recluse at home and in college, a "bookworm" with no "dates" and no friends who feels the situation keenly.

Boy of 18, a serious-minded, hard-working chap who does not know where he is going but is trying hard. He has few friends and is aware of his handicaps. He is thinking much about the future and has called three times upon his pastor to talk over his problems.

Man of 23, with some college training, is engaged to be married but is having difficulty securing work. He is doing a lot of worrying.

Boy of 20, a student in college but still a "sissy." He is shallow, self-centered, going through a personality change in a struggle to grow up.

Boy of 19, badly deformed and with a high-pitched, squeaky voice. He is ambitious, went to college, but has an extremely difficult situation.

e. THE REORGANIZED

There are four persons who in the face of mounting difficulties or threatening defeat have achieved some sort of reorganization.

One is a badly disfigured woman. Her solution has been found in religion of the Four Square Gospel variety. Through it she has found comfort and peace of mind. She enjoys talking about religion and spends a good bit of time writing poetry.

Another is an alcoholic who was converted twenty years ago. At the age of sixty-seven he is still going straight. The community, however, looks upon him as a religious crank. He is said to be bigoted, belligerent, and hard to live with. This man attends church faithfully in another village.

The third is another reformed alcoholic, now a man of fifty. He once held a responsible position, but lost it because of his excessive use of liquor. He is now on the "water wagon" and is saving his money. He has to take a good bit of chaffing from the old crowd and is said to be set in his opinions and harsh toward inebriates. To what extent religion was a factor in his reformation is not clear. His present job keeps him from attending church.

Finally there is a mother whose life centered around an only son, a very able and well-liked man. When this son was stricken with a fatal disease, she turned to Christian Science and against the protests of the family installed a Christian Science nurse. Although the son died in agony, her faith in Christian Science has remained unshaken. She has stopped attending the community church.

2. The Omnipresence of the Mentally Ill

A review of our findings from another angle reveals even more clearly the seriousness of the mental health situation. Two persons were definitely psychotic; two others had been inmates of a mental hospital and were still far from well; four were near-psychotic; six were psychoneurotic; nine were seriously alcoholic, two of them having been in institutions for alcoholism. At least eight were mentally subnormal. There was one drug addict, one sex pervert, one cretin, one hydrocephalic, and three seniles. Together with the difficult, the distressed, the outlaws, and the ne'er-do-wells, these persons constituted a full third of the population of the village.

In interpreting these findings it is important to bear in mind that the American country village has today become a haven of refuge for many inadequate persons. With the passing of its importance as a trade center many families have moved away. Rents are therefore cheap and the houses are often filled by families unable to make the grade elsewhere. For this reason the percentage of mental illness is probably greater than in the country as a whole. It is, however, to be noted that of those included in this study of Springville 75 per cent had been born and brought up in the community and not more than 18 per cent had moved in within ten years. It is also to be noted that

46 per cent were classed as of comfortable economic status, 39 per cent marginal, and 15 per cent poor or on relief. These figures suggest that the haven-of-refuge explanation must be accepted with caution.

However that may be, several things stand out clearly. In the first place, attention is drawn to the number of persons living in this village who would not be permitted to remain at large if they were living in a city. Where urban communities tend to commit a large proportion of their mentally ill to institutional care, the country community carries most of its own burden. One will also notice the shading off from the definitely psychotic to the less severe forms of mental illness.

These findings suggest, furthermore, an explanation of the marked increase in hospital population during the past forty years. If the figures for Springville seem high, it is because a competent observer had here an adequate opportunity to observe. So also in the country at large, the increase in the number of patients in mental hospitals is due chiefly to the growing awareness of the problems which they represent.

3. THE STATIC CHARACTER OF SPRINGVILLE'S RELIGION

The religion in operation in Springville is clearly religion of the static, or epimethean,[3] not religion in its creative phase. This does not mean that progressive spirit is lacking. Evidence of its presence is found in the fact that eighty laymen organized a community church notwithstanding denominational protests. We must understand rather that the vision and enthusiasm of religion's creative stage have been transformed into custom and habit. The mores have become so firmly established that, despite the new ideas which come flooding in through radios, movies, and newspapers, and despite the spread of education, there is surprisingly little disposition to question or chal-

[3] W. H. Sheldon, *Psychology and the Promethean Will* (New York: Harper & Brothers, 1936).

lenge the basic assumptions in matters of right or wrong and of theological belief.

There were indeed not a few persons whose conduct had been irregular and who were in consequence more or less ostracized. Some of these had reacted by charging church people with hypocrisy and even by disparaging the church and railing at things religious, but it was noted that many of them encouraged their children to go to the church school. It was therefore concluded that they were not really *pagans*, but rather persons who had failed to measure up to the community requirements and who had adjusted themselves as best they could to community judgments whose justice they inwardly accepted.

The static character of Springville's religion is further indicated by the fact that only four persons were found whose lives had been reorganized and not one of these owed that reorganization to the local church. One was an alcoholic who had turned over a new leaf, apparently without much religious help.[4] The other three had had recourse to religion, but it was religion of another kind, in one case Christian Science, in the other two something of the Holiness variety. It is not necessary to place too high a value upon sudden conversions to regard their absence within the membership of a church as evidence that that church is placing its reliance upon the processes of education and steady growth. The evangelistic zeal which has characterized most religious movements in their formative stages is in these churches not greatly in evidence.

4. How the Community Standards Are Implanted By Church

This resistance to the impact of new ideas may be explained by the consideration that moral and religious education is dependent not so much upon formal instruction as upon praise and blame for actual conduct on the part of those whom one admires and whose authority one accepts. The fact that Springville is a small, homogeneous com-

[4] The fact that he is said to be intolerant of inebriates suggests that he has relied upon his own "will power" to mend his ways.

munity with abundant opportunity for working and playing together goes far toward explaining the acceptance of a common set of standards and the tenacity with which these standards are held.

Among the institutions and agencies which have had a part in the internalizing of these group standards the church may be regarded as the most important. It stands as the symbol of a supreme loyalty, of which the standards are but functions. It demands complete commitment to that loyalty. It calls for an expression of that commitment through regular assemblage and sacrificial service. And it provides for a constant reconsideration of the implications of that commitment in the light of changing conditions.

The church is built upon the family unit. Where other institutions in Springville minister to special groups, such as farmers, businessmen, women of certain interests, adolescent boys, adolescent girls, the church ministers to all ages and all classes. In earlier years families used to come in a body and sit together in the family pew. While this practice is not so common today, still the church is founded upon the family and it is chiefly through the family that its ideals are made effective in human life.

The importance of the family in the determination of personality adjustments is indicated by a re-examination of the data. Of the 322 persons included in this study there were 82 whose parents were included and 87 parents who had children that were also included. It was found that for those parents who were classified as *faithful* the number of well-adjusted (*faithful* or *complacent*) children was 15, and the number of maladjusted children (*pagan, difficult, defeated, distressed,*) was only 2. For those parents who were classified as *complacent* the ratio was 9 to 5, and for those who were classified as *maladjusted* the ratio was 3 to 5.

The contrast is much more striking if only those parents are considered who were given the same rating. The 7 couples who were classed as *faithful* had 12 children. Of these 10 were classed as *faithful* and 2 as *complacent*. Nine couples who were classed as *complacent* had 16 children. Of these 3 were classed as *faithful*, 8 as

complacent, and 3 as distressed. The 4 couples classed as maladjusted had 5 children. Of these 2 were complacent and 3 badly
maladjusted.

Looking at it from another angle, it was found that of the 82 persons whose parents were also included in this study 20 were classified
as faithful. Of these 14 had at least one parent who was classified as
faithful. There were 31 who were classified as maladjusted. Of these,
26 had at least one parent who was also maladjusted.

While the number of persons included in this study is insufficient
to satisfy statistical requirements, these findings are supported by
those of other studies,[5] and there is justification for concluding that
the adjustments of children tend strongly to follow those of their
parents.

Such a conclusion is of course in line with what is being discovered
today regarding the tremendous influence of the parents upon the
attitudes of the child. The young child is dependent upon the
parents for protection and for love to a degree which is never repeated in the course of his existence. From this early relationship,
more than from any other source, comes his idea of God and his
moral standards. This modern view is in accordance with the teaching of the Church's Founder. It is of the very essence of the Christian religion that it looks upon God as a Father and upon men as
brothers. The church is itself a family.

Springville's school, in accordance with the traditional American
plan for the separation of church and state, gives no religious instruction. Neither does it make any provision for the formal teaching of
ethics. The community appoints its own teachers, however, and the
character and the religious attitudes of these teachers do not escape
inspection. The principal of the high school and his wife were active
participants in the church, and most of the teachers, although they
were not residents of the community, identified themselves with the
local church. This means that the standards of praise and censure in

[5] Boisen, *Exploration of the Inner World* (New York: Harper & Brothers,
1936), Chap. IX.

the schoolroom and in the supervised playground and recreational activities of the school would conform to the community standards.

Opportunities for social intercourse and for the administering of praise and blame are provided through formal organizations and also through many informal gatherings. Among the former are a businessmen's club with some 50 members, a Masonic lodge with 20 members, an Eastern Star lodge with 20 members, an Odd Fellows lodge with 10 members, an American Legion post with 17 members, a Legion Auxiliary with 12 members, a bridge club with 16 members, Cub Scouts with 8 members, 4-H Club for girls with 12 members, the Junior Choir of the church with 46 members, the Ladies' Aid Society, and the Missionary Society. In addition, the high school has its various athletic, musical, and dramatic organizations.

Springville thus gives evidence of the effectiveness of praise and blame in the determination of the standards and attitudes of men. Mrs. Grundy is an excellent policeman, but like most policemen she has some faults. She is much quicker with censure than with praise. This is due to the fact that censure is a common protective device. The loafer in the poolroom who criticizes the President feels himself in some measure superior to the President. He is thereby bucking up his self-esteem. So also the malicious gossip is motivated by the desire to prove that other persons are inferior to herself. Control by censure means control by fear. It means emphasis upon the "Thou shalt nots." And that means a static morality and a static religion.

The control by fear may also help to explain the large amount of maladjustment which was found in Springville. The person whose standards are determined by fear has not really accepted those standards. He is therefore not free. His conduct is controlled by something which is still external to himself, something which he often resents. That resentment, if it does not eventuate in an open break, is likely to give shelter to interests and conduct of which the better self does not approve. There is likely to be a mixture of love and hate toward the representatives of authority which will mean a divided self and therefore a sick soul. Mrs. Grundy's guardianship is likely to be ineffective when the young man from the village visits the big city and the forbidden indulgence which he is afraid to acknowledge then becomes a source of serious trouble.

5. The Altar Fire

In the ancient story of the destruction of Sodom it is recorded that Abraham interceded in behalf of the doomed city. He told the Lord it would not be just to destroy the righteous along with the wicked. The Lord agreed. The question then arose as to how many righteous persons it would take to save the city. Starting with fifty, Abraham gradually reduced the number until the Lord agreed to spare the city if even ten could be found.

Judged by this standard Springville is not in danger of destruction. It is smaller than ancient Sodom and within it are found more than fifty persons who were classed as righteous.

The question now is how the presence of this nucleus of the faithful contributes to the well-being of the community. Three considerations suggest themselves.

First, the task of organized religion is to transform into custom and habit the new vision and quickened purpose of its creative stages and thus transmit them from one generation to another. In such a community as Springville it is the group of the faithful which is entrusted with that task. Even though that group may be dwindling in numbers, and even though its beliefs and practices become formalized, it is no small matter that the altar fire is kept burning.

It is also to be recognized that within this group of the faithful are those who best exemplify the virtues of honesty, industry, efficiency, and kindliness, virtues upon which the health of the community is based. Within this group are some of the community's most devoted and capable servants, those who are most likely to give employment or financial assistance to the able-bodied and the helping hand to those who are in trouble. It thus meant not a little to Springville that during the tragic years of the depression, when the banks in neighboring towns were failing, the local bank, honestly and efficiently administered by one of this group, did not go under.

It is part of the genius of the Christian Church that it provides for the renewal of the vision and the replenishment of the fire. In contrast with other great religions which make no provision for religious assemblage, in contrast with the modern lodge, which has its assemblages and its religious rituals but no provision for instruction, the church has not only its regular assemblages but also its pulpit and its church school. The sermons may frequently be dry and the church school teaching sterile, but the way is left open for the prophet when he comes.

RECONSIDERATION

1. Springville may be regarded as representative of an American face-to-face community in which the religious impulse has been largely transformed into custom and habit.

2. Among the institutions of the community, the church is the only one which is built upon the family as a unit and which brings people together on the basis of their highest loyalties. As such it has had no small part in the maintenance of the community standards and attitudes.

3. Very striking is the fact that in spite of radios and movies and newspapers there is little disposition, even among the poolroom habitués, to question the customary assumptions in matters of right and wrong. This may be accounted for by the fact that the community is a homogeneous one with abundant opportunity for working and playing and associating together. Praise and blame for actual conduct have then full scope as determinants of moral attitudes.

4. The moral attitudes thus determined are of the static rather than of the dynamic type. They emphasize the "Thou shalt nots" and are enforced by fear. This may be a factor in the high proportion of personality maladjustment and mental illness in this community.

5. In all probability this community may be taken as fairly repre-

sentative as regards the amount of personality maladjustment. If that amount seems high it is only because a competent observer had here an adequate opportunity to observe. The suggestion therefore follows that liability to mental illness may be looked upon not as an evil but as the price we have to pay for being men and having the power of choice and the capacity for growth.

6. In the small groups of the distressed and of the regenerated [6] we have a suggestion which will receive attention in a later chapter: that mental illness itself may not be an evil but a desperate attempt at reorganization, or cure.

7. The church in this community is a conservative institution in the best sense of that word. It keeps the altar fire burning and provides for the rethinking of its beliefs and for the maintenance of the ideals which are mankind's distinctive heritage.

[6] Variant groups of the mystical type always have a difficult time getting started in small communities such as Springville, and individuals who undergo experiences of the dramatic type are less likely to receive social support from those who understand than in larger communities.

IV. Crises in Personality Development

THE enormous amount of mental illness which we found in the small village considered in the last chapter led to the suggestion that mental illness may be the price we have to pay for being human and having the power of choice and the capacity for growth. This chapter presents evidence in support of that suggestion. It attempts to show that certain forms of mental illness are themselves manifestations of healing power. These forms, to be sharply distinguished from those in which some adaptation to defeat and failure has been made and accepted, are associated with periods in the development of the personality in which fate hangs in the balance and destiny is in large measure determined.

In such periods of crisis religious concern is much in evidence and the creative forces are exceptionally active. So also are the forces of destruction. These are periods of seething emotion which tend either to make or to break. We therefore frankly acknowledge that religion is associated with mental illness. This follows from the fact that religion is concerned with that which is not yet but ought to be both in personal character and in social order, and that it is ever religion's task to disturb the consciences of men regarding the quality of the life they are living and the failure to achieve their true potentialities.

For light upon this problem we turn to the laboratory of life and examine the experiences of those who are breaking or who have broken under the strain of moral crisis. From them we may learn that crisis experiences are associated with religious quickening, and tend to set in motion forces which have the capacity to transform the

41

personal and social life. We shall try to discover the conditions under which religious concern is likely to appear and the conditions under which defeat or victory is likely to result.

1. TYPES OF PERSONAL CRISIS

a. CRISES IN NORMAL DEVELOPMENT

Crisis periods are characteristic of normal growth. Any individual in the course of development is sure to pass through some critical periods: coming of age, getting married, birth of children, advent of old age, bereavement, and death. In the development of the religious life such crisis periods are likely to be of decisive importance. The man who normally goes his way somewhat carelessly, occupied with his daily work, with the sports page, or with the movie offerings, doing little serious thinking, may at such times feel himself face to face with life's ultimate issues. His eyes may be opened to unsuspected possibilities and he may accept for himself a role which completely changes his course in life.

Evidence of the religious significance of these normal crises in personal development may be found in the extent to which they are associated with religious ceremonies. Civil marriages and mortuary chapels in America may be increasing in number, but funerals and weddings are still prevailingly functions of the church. And not only in America but also in non-Christian lands religious ceremonies are associated with marriage, with the birth of children, with the burial of the dead, and, especially among certain primitive peoples, with coming of age.

But religious quickening does not always occur at such times. There are many who, passing through what should be crisis periods remain blind to the issues at stake. Some come to grief. One very large group, found in every mental hospital, has been given the label "dementia praecox" because the types of reaction which it represents seemed to be associated with adolescence. Serious disturbances are also associated with the birth of children; and they are not limited to mothers; they befall fathers also. The onset of old age is another critical period in which a new level of development must be achieved. It also is associated with liability to disturbance.

b. SITUATIONAL FRUSTRATION

Frustration may be a condition of growth. It is generally recognized that, if we got everything we wanted when we wanted it, we would not become men. There would be no thinking and no feeling. Character and personality develop through the overcoming of difficulties. So also do cultures.[1]

Even serious frustrations may bring blessing with them. But they also bring danger. Such experiences as disappointment in love, domestic tragedy, vocational failure, business reverses, and chronic illness or disability may result in religious quickening. There are those who come through with flying colors. There are also those who take to drink, those who accept the situation with listless resignation, those who go to pieces, and those who pass into a physical decline.

Here, for example, is a man who was faced with a serious domestic tragedy. He was a minister of religion, an Armenian who came of a long line of village priests. As a boy of twelve he had seen both his parents massacred. After completing college he took a church and married a beautiful but illiterate woman. He then came to America leaving his wife and children in the old country. Within three years he was able to send for them. When they arrived, in company with an uncle of his, it was at once apparent that something was wrong. Three months later the wife gave birth to a child by this uncle.

What is a man to do in such a situation? There have been those who, in the face of very similar tragedy, have emerged with blessing. It was thus that the prophet Hosea discovered God's love for His erring people. Not so this man. His reaction was outwardly proper. He made quiet arrangements for a divorce. He gave up his church

[1] See Arnold J. Toynbee, *The Study of History*, abridged edition (London: Oxford University Press, 1947). The concept of a "time of troubles" as the creative stage in the development of every great civilization is a central thesis in this important book.

and took a teaching position. But deep bitterness, rooted perhaps in his tragic childhood, took possession of him. Finally he attempted to shoot his eldest daughter.

In the hospital where he was sent he was neat, orderly, intelligent, and somberly prepossessing in appearance. But he was always bitter. The more one did for him, the more he demanded. It was clear that with his church he had also given up his religion. While he still loved to talk theology, that theology was of a peculiar sort. The golden rule, which he was always quoting, was invariably in reverse. It was what others ought to do for him, not what he should do for others.

One can sympathize with this man in the bitterly trying experiences through which he had passed. It was easy to understand his reaction, but that reaction was nonetheless malignant. He was regarded as one of the most dangerous men in the institution and because of his extreme bitterness no hope could be entertained for his recovery.

This case is of interest because we see many similarly embittered persons in this war-torn world. It also exemplifies a reaction pattern common not only in mental hospitals but in any normal community. There are many who in the face of life's frustrations develop malignant attitudes and become so set in their ways that little can be done to change them. In this case some measure of self-respect was maintained and the personality was thus preserved, but only at the cost of isolation from human fellowship.

In one respect this case is not typical of situational disturbances. The outlook is extremely gloomy. Among the cases which come to a mental hospital a classification of "situational psychosis" usually carries with it the hope of a favorable outcome. It is only when situational frustration is combined with deep-seated weakness of character that the outlook is hopeless.

c. INTRAPSYCHIC CONFLICT

Why did this minister adopt such an unfortunate way of dealing with his problem? Of one thing we may be sure: the more serious nonorganic disorders which come to a mental hospital are to be explained, as a rule, not in terms of the immediate situation but rather in terms of some defect in the structure of the personality. The experience of seeing his parents massacred must have been a factor in this man's bitterness. We may suspect that there were other factors. There may have been long-standing conflict between the loyalty which he professed and interests which should long since have been outgrown. His bitterness may then have served as a defense against some sense of personal failure and unworthiness. Crisis experiences reveal hidden elements of strength and of weakness. In bereavement, for example, exaggerated display of grief is often due to a lurking sense of guilt rather than to deep affection. In any case the symptoms of a neurosis may be best explained as reactions to an accumulation of unassimilated experience which, like ill-digested food, gives the sufferer no peace until in some way it is taken care of.

2. REACTION PATTERNS

Among the various ways of dealing with trial and frustration and the sense of personal failure we may recognize a number of common patterns.

First of all is that of throwing in the sponge. It is represented by those who in the face of growing uneasiness and difficulty merely shut their eyes and drift, getting perhaps easy satisfactions through drink or daydream. In such persons there is little religious concern. Their end is progressive disintegration.

Another pattern is that of "saving face" and keeping up appearances. It is represented by those who refuse to admit defeat or error and resort to various concealment devices. Like the Armenian minister they may dwell on their grievances and become suspicious and bitter. They may exaggerate their own importance and build their world on the basis of some grandiose idea of themselves. They may take refuge in physical incapacitation, securing for themselves sympathy and attention. Religious concern is little in evidence in this group, least of all in those who are embittered and who blame others for their difficulties. And few such persons recover.

There are also those who escape into activity, those who resort to various compromises, those who substitute minor for major virtues and minor for major loyalties. The list could be extended, for many are the devices by which frail human nature seeks to live at peace with itself and come to terms with evils it is unable or unwilling to renounce. Not infrequently religion itself is employed to this end.

There is also an important group composed of those who accept responsibility for their shortcomings and failures and blame themselves rather than others. Such persons may develop severe anxiety. They may even become acutely psychotic. But some of them make excellent recoveries and religious concern is characteristic.

These patterns of reaction to the sense of personal failure and the types of adjustment to which they lead are shown in schematic form in the accompanying chart.

It is here assumed that the sense of personal failure, which is taken as the primary difficulty, is not necessarily an evil. When frankly recognized and intelligently handled, it becomes a precondition of growth. It is only when concealment is resorted to or when no effort at rectification is made that the malignant forms of mental illness are likely to develop.

This chart reads down and also across. Horizontally we have different levels of adjustment, while the vertical columns represent the different aspects or determinants of behavior. Clear awareness of difficulty and its frank acknowledgment may result in a constructive solution. There may be normal growth in the direction of socialization and unification on a basis conceived as abiding and universal. Such a solution, regardless of the symbols employed, should be recognized as religious. There may also be socialization on the level of the contemporary and local, or even on the level of the delinquent gang. Or, again, the reaction modes of bluffing and shifting responsibility may result in systematized delusions of persecution or of self-importance. Similarly, the reaction of withdrawal and surrender to the regressive tends to eventuate in loss of hope and progressive disintegration of the personality.

The two central columns represent the type of development by which the end stages are reached, the one gradual and the other eruptive. The one signifies the logical working out of the particular patterns employed, the end results of a particular style of life. The other represents a more or less desperate attempt at reorganization in the face of accumulating difficulties. It signifies, in other words, an attempt to break up established habit patterns and it may be followed by almost any type of adjustment from hopeless dissolution or delusional reorganization to that of prophetic insight.[2]

Our chief interest in this study is in these attempts at reorganization in which the better self is struggling for possession. It is the thesis of this book that crisis experiences have profound religious significance. Mental disorder as well as religious experience may be a manifestation of the power to heal, and religious experience as well as mental disorder may involve emotional upheaval.

We turn, therefore, to a type of reaction which is neither drifting nor concealment nor compromise but a desperate attempt at reconstruction. We shall examine first a case of religious conversion, then a case of acute schizophrenia.

3. RELIGIOUS CONVERSION

This case is an episode in the life of a man named Rudolph, who at the age of forty-three came to the hospital after an attempt at suicide. According to his story he was born in Germany of respectable, middle-class parents. His father, he said, was very strict, ready to knock any foolishness out of his head. His mother he described as kindhearted and "awfully soft." In later life she was very religious. He himself finished grammar school at the age of fourteen. His scholastic standing was high and his teachers wanted him to study for the teaching profession. He chose, however, the trade of carpenter. At the age of sixteen he came to America.

It is clear from his account of himself, as well as from the testi-

[2] A more detailed consideration of this chart may be found in my *Exploration of the Inner World* (New York: Harper & Brothers, 1936), pp. 147–62.

mony of those who knew him, that Rudolph was a good boy, well-meaning and conscientious, perhaps to a fault. The first requirement in moral and religious education had therefore in his case been fulfilled. He had accepted as his own the standards of his parents and of organized society. But the second requirement had not been achieved. He had not brought himself into harmony with the standards he had accepted. He was having trouble with that drive which must somehow or other be brought under control before the boy can become a man. From his twelfth year on he had struggled with the problem of masturbation. He felt "unspeakable worry" over it, and he often cried about it at night. About a year after his arrival in this country the tension became so acute that he was driven to consult a physician. The latter, after listening to his story, advised him to try religion.

Rudolph had at this time become rather shaky in his religious faith and had wandered far from the admonitions of his pious mother, but he now determined to investigate. It so happened that a series of revival meetings was at that time under way. He therefore began his investigation with these meetings. Here is his account of what happened:

One day while Mr. Moody was preaching and I had spent all my nights in prayer, and I had prayed and cried—yes, cried; I was a regular baby. But at any rate, while Mr. Moody was preaching about God being a Father and about his being ready to forgive us for our past, if only our purpose is good—I can't explain it; it was a natural phenomenon that came over me. I had gone there a downcast individual, not a young man, but an old man. When I came out I felt as though the very sparrows in the trees were singing songs. Everything was changed, and it seemed such a real experience. I can't account for it today, but I know this: I was happy for many years after that and I was more successful in my work.

The story of the years that followed, of Rudolph's enthusiastic participation in church work, of his fall from grace, of his marriage to a faithful member of this church—a wife of whom he stood very much in awe—of his desperate attempts to maintain his self-respect by means of compromise devices, and of his final attempt to take his own life, contains many points of interest but is not directly pertinent to our problem. We are concerned here with his conversion experience and with the change it wrought in his life. The fact that there was backsliding which brought him eventually to the hospital later on does not alter its significance as a constructive solution of a crisis in this man's adolescent struggle. That it was representative of a well-known type of religious experience can be established at once by a reference to Starbuck's study of religious conversions.[3]

From the standpoint of our inquiry the first point to notice in considering this experience is that the period preceding his visit to the doctor was for him a time of grave peril. He was at that time a candidate for a mental hospital. He was in a state of anxiety which might easily have passed into an acute panic.

It is also to be noted that in Rudolph's own words he suffered "unspeakable worry." That is a telling phrase. It is an exact characterization of his real difficulty in the light either of Mead's social interpretation of the personality [4] or of orthodox Freudian doctrine. The realm of sex was for him something at once fascinating and terrifying. It aroused in him desires and tendencies which he could not control and of which he was afraid to speak. It had therefore remained for him unassimilated to the point of acute mental indiges-

---

[3] Edwin D. Starbuck, *Psychology of Religion* (New York: Charles Scribner's Sons, 1899), Chap. 12.

[4] According to Mead all animate life is essentially social, but what distinguishes the human from other forms of social organization is its dependence upon language. Where bees and ants co-operate because of the way they are built, the human being incorporates the social organization within himself by means of verbal symbols and co-operates through inner self-direction. Desires and cravings which cannot be put into words because they are disowned thus remain unassimilated and behave much like ill-digested food. Far from being "unconscious," they give the sufferer no peace until they are taken care of some way. Mead's theory has implications of enormous importance for the psychology and sociology of religion and will be basic to this study. It will be referred to repeatedly both explicitly and implicitly. For the best presentation of this "social interactionism" see his *Mind, Self and Society* (Chicago: University of Chicago Press, 1935), particularly Sections III and IV. See also Ellsworth Faris, "The Social Philosophy of George H. Mead," *American Journal of Sociology*, November, 1937, vol. 43, pp. 391 ff.

tion. The essence of the difficulty lay then not in some mysterious disease process but in the internalized social relationships. There was serious intrapsychic disharmony. He felt himself estranged from that which was supreme in his system of loyalties, that which for him was symbolized by the idea of God and which is operative in the lives of all men whether they recognize it or not.

It is also pertinent to our inquiry to note not only that Rudolph had reason to worry but that worry in this case served a useful purpose. It drove him to make a visit to his doctor. Not to worry in the face of a really serious maladjustment of this sort would have been the really ominous reaction. The true evil in this case was the short-circuiting of the sex drive and the consequent failure to attain to the next level of development. The "unspeakable worry" was thus not an evil but a manifestation of nature's power to heal analogous to fever or inflammation in the body.[5] The conclusion follows that the old theological doctrine which regards the conviction of sin as the first step in the process of salvation is not entirely mistaken.

From these considerations it may be seen that Rudolph went to Mr. Moody's meetings all set for something to happen. He had mustered up his courage and had gone to see his doctor. To him he had spoken of the "unspeakable worry." The cure was therefore already in process, because the real difficulty had been brought out into the open and discussed with a sympathetic physician. But this physician had advised him to try religion. All that was now necessary was the right suggestion; and that Mr. Moody gave. He talked about God's being a Father and about His being ready to forgive us for the past if only our purpose is good. This, at least, is what Rudolph picked out and remembered down through the years from among the many things which Mr. Moody said. Perhaps some other suggestion might also have served, but we may recognize in these words the essence of

[5] Many psychiatrists would not agree. I have discussed this problem at some length in my *Exploration of the Inner World*. The basic evidence will be found in Chap. I. See also my "Therapeutic Significance of Anxiety," *Journal of Pastoral Care*, 1951, No. 2.

all good psychotherapy and the essence also of the gospel of Jesus and of Paul.

In order to appreciate the significance of this suggestion, we must bear in mind that in the task of internalizing the group attitudes and values, which is essential in all education, there are two chief instruments, fear and force on the one hand and love and admiration on the other. In most cases there is a mixture of the two. In Rudolph's case there was a love for his mother, but he described her as "awfully soft." We wonder, therefore, how much he admired her and we are sure that he did not fear her. How much he loved his father is not clear, but he certainly feared him and he probably admired or at least respected him. In any case it is evident that he accepted his father's authority and that his moral attitudes were governed chiefly by fear. His was a morality of the "Thou shalt nots." It was a static rather than a functional morality.

Now the essence of Mr. Moody's message, which was derived from the teaching of Jesus, was that the universe is governed not by force and fear but by a love that looks upon the heart and is ready to forgive even to the uttermost. In the eyes of love the important thing about any individual is not what he is now but what he is in process of becoming. Even the most faulty person is good and worthy of honor insofar as he is doing the best he can with what he has to work with, insofar as he is moving to become better.[6] The insight that God is a Father and that He is ready to forgive our past if only our purpose is good thus went to the heart of Rudolph's problem. It changed the basis of his self-judgment and set him free to strive for the attainment of his true objectives in life.

Good psychotherapy depends precisely upon this principle. The psychotherapist must see the patient with the eyes of sympathetic understanding. This does not mean that he may not pass judgments. On the contrary, his first task is that of diagnosis, for which he must

[6] John Dewey, *Reconstruction in Philosophy* (New York: Henry Holt & Co., 1920), pp. 176 ff.

be an accurate judge of character. He may and often must condemn a patient. That is, he may be compelled to decide that a case is hopeless and does not warrant intensive treatment. But if he is to help the patient, he must be quick to see the possibilities of usefulness amid the wreckage of apparent failure and the promise of beauty in what seems commonplace and unlovely. He must be equally quick to see through the shams and self-deceptions which are sheltering forbidden desires and are thereby blocking growth. His task is to reinforce or to kindle the patient's faith in himself and to help him to deal honestly with his frailties, so that he may make a better job of his life. He must therefore make accurate judgments, but he must do so as a trusted friend, seeing always through the eyes of the patient.

These considerations are in line with the principle that psychotherapy is dependent upon the interpersonal relationship between physician and patient. Wherever the patient trusts the physician to talk with him about his real difficulties, and wherever the physician is able to think *with* the patient sympathetically and intelligently, results are likely to follow. Technique is of secondary importance.[7] One physician may stress dream interpretation, another free association, another moral re-education; another may even hand out advice or make use of hypnosis. The significant fact from the standpoint of this inquiry is that the evil to be dealt with in any such crisis experience as Rudolph's is the sense of inner disharmony due to the presence of some "unspeakable worry" and that in some form or other there must be confession and forgiveness. The unsocialized, and hence unassimilated, interest must be resolved and the sufferer must be able to feel himself restored to the fellowship of the best. Mr.

[7] C. Macfie Campbell, "Psychotherapy," in *Boston Medical and Surgical Journal*, September 17, 1923.

See also Otto Rank's observation: "My technique consists essentially in having no technique, but in utilizing as much as possible experience and understanding that are constantly converted into skill but never crystallized into technical rules." (*Will Therapy* [New York: Alfred A. Knopf, Inc., 1936], p. 149.)

Moody thus gave just the right suggestion. The immediate effect was a release of tension. Rudolph's wording is cautious, but it is clear that like others who have had this experience he felt himself forgiven directly by God. It was thus an experience of the mystical type. As in all such experiences it came with a tremendous emotional impact and resulted in a profound alteration of outlook and attitude. In his case the emotion was one of joy and hope and the change was for the better. He had now a new role in life. He was forgiven and he had something to live for and work for.

In order to understand the significance of this experience in its relation to this inquiry we need to look a little farther. We have seen that Rudolph, before he went to see his doctor, was a candidate for a mental hospital. We have also seen that there was subsequent back-sliding and that twenty-five years later he actually became a mental patient. We are thus reminded that crises in the struggle for personal self-realization do not always issue happily. This is something which students of religion have too often ignored. Thus Starbuck, in his important study of religious conversions, arrived at the conclusion that in a considerable number of his cases there was an eruptive breaking up of evil habits consequent upon the sense of sin and the turning of the vital energies into new and constructive channels. It seemed to be nature's way, he said, to heal the breach between the ideal self and the actual self not by lessening the conflict but by heightening it. When, however, a medical writer called attention to the fact that the sense of sin thus described was also a factor in mental illness, Starbuck did not see in this a lead to be followed up. He saw rather a charge to be refuted. He took the psychiatrist to task for claiming everything in sight and devoted an entire chapter to the attempt to draw the line between the normal and the pathological in religious experience.[8] Our inquiry is proceeding on the assumption that the mental patient has much to tell us about religion, not only in its individual but also in its collective aspects.

[8] *Op. cit.,* Chap. 13.

4. Acute Schizophrenic Reactions

The following case of acute mental disturbance represents a crisis experience which is of peculiar interest from the standpoint of this study.

The patient in question was brought to the hospital because of an attempt at suicide. He had been found in his home with the gas turned on and both wrists cut. According to the commitment papers, the motive was self-sacrifice. He wanted to relieve the world of its sin. The onset of the illness, according to the patient, was "quite long—it was a whole week." The wife states that she had not noticed anything out of the way until two days before. There had been a previous commitment thirteen years before. Then also the onset had been sudden, the disturbance severe, and the duration brief.

In appearance Oscar, as we will call him, was a stocky man of fifty-three with barrel chest and heavy muscles. When he was first seen, the disturbed condition had already passed. For one who had emerged from so searching an ordeal he showed a surprising degree of quiet self-assurance. He talked frankly of his experience in a sensible and matter-of-fact manner.

The case history showed that he was of good, middle-class Swedish stock, second in a family of nine, of whom seven were boys. All of the children lived to maturity and have given a good account of themselves.

Oscar considered himself to have been a fairly normal boy. He went through seven grades of school without repeating any grades, but his scholastic standing was only fair and he hated school. In a fight, however, he was "not so dumb." He could lick any boy in his room. After leaving school he served an apprenticeship as a mechanic and worked for a time as a journeyman. Then at the age of twenty-one he went to sea. After seven years of roving he settled down in the United States and at the age of thirty-one he married. His vocational record was excellent. His trade, however, was a highly specialized one and the assignment of jobs was determined by the union. For this reason he was often idle.

Of his sex adjustments he talked frankly. There had been the usual difficulty with masturbation in the adolescent period, but he thought it had not been excessive. While at sea he sometimes went with his mates to houses of prostitution in some of the ports they visited, but he contracted no venereal disease and apparently he kept within the limits of respectability as judged by his particular group.

His wife at the time he met her was a working girl. He became interested in her and then discovered that she came from his native town in Sweden. According to him the marital adjustments had been happy on both sides. The wife also admitted no irregularities. One inferred, however, that the home was somewhat of a matriarchy. The wife was a quick, attractive, businesslike person, accustomed apparently to having her own way. She said of him, "He always says anything I say is all right." He said of himself that he had good will-power and that whenever he wanted anything he did not hesitate to assert himself. One got the impression that he did not choose to assert himself very often.

Oscar and his wife were both brought up in the Lutheran Church. Of his early training he said that he was dragged off to church and Sunday school and that he hated it. He "never did grab anything in religion." He claimed to be something of a freethinker. In politics he inclined toward socialism. In religion he came from Missouri. He wanted proof before he was ready to believe. Neither he nor his wife was ever active in church.

According to the wife the first indication that anything was wrong was an increasing self-absorption and loss of sleep. She noticed this first on Friday. By Sunday he had become extremely agitated. He kept pacing the floor, moaning and lost in thought. When spoken to, he was irritable, especially toward her. He asked her to go away and leave him alone. This she finally did. The suicide attempt was made during her absence.

Oscar was quite ready to tell of his experience and allowed me to get it down pretty much word for word. Here is his report:

I must give it to you in order. You can't understand unless we go back to the beginning thirteen years ago. You must know how the whole thing started, how I made a sort of bet with God. I was at a socialist meeting one night. A man there spoke of Jesus and of his giving his life for others. He asked if there were not many other men who would be willing to do that.

That night I was thinking about what the socialist speaker said and that I would gladly give up my life for my family alone. In the night I was waked up and a voice said, "You must be put to the test to see if you will really give up your life." It seemed as though God were right in front of me, and the voice seemed to be God's voice, and words from the Bible came into my head. I began to feel very nervous. It seemed as though something were getting into me. I did not tell my wife. I felt she would not understand. I got up and ran out into the street in my underwear. Of course that was a very strange thing to do, but it was just like the old Greek who found out how to weigh a ship. He was in his bathtub at the time the idea came to him and he got so excited that he jumped up and ran out without anything on. You get an idea so big it just carries you away. But a policeman brought me back and I slept until eight or nine o'clock in the morning.

I think it was the same night that blood came into my mouth and something said it took almost two thousand years to produce a man like me. I had lived for two thousand years. It was just like I had gone through many generations. Sometimes I was born rich and sometimes I was born poor. . . .

About a week after that I was sent to the hospital. After that dream I was nervous. I had a feeling like when they bind up your arm and give you a blood test. I was sort of filled up. It was a queer feeling—something you don't understand what it is. I had the feeling that there were two sides and that I had to go to one side or the other in order to get salvation. . . .

In the hospital I was put in a strait jacket. The first night I had a dream. I seemed to be crucified and the whole room was full of devils. They were trying to hurt me, but I was full of power. You see I was in a delirium. I dreamed I was dead. I dreamed I was laying in the grave just like Jesus did.

In about three days my mind came back and I was released at the end of three weeks. I got along very well after that. I had steady work and there was nothing to worry about. During the last three years work has been scarce and there has been plenty of time to think. No, I had not been thinking much about religion. My wife was told at the hospital that the trouble came from reading the Bible, so I put the Bible in the attic. I didn't want to make her nervous. And I didn't go to church. The last attack came when something told me to go and get the Bible. I had started then to pray to God. I had been feeling lonesome and I had it in my mind that there is a God. Then it came to me that I had a second installment to pay. I had to finish paying my bet with God. I came then into a state of fear. Something said to me, "Are you willing to commit suicide?" And it was just like I had to do it. I turned on the gas. That was for my wife. Then I slashed my wrists, one for one daughter and the other for the other daughter. But everything I have done before came to a good end and I have the feeling that this will too. I just felt that I had to do it to keep my promise. I have the feeling now that I am a new man. All this is over. I have done my part.

No, I didn't hear anything. It's just like when you sit and think. Something comes to you. Sometimes it comes quick just like something talk to you. I suppose it comes from God. I can't see any other explanation. Yes, it came from the best part of myself.

Yes, I did say that when this came on it was just like I hypnotized myself. When I talk with a doctor I talk about self-hypnotizing. A doctor understand that. He don't understand about religion.

Did I think of myself as Christ? Yes, I guess I did. That was before I understand. You get happy and you wake up and think you are it. You get puzzled as to who you are.

My plans? I want to get to work as soon as possible and get along the same as before. I don't want to take any more of them fits. When this thing came on, I thought I was going to have to preach, but the voice said, "You was going right the way you was. I don't need you to preach. I have other men I can send to do that."

Oscar's case is typical of the acute phase of those profound disturbances of the personality which are known as schizophrenia, or dementia praecox. It is typical not in the sense that it is the usual picture, but rather in that it presents a constellation of phenomena which statistical studies have shown to be related and presents them freed to an unusual degree from complicating features.

Here is a desperate attempt at reorganization which was actually in some measure successful. It occurred in a man who had many assets and relatively few liabilities. He was well adjusted vocationally.

He was happily married and had two attractive daughters to whom he was genuinely attached. And he was unusually free from the malignant attitudes of suspicion, hostility, and eroticism. More than that, the disturbance developed quite abruptly. As in the case of Rudolph, it followed a period of preoccupation and sleeplessness and it began with an "idea so big it just carries you away." He thought that God was talking to him. Then as he obeyed the prompting to sacrifice himself for the sake of his family, he found that he was a far more important person than he had ever dreamed. He had lived two thousand years. He was one with Christ. Sometimes he had been born rich and sometimes he had been poor. A great responsibility was resting upon him, that of relieving the world of its sins. He thought he was going to have to preach, but the voice said to him, "You was going right the way you was. I don't need you to preach. I have other men I can send."

Among our excited schizophrenics ideas of prophetic mission are characteristic, and not always does the voice give such sound advice. Characteristic also is the idea that God is talking to them or that the devil is on their trail. Usually the disturbed period begins with some supposed manifestation of the superhuman which shatters the basis of their accepted beliefs and judgments. Such a patient does not know what to believe. There is utter perplexity regarding the very foundations of his being. "Who am I?" "What is going to happen?" become for him questions of life and death to which he sees new answers.

In many cases his eyes are opened to the fact that he is more important than he had ever dreamed. "It comes to him," or "something tells him," or "the voice says" that a great responsibility has been resting upon him and that his failure has brought misery to those he loves. Perhaps the entire world has been hanging in the balance, its fate dependent upon him. He has been remiss and it is now about to be destroyed; but there is still a chance to save it. To accomplish this he must sacrifice his own life. His readiness to do this is commonly followed by the sense of being identified with God or with

Christ. It may also come to him that he is about to be reborn or that he has lived before in previous incarnations.

We find such ideas in case after case in disturbances of this type. They crop out spontaneously regardless of previous indoctrination. Where we find one we are likely to find the others also. Such disturbances are to be regarded, according to my view, not as evils but as problem-solving experiences of a desperate and dramatic variety.[9]

What now was the particular problem with which Oscar was grappling? The key may be found in the beginning of the first disturbed period. He had gone to a socialist meeting and the speaker had asked if there were not other men besides Jesus who were willing to give their lives for others. That night, he tells us, he kept thinking about what the socialist speaker had said, and the question came to him, "Would you be willing to give your life for your wife and family?" It came to him that he must be put to the test.

We must, of course, be careful not to draw too many inferences from the immediate occasion of a disturbance. We know that we have to do with an accumulation of inner stresses, especially in the acute disorders, and that the upsetting factor may be the merest touch. But this factor must have some relationship to the central problem. We notice, then, that the question with which the disturbance began had to do with Oscar's relationship to his wife and family. Examining the story from this standpoint, what do we find?

The picture seems fairly clear. Here is a reasonably steady, self-reliant person who, after serving his apprenticeship as a mechanic, goes to sea. There are in this period some irregularities, but nothing which goes beyond the bounds of respectability as judged by his group. After several years of wandering he marries a young woman

[9] I have reference here to the type of schizophrenia which is usually labeled "catatonic." A more extended consideration of schizophrenic thinking will be found in my *Exploration of the Inner World*, Chap. I; and in my articles, "The Form and Content of Schizophrenic Thinking," in *Psychiatry*, May, 1942, pp. 23–33, and "Onset in Acute Schizophrenia," in *Psychiatry*, May, 1947, pp. 159–66. See also H. S. Sullivan, "Conceptions of Modern Psychiatry," in *Psychiatry*, February, 1940, pp. 1–117, especially Lecture IV.

from his native town in Sweden whom he meets in America. She is an attractive person of considerable force of character.

With his marriage, his entire manner of life is changed. He becomes now a devoted husband and father. His evenings are spent at home or at least in the company of his wife and daughters. Aside from his labor union, he belongs to no organizations. It is therefore clear that his wife is now supreme in his system of loyalties. His entire life is built around her, and his love for her has for him been a substitute for a religion.

There is in this nothing unusual. Sex love, as Professor Hocking points out,[10] is closely associated with religion. It is not that religion can be explained in terms of sex, but that sex love at its best approaches religion. Both want somewhat the same thing: union with the idealized Other-than-self. But it is also true that sex love seeks something beyond the finite object of affection and that it cannot be satisfied with the finite. This is the law which is exemplified in the old story of Dante and Beatrice. It seems fair to assume that it was operative also in the case of this simple mechanic.

It was not sufficient for him to have reorganized his life around his love for his wife. He had undoubtedly, after the manner of lovers, sworn his readiness to give up everything for her; and his picture of himself was that of a devoted husband and father. But the actualities would be sometimes a bit trying. As a rugged, self-reliant male he found it not always easy to submit to her domination. Probably he became uncomfortably aware of attitudes within himself which were at variance with the devotion he professed. The socialist speaker had asked a question which for him was a live one. We may hazard the guess that the source of strain in this case was not merely the sense of guilt due to the presence of repressed hostility so much at variance with his accepted role but also the need of achieving a higher level of adjustment. I refer to the level represented by the psycho-

[10] *Human Nature and Its Remaking* (New Haven: Yale University Press, 1923), Chap. 42.

analytic doctrine of autonomy and the Christian doctrine of the sovereignty of God.

During the fourteen years which elapsed between this man's release from the hospital and his death from carcinoma, he passed through a period of stress when he returned voluntarily to the hospital. This occurred six years later in a period of enforced idleness. He was, however, adjudged "not insane" and remained only a week. Aside from this period he worked steadily and there is reason to believe that a higher level of adjustment was in some measure achieved. Cases of profound mental disorder with clearly constructive solutions are the exception rather than the rule, but they form a continuum with cases of dramatic religious experience. They have thus great significance.

In reactions of another type the patient sees no way out. The situation seems to him utterly hopeless. He himself must therefore die; or perhaps he is already dead with nothing to hope for but rebirth. The picture then is one of depression, or stupor.[11]

In still other cases ideas of mysterious hostile forces are dominant. Ideas that evil forces are at work and that great danger is impending are common in acute disturbances, and when the prevailing attitude is one of bitterness, as in the case of our Armenian minister, when there is a marked tendency to transfer blame onto other persons and to nurse grievances and suspicions, the chances of recovery are anything but favorable.[12]

During the stormy phases of schizophrenia there may be no serious disarrangement of the thinking processes. Seeming incoherence is often due to the very quickening of the mental life, to the tendency to accept as valid all the ideas that come surging in, and to the difficulty of keeping pace with the thoughts. In such states meaning far outstrips symbol. Not only does the excited schizophrenic have to find new words to express the strange ideas which come thronging in

[11] August Hoch, Benign Stupors (New York: The Macmillan Company, 1921).
[12] H. S. Sullivan, op. cit., pp. 75 ff.

upon him, ideas for which the conventional language is inadequate, but he has no longer any language of which he is sure. Only one thing appears certain: things are not what they seem. In everything that happens he sees hidden meanings.

A patient of this type once came to me in great excitement. There was something strange going on in the ward. Every time he placed a certain brush in a certain position in the water section, someone would change it. What could this mean? he wanted to know. The answer was obvious. Another patient shared his idea that the brush meant something important, without knowing just what, and had therefore watchfully changed its position.

The way one walks, the rubbing of the nose, the crossing of the knees, the arrangement of the chairs on the ward and of the knives and forks on the table, the color of a necktie, the smoking of a cigarette are all supposed by many of these patients to have meaning. They feel themselves in a mysterious universe surrounded by friendly and unfriendly forces, and they are trying to decipher the code by which one can communicate with the friendly forces without giving oneself away to the ever-watchful enemy. This code is sought in supposedly significant gestures.

It is important to recognize that the acute disturbances, though gravely serious, are transitional. Like the conversion experience, as exemplified in the case of Rudolph, they are manifestations of nature's power to heal. They tend either to make or to break. If the problem is more or less solved, the patient returns to his normal condition, sometimes changed for the better, usually somewhat damaged in his self-esteem. In many cases there is no reconstruction. Instead the patient loses faith in himself and gives up the fight. We have then a progressive fragmentation of the personality. In other cases the personality is rebuilt on the basis of beliefs regarding oneself implanted during the disturbed period which others do not accept.

An instructive case is that of a Polish longshoreman with a superb physique and an excellent industrial record who, after a period of anxiety regarding his sexual potency, went to a Pentecostal meeting and got the "baptism of the Spirit." Within a couple of days he passed into an acute schizophrenic condition in which it was told him that the end of the world was at hand and that he was the Christ of this present age. In the hospital where he was sent he prostrated himself upon the floor with his arms outstretched at right angles to represent a cross. He performed many other symbolic acts.

From this condition he emerged in about ten days, making a recovery apparently as satisfactory as that of Oscar. He talked rationally and was even ready to laugh regarding the queer ideas he had had. But in about three weeks there was another disturbance, then another recovery, then a third disturbance. From this he emerged with the unshakable conviction that he was indeed the Christ of this present age and that a new era was at hand. Upon this new role he rebuilt his life. The strong emotion passed and he became a remarkably well-unified person, free from all bitterness and from ideas of persecution. Very striking in him was a certain quiet reserve of strength which was felt even by his fellow patients on the disturbed ward, where he was kept because of his refusal to work. But his universe was little bigger than himself. To an unusual degree his system of delusions had succeeded in preserving the integrity of his personality, but only at the cost of a really satisfactory social adjustment.

The freedom from bitterness and from ideas of persecution is unusual in such delusional reconstructions, but common to them all is the reliance upon the reasoning processes for the maintenance of the integrity of the personality and for keeping the head above water. There is in such cases no breakdown of reason but rather its accentuation. This is reflected in the coherent thinking characteristic of this type as distinguished from those cases in which the personality has gone to pieces and in which we find the "word-salads," the disjointed sentences, and the disorderly thinking so often mistakenly regarded as characteristic of all schizophrenic patients.[13]

[13] Boisen, "The Form and Content of Schizophrenic Thinking," *Psychiatry*, May, 1942, pp. 23–33.

5. MYSTICISM AND THE PATHOLOGICAL

A somewhat extended consideration has been given to these less familiar, though common, types of experience because they represent personal crisis in its most easily accessible and striking forms. They also throw a flood of light upon the social basis of the personality, upon language as a factor in personality structure, and upon the social significance of the idea of God. They tell us what happens when an individual feels himself cut off from the inwardly conceived fellowship of the best. They tell us what happens when he feels himself face to face with a social order which he regards as superior and different and when his concept of himself is radically altered. They tell us of the imperative need of organization in the personality and of faith in oneself.

In the light of these experiences we see that the idea of God stands for something which is operative in the lives of all men, even though they may not call themselves religious. It is the symbol of that which is supreme in the interpersonal relationships and corresponds closely to what Mead has called the "generalized other." It stands also to the individual in the time of his extremity for that fellowship without which he cannot live and of which his system of values is merely a function. These considerations help us to understand the emotional impact of experiences which are interpreted as manifestations of the divine. The ancient Hebrew question, Can a man see God and live? suggests that men have long recognized the destructive aspects of mystical experience as we see it in the acute disorders.[14] But they have also recognized it as constructive and have given credence to those who, like our Polish longshoreman, have emerged from such an experience with the deep conviction that they have found ultimate reality.

No little attention has been given by psychiatrists and anthropolo-

[14] The term "mystical," as used in this book, denotes an experience interpreted as direct contact with the superhuman. According to Coe (*Psychology of Religion* [Chicago: University of Chicago Press, 1916], Chap. 16), the distinguishing characteristic of the mystical is "automatisms" interpreted as possession.

gists to certain resemblances between the form and contents of schizophrenic thinking and the thinking of primitive peoples. There is, they point out, a tendency to think in concrete pictures instead of abstract ideas and a profuse employment of images and symbols. There are also certain common ideas, such as rebirth and previous incarnation, divine vocation and mystical identification, salvation through sacrifice and the tendency to believe in mysterious and uncanny forces and in possession by good and evil spirits. A number of explanations have been offered,[15] but those which seem most reasonable in the light of our findings are to be found in the meaning of the mystical experience and in the credence given by primitive peoples to their holy men.

The first consideration is the fact that mystical experience greatly enlarges the field within which intuition is valid.[16] The mystic gives relatively great weight to the ideas which come darting into his mind as compared with the organized beliefs which govern the conduct of the group. Primitive peoples do somewhat the same thing. They have not yet learned to recognize the operations of natural law and are inclined to be guided by their dreams and by their intuitive promptings, and to see mysterious and superhuman forces in all that happens. Inasmuch as acute schizophrenia usually begins with an experience which is interpreted as a manifestation of the superhuman and with the consequent breaking down of accepted beliefs, the schizophenic's reasoning will proceed upon somewhat the same basis as that of primitive men. Looking for hidden meaning in all that happens, distrusting the accepted language, he will inevitably avoid abstract ideas and will make wide use of images and symbols.

A more important factor is the prestige accorded to the shamans, or holy men, among primitive peoples. Some of these are frankly

[15] Alfred Storch, *Primitive Archaic Forms of Inner Experience and Thought in Schizophrenia*, translated by Clara Willard (New York: Nervous and Mental Disease Publishing Company, 1924). William Alanson White, "The Language of Schizophrenia," in *Schizophrenia (Dementia Praecox)* (New York: Paul B. Hoeber, Inc., 1928), pp. 323–43.

[16] Henri Delacroix, *Études d'Histoire et de Psychologie du Mysticisme* (Paris: Felix Alcan, 1908), pp. 376 ff.

magicians who exploit the credulity of their people. Commonly, however, they are persons who lay claim to psychic powers.[17] The authority they claim is that of the superhuman. This means that many of them have passed through some searching experience of a more or less schizophrenic type and have emerged with the conviction that they have tapped the sources of spiritual power. Inasmuch as experiences of this type tend to yield similar ideas among men of all ages and races,[18] we need not wonder at finding some of these ideas current among those who accept the word of the holy man and believe in his psychic authority.

We are thus enabled to understand why it is that crisis experiences of the more dramatic type are likely to have both mystical and pathological features. Because they compel men to think and feel intensely about the things that matter most there is intense religious concern, and because they may involve drastic reorganization, pathological features are likely to appear. It is a matter of no slight significance that manifestations of nature's power to heal in the realm of personality disorder are felt as something social.

It is not, however, to be inferred that mysticism is always associated with the pathological. Professor Eliot Dole Hutchinson has called attention to the fact that the phenomena of mysticism are related to the achievement of insight in the realm of religion and as such are closely related to creative thinking in other fields.

The scientist, the artist, the thinker of whatever variety, has before him a problem involving some production or decision. For months or years, it may be, this problem remains unsolved, this creative intention unfulfilled. Attempts at solution have ended only in bafflement. But suddenly, usually in a moment when work has been abandoned tem-

---

[17] G. A. Coe, op. cit., Chap. 11.

[18] C. G. Jung, Psychology of the Unconscious, translated by Beatrice Hinkle (New York: Dodd, Mead & Co., 1925); also Storch, op. cit. The interpretations of these two authors may be questioned, but the facts they present seem fairly well substantiated. We are, however, in need of additional studies of psychotic ideation in different cultures. For further studies of schizophrenic ideation in our culture, see footnote 9, this chapter.

porarily, or attention has been absorbed by irrelevant matters, there comes an unpredicted *insight* into the solution. As if "inspired," or "given," ideas arise which constitute a real integration of previously accumulated experience. An answer, a brilliant hypothesis, a useful "hunch" paves the way to artistic or scientific advance. Exhilaration marks such moments of insight, a glow or elation goes with them, a feeling of adequacy, finality, accomplishment. The content of these insights is either lost through inattention, or, if caught and held by explicit formulation in consciousness, takes full form only through subsequent verification and criticism.

Thus the pattern of insightful thinking involves a period of preparation; a period of renunciation or recession, a period or moment of insight, and a period of verification, elaboration, or evaluation.[19]

The distinction between religious insight and scientific or artistic insight is to be found in the nature of the problem which is at the focus of attention. In the case of the artist and especially of the scientist the new insight will pertain to something objective which can be more or less readily verified by others and fitted into the structure of tested and organized experience. In the case of the mystic the new insight is often intimately personal and has to do with his own role in life. It is therefore not so easily subject to verification and it involves tremendous affective reactions.

Pathological features will then be most in evidence when the problem concerns the individual's own role in life and when it is complicated by serious maladjustments and a pronounced sense of guilt and personal failure. The insights which come under such conditions have to do with the unsuspected importance of the individual and with the resources at his command. Such insights may be true, for the infinite complexity of the human being is one of the indubitable revelations of modern science, but they are likely to throw the individual off balance. He will at first be seriously disorganized, and if he succeeds in effecting a reorganization his faith in himself may not take sufficient account of his social relationships. Our Polish long-

[19] "The Phenomena of Insight in Relation to Religion," *Psychiatry* (November, 1943), VI, 347–87.

shoreman who thought himself the Christ of this present age had perhaps received the same insight which led Paul of Tarsus to speak of the Christ that lived in him. But he failed to achieve the perspective which would enable him to adjust to the world of men about him. He retired instead into a tiny world of his own.[20]

The outcome of an acute crisis experience depends upon the nature of the problem, upon the liabilities and assets of the person involved and upon the social situation to which adjustment must be made. In the case of such men as Isaiah and Jeremiah and Jesus of Nazareth, the problem upon which they were intent had to do with the fate of their people rather than with personal difficulties of their own. In such cases the vision is likely to be relatively clear and the pathological features at a minimum.

RECONSIDERATION

This chapter has shown that crisis periods tend to be associated with religious quickening. Men are naturally lazy. They do no more hard thinking than they are forced to do. In periods of normality, therefore, they do their thinking in an accepted currency of ideas, and their attention is free to apply itself to the commonplace duties of life. In time of crisis, however, when their fate is hanging in the balance, they are likely to think and feel intensely. Under such con-

[20] It is to be noted that the stages of development in acute schizophrenia resemble closely those which Professor Hutchinson recognizes in normal insightful thinking. We find in common a period of preparation or frustration, an unpredicted insight which comes as "inspired," or "given," and carrying authority because of the way in which it comes. We find also a period of elaboration and criticism represented in the flood of new ideas and the consequent strain upon the critical faculties. What is not so clear is the period of "renunciation," or "recession." Instead of the temporary turning of attention to irrelevant matters we have in the schizophrenic experience a period of narrowed attention and intense preoccupation. The explanation may be found in Professor Hutchinson's suggestion that the temporary giving up of the problem which he finds in normal creative thinking serves as a protection against mental unbalance. It would follow then that the schizophrenic condition results when in some desperate problem-solving effort the creative intuitive forces take possession at the expense of the organized self. (See Boisen, "Onset in Acute Schizophrenia," Psychiatry, May, 1947.)

ditions new ideas come flashing into the mind, often so vividly that they seem to come from an outside source. Crisis periods have therefore creative possibilities. They are also periods of danger. They may either make or break.

Crises are likely to arise in the normal course of development. Coming of age, getting married, birth of children, and bereavement are experiences which few persons escape. And few escape more or less serious situational frustration. The more serious crises are those resulting from inner stress and maladjustment in which the sense of estrangement from the inwardly conceived fellowship of the best is the primary factor.

The emotional disturbance which often characterizes such experiences is not to be regarded as an evil, even when it becomes definitely pathological. In the face of difficult life situations and serious personality maladjustments, the really malignant reactions are those of withdrawal and concealment in its various forms. Anxiety and self-blame, insofar as they represent the honest facing of the facts, are likely to result in constructive solutions, even though they may induce actual psychosis. Such disturbances may be regarded as manifestations of nature's power to heal. They are characterized by marked religious concern and, when severe, by a constellation of ideas which crop out spontaneously, apparently without regard to the individual's particular culture: ideas of death, of rebirth, of previous incarnation, of cosmic catastrophe, of cosmic identification, and of prophetic mission.

Pathological experiences are frequently attended by religious concern, and religious experience of the dramatic type by pathological features. This is explained by the fact that both may be attempts to solve some difficult and vital problem. When the outcome is constructive, we are likely to recognize it as religious experience. When it is destructive or inconclusive, we call it "mental disorder."

The outcome of an acute disturbance is dependent upon the assets and liabilities which the individual brings to the crisis experience. The nature and value of the insights which come to him will depend upon the problem with which he is grappling and upon his own previous preparation.

In these considerations we have the key with which to approach the problem of religion in its relation to personal and social organization.

V. *Economic Distress as Social Crisis*

1. THE RISE OF THE PENTECOSTAL SECTS IN THE 1930's

This chapter undertakes to show that social crises are subject to the same laws which govern personal crises. They also are periods of stress and danger. They also are likely to be marked by religious quickening in accordance with principles which help to explain the rise of the Holiness sects in Blankton.

We may begin by noting that the rapid growth of these Holiness sects coincided roughly with the economic depression of the 1930's and that there was in this period no demonstrable increase in mental illness.

It was anticipated that following the crash of 1929 there would be a considerable increase in the number of mental breakdowns. Such, however, was not the case. There was indeed an increase in the number of hospitalized patients, but not more than could be accounted for on other grounds, such as the greater difficulty in hard times of supporting nonproductive members of the family group and the further difficulty of finding employment for patients who had improved and were ready to go out. Such factors would increase the number of commitments and decrease the number of discharges sufficiently to explain the increase in hospital population.[1]

On the other hand, the Holiness sects grew rapidly. In a decade in which the old-line Protestant churches showed an 11 per cent decrease in membership, from 26,000,000 to 23,000,000, the Holiness sects of the more sedate variety increased 50 per cent and the more

[1] Paul O. Komora and Mary A. Clark, "Mental Disease in the Crisis," *Mental Hygiene* (April, 1935), XIX, 289–330.

radical Pentecostal groups more than trebled. According to the
United States Census they grew from 88,000 in 1926 to 298,000 in
1936.[2] The aggregate membership may not have been large but the
growth of these sects was nonetheless sufficient to cause much concern in the minds of the leaders of the older churches. They wanted
the explanation of this growth. They took it as an indication of needs
which were not being met by our major churches. It was thus that I
found myself drafted for the task of investigating the situation.

The Holy Rollers, with whom we are here particularly concerned,
are sects which cultivate an extreme form of mystical religion. They
belong to the general group of Holiness sects, holding in common
with them the doctrine that in addition to the experience of "conversion" the true Christian must also have the experience of "sanctification." They speak of this as the "second blessing." As distinct
from the other Holiness sects, the Holy Rollers believe that it is also
necessary to be "baptized by the Holy Spirit" in accordance with the
account of the Day of Pentecost as given in the Book of Acts. For
this reason the word "Pentecostal" appears frequently in their official
names. Evidence of this baptism of the Spirit they find in the phenomena of "speaking with tongues."

In the pursuance of my assignment, I chose certain limited areas
for special study, being guided by two considerations. In the first
place, at the time I undertook the study, no recent religious census
was available. The use of sample areas seemed, therefore, the best
means of getting some idea of what was happening. In the second
place, I have long been convinced that it is impossible to understand
such groups except as we see them in operation in a particular setting.
Census figures and denominational year books are useful, but they
remain lifeless except as they are supplemented by an examination

[2] The census report for 1936 is to be accepted with caution. The figures were
secured through reports from individual churches obtained by correspondence
and the returns were far from complete. It is thus generally agreed that the decreased membership in the major church bodies is due to the incomplete reports
rather than to an actual falling off. However, if the reports from the older established churches are incomplete, those from the loosely organized Pentecostal
bodies would be far less complete.

of the functioning organizations and of the persons who compose them.[3]

My sample areas indicate that the actual growth of these sects has been far greater than the census reports indicate. Out of a total white Protestant church membership of 98,000 in the sample areas,[4] there were 11,000 who belonged to the Holiness group, and of that number 6,200 were Pentecostals. In other words, in the areas studied the Holiness membership was about 11 per cent of the total white Protestant church membership, or more than three times what the census report indicated.

The spontaneous character of this movement is an outstanding impression which has remained with me.

There are indeed several strongly centralized organizations which conduct a vigorous missionary campaign and even make use of high-pressure salesmanship. The leaders are generally men of limited education but real earnestness and often of considerable ability. Some of them derive their support from the organization, but many of them, particularly the local leaders, earn their living in other ways.

While the form of organization is usually patterned after that of

[3] According to the *Year Book of American Churches* for 1953 the present membership of the Pentecostal sects is now well above 1,200,000, at least if the Negro groups are included. The larger bodies include the Assemblies of God with 370,000 members, the Church of God (Cleveland, Tenn.) with 127,000 members, the United Pentecostal Church with 125,000, the Church of the Foursquare Gospel with 78,000 and the Tomlinson Church of God with 56,000. The largest Negro body is the Church of God in Christ with 328,000. There are a number of smaller bodies and many "Free Pentecostals" which have no national organization.

The other Holiness groups have an aggregate membership of about 600,000. Their larger bodies include the Church of the Nazarene with 243,000 members, the Salvation Army with 230,000, the Church of God, Anderson, Ind.) with 110,000, and the Christian and Missionary Alliance with 56,000. There are also a considerable number of loosely organized "Bible churches," "gospel tabernacles," and "interdenominational tabernacles" which are usually of the Holiness persuasion.

[4] These sample areas included Gibson County, Tenn., Coles County, Ill., Monroe and Lawrence counties, Ind., Chester County, S.C., Lee County, Ala., Vernon and Stone counties, Mo.; also Springfield, Mo., Princeton and Richmond, Ind., Cleveland, Tenn., and Athens, Ohio.

the Methodist Church and much authority is given to the leaders, these Pentecostal sects are essentially laymen's movements. They believe with George Fox that to be bred at Yale or Princeton is not sufficient to fit and qualify a man to be a minister of Christ. Their leaders are drawn from the ranks of the laymen. Throughout it is the zeal of the laymen which carries the burden of the work. As in Blankton, these sects spring from the common soil of human nature and are to be regarded as the spontaneous expressions of the religious fervor of the common people. Most of the members tithe conscientiously and make many genuine sacrifices in behalf of their cause.

Of particular interest are the innumerable Free Pentecostal groups that are scattered throughout the country. These have no national organization. Someone gets a call and gathers unto himself some followers. His organization grows and perhaps gives birth to other organizations and other calls to preach. In many cases a Free Pentecostal organization owes its existence to the fact that some would-be preacher is not recognized by the existing organizations as the tendency develops to raise the educational standards of their ministry.

According to the yearbooks of several of the Pentecostal bodies, they began with a great outpouring of the Spirit, which started in Texas in 1901 and then moved to Los Angeles. There in 1906 there was an especially great awakening with evidences of "Pentecostal power." This outpouring of the Spirit resulted in the formation of a number of groups of believers who took different names, such as the Apostolic Faith Assembly, the Full Gospel Assembly, and the Assembly of God. The Free Pentecostals are probably to be regarded as the continuation of this process, and the national organization as amalgamations of spontaneously formed smaller groups of kindred spirit. The Nazarenes thus were made up of eight distinct organizations which originated in the 1890's through the influence of the Holiness movement in the Methodist Church. The Assembly of God likewise is said to have sprung from the union of a number of independent revivalistic congregations, most of which sprang up during the Roosevelt panic of 1907.

The congregations which one sees in most Pentecostal gatherings are relatively youthful. Time and again I have been struck by the small proportion of gray-haired persons among them. Clearly they were drawn from the working classes. A considerable proportion of them seemed to be country people who had moved into town to work in shop or factory. Among them were many fine types: attractive women, and men of rugged physique, clean-cut features, and pleasant expression.

2. WHAT THEY TEACH

The doctrines one hears in the Pentecostal services are those of orthodox Christianity. These doctrines may not be expressed in systematic or scholarly fashion, but they are implicit in all of the preaching. To these sects the Bible is the literally inspired Word of God. Jesus is God, born of a virgin. He died for our sins in order to free us from the wrath to come. Man himself is totally depraved. There is no health in him and no hope of salvation except through conversion and regeneration.

Although arising among the underprivileged and rooted in the social and economic injustices of our present-day civilization, the Pentecostal sects concern themselves not at all with the problem of social betterment. They are not seeking to save the world but to save individuals out of a world which is getting worse and worse. They believe that the second coming of the Lord is near at hand and in their preaching they have much to say about the signs of the times. In any case salvation for them has to do largely with the life to come. In the convention of the Church of God in Chattanooga, Tennessee, nine of the eleven hymns used in one evening service had otherworldly themes. Among them were the following first lines: "That home of the soul over there"; "When we cross the great divide"; "Somebody's going to be left behind." At one point a girl of seven sang as a solo "I'll never feel at home in this world any more." An examination of the hymnbook showed that 75 of its 170 hymns related to the future life.

Occasionally one hears derogatory reference to education and educated people. Here, for example, are some remarks I picked up in a Negro Pentecostal meeting in Boston thirty years ago:

Say, you know we Holiness folks don't fit in nowhere. It's cause we've got Jesus in us.

Paul was an educated man, but these men we are talking about was ignorant men. Jesus chose twelve ignorant men and only one educated man. Not many wise, not many mighty are called. God will take a man from out of the gutter and clean him up and set him before kings.

We're farther from God today than ever. What did we see in the war? Priests and ministers on both sides standing up and asking God to kill the other side. And they were educated men! German priests and ministers asking God to kill Englishmen and Frenchmen and Americans; and French and English and American priests and ministers asking God to kill Germans. What was God to do? And they were educated men!

You see the trouble is today that every dog is after his own tail. The Irish is stuck on his self. The white man he look out for his self and the black man for his self. And the Japanese, he stick out his chest and look out for his self. Education does not keep people from being fools.

For the most part the emphasis is ethical and practical. The following testimonials given in another Negro Pentecostal meeting in Boston are fairly representative.

A young Negro woman is speaking:

I praise God tonight because I've been an overcomer all day. You know, I used to work in a hotel and there every day we had to punch in so's to get our pay. I feels like punchin' in tonight so's to get my reward. I want to bear witness that I've lived a righteous life today and I'm so happy. It's a wonderful thing to have God in a good humor with you. When Jesus came to me the praises just leaped from my lips and I didn't seem to have nothing to do with it.

An older woman follows:

I feels like punchin' too. I want to bear witness that I've done my part. I've got the power. Hallelujah, Jesus. I've got the power of glory.

Another elderly woman gives her testimony and closes with this admonition:

Without holiness no man shall see God. We can't drink whiskey and do this and that and receive the Holy Ghost. But God has the power to save from all sin. God can take a man who is a drunkard and this thing and that thing and pick him up and clean him up.

The next speaker is a young Negro man:

I want to praise God tonight 'cause work don't take the joy of the Lord out of my soul. . . . Some of us here tonight, if we hadn't come here, might be locked up now in that big hotel they keep down on Charles Street. It don't worry me, what they call me, "Holy Roller," "Holy Jumper," anything they like, so long as they put the holiness in. . . . I used to be a Roman Catholic. For five years I studied how to go round and hold up the priest's coattails. . . . Lots of people let father and mother work hard and save money to send them to college and then they don't come out nothing but educated fools. I praise God tonight 'cause He taught me. I went to the Holy Ghost college.

It is to be noted that for at least one of these speakers holiness was not the assertion that they were free from faults. It was rather the assertion that "we must not sin. We can't do this thing and that thing and have the Holy Spirit."

At a somewhat more sophisticated level the holiness doctrine has reference to a permanent change of heart. The conversion experience means the obtaining of pardon and peace, but it does not free the convert all at once from the old nature. This keeps rising up against him until the "second blessing" comes. This is a state of grace in which one is freed from the consciousness of willful transgression to strive for the overcoming of his imperfections.

It is important to recognize that the doctrine of holiness, which is common to all these groups, is primarily a matter of religious experience. These people are commonly austere in their piety. They forbid such amusements as card playing, dancing, and theatergoing, but they are not interested in virtue for its own sake. They are interested rather in that sense of fellowship with the Greater-than-self which we call "mysticism." Their austerity is either just a means toward obtaining and keeping that experience or else an expression of their faith in the potency of that experience.

While rigidly conservative in their doctrinal position, these sects are anything but conservative in spirit. They are made up of persons who are taking their religion in earnest, persons who are seeking or who believe that they have found new sources of spiritual power. For many of them it is no easy course which they have chosen. It has meant for them a defiance of convention, a break with the past, a venturing forth upon uncharted seas. They are radical mystics, but, as often happens, their mystical experiences have given emotional validation to traditions familiar from childhood, traditions to which most men merely pay lip service. Ask them what religion means to them, and their answer will be in substance, "We have found God. We know through our own experience that He lives and works today just as much as ever He did."

3. The Experiences They Value

Among the various groups there are differences regarding evidences of the work of God. Some lay great stress upon divine healing. The Tomlinson Church of God, for example, in its general convention in Cleveland, Tennessee, makes the healing service the feature of the week. However, the major emphasis is mostly on salvation from sin, on the healing of the soul rather than the body. All of them find the supreme evidence of the divine presence in the sense of release from the burden of guilt and in experiences interpreted as possession by the Holy Spirit. The Pentecostals have the peculiar belief that the presence of the Holy Spirit is manifested by the phenomenon of "speaking with tongues." This is accompanied by other abnormal manifestations such as dancing, jumping, jerking, thrusting up the hands, falling on the floor, and even passing into a state of unconsciousness.

The significance of the experiences which they thus value and cultivate may best be revealed by looking at them through the eyes of one of their converts.

The man in this instance was a middle-aged white man of no little ability and fair education who held a responsible job and served as deacon and also as Sunday school superintendent in a fairly strong Congregational church in New England. Dropping in one evening at a Negro Pentecostal mission, Mr. T. became deeply impressed. He continued to attend and finally he himself had the experience of being baptized by the Spirit. This experience he valued so highly that he wrote a lengthy account of it under the title of *My Baptism* and published it at his own expense. A member of the mission gave me a copy. Here are some extracts:

They came forward at once, some twenty of them (in response to the altar call) and kneeled about the altar, and then began the strangest prayer I have ever experienced. Some one began singing, "Savior, lead me lest I stray"; others joined in and the song seemed finally to dissolve in a prayer of many voices, mingled with groans, moans, shouts and cryings and the fantastic musical wail so peculiar to the colored race. This prayer lasted about twenty minutes. It was brought to a close by an ardent prayer from the black man on the platform. When they arose their faces were beaming with joy. Some one started singing, "Who shall abide in thy tabernacle? He that walketh uprightly and speaketh the truth in his heart." It was begun by a voice a bit out of tune, but taken up by the others it soon improved in tone and form, and with the staccato of clapping hands and the even tinkling of tambourines it became rhythmically irresistible. Again and again they sang it with swaying bodies and beating feet, gaining in power amid the shouts of "glory." Suddenly a woman on my right shouted, "Praise him! Praise him!" Jumping up she began to dance, seemingly without thought as to any one's opinion of the propriety of the act. I was convinced that she was in the grip of some outside power, for she was of such ample proportions physically as to preclude such exhibition under normal conditions. One after another joined her until a dozen were on the floor singing and dancing until the place rocked with their joy.

Then came the testimonies. The first to speak was a young colored woman, who said, "I want to praise God for his wonderful way with me. I used to be in the world and loved to dance and play cards and go to the theatre and such like, but praise God, He has changed my life— Glory to Jesus. He has saved my soul from hell through the blood of the cross, and not only that, but He healed my body. I followed the world and its pleasures so hard that I was taken sick. The doctors said one of my lungs was gone and my case was hopeless. I became a mere skeleton, but—Glory to God—I took my case to Jesus and he healed me, Halle-lujah, Praise Him—He surely can put flesh on the bones." And she surely looked it!

Well, one by one they testified to the knowledge of a walk with God. From the first I felt wonderfully at home in that humble room. The voices seemed to ring true. Men clearly of little education (as the term goes) preached sermons that were marvels of pointed truth and convinc-ing power, and sinners came forward during the preaching and knelt at the platform, calling upon God.

On one occasion an ignorant colored woman (as the world counts wisdom) addressed the meeting and under the power of the Holy Ghost she broke forth with the marvel of an unknown tongue, a tongue that the intelligent observer could easily perceive was classic. Although I could not understand the utterance, I detected at once its Latin origin. When this demonstration ceased, the sister said, "Now you all know that wasn't me. I can't speak my own language right, much less a foreign one. That wasn't me. That was the Holy Ghost." The leader then called for an interpreter. A sister rose and said, "I am not an interpreter but I can speak the Spanish language and the sister spoke in that tongue. I didn't get it all, but the last phrase was, Glory to the precious name of Jesus."

After two months of faithful attendance at this little mission, Mr. T. finally responded to the altar call. Two evenings later he was back again in the mission, going through a terrific struggle. He describes it as follows:

Praise God's great name forever. The prayers of the righteous prevailed that night; for the struggle ceased and Satan was defeated.

I remember that I lay face downward on the floor, my left hand be-neath me. I have the habit of drumming with my right hand during family prayers on the chair seat. I began to do it then, moderately at the beginning, then faster and faster until the beats became unthinkingly rapid. Then the movement of my hand changed. I struck my forehead with my open palm—slowly at first but increasing in force and rapidity until it seemed that my head would be beaten in. Just at the point where seemingly I was killing myself a strange thing occurred: I lost conscious-ness. How long I remained in that condition I do not know, but this I do know, that in that interval the power of God possessed me entirely; for upon regaining my understanding and feeling, I was flat on my back— my legs and my arms at 90 degrees with my body, even as Jesus was on the cross—for had I been nailed to that blessed floor, I could have been no more powerless to move.

My eyes were still closed but a light was blinding them even through closed lids and through the white radiance there shot and leaped tongues of yellow fire apparently just above my head. After a little while the flames died away and I was permitted to open my eyes. I imagined myself in another world, but as my vision returned, I saw the old rusty stove pipe and I knew that I was in the House of Prayer. I saw that I was surrounded by shining black faces, lighted up as it were by the glory of God.

Then I said, "So this is it—well, praise God—Holy, Holy, Holy, Lord God Almighty." Then I began to have intervals of liberty—for waves of glory swept over me and when they came I praised God with a loud voice and in the spirit I clapped my hands and rejoiced. I should judge that I was under the spell of that holy joy for, say, twenty minutes.

For the first time in my life I knew the inexpressible rapture of being entirely controlled by the power of God and it was wonderful past describing.

After a long and glorious season of uncontrollable praise, there came a gradual subsiding and a blessed quietness and in that holy calm I gave honor to the new power, the Holy One, in words that I formed not and which I shall never forget—"Wonderful, wonderful, wonderful, wonderful; the Holy Ghost, the Holy Ghost, the Holy Ghost; praise Him, praise Him, praise Him, praise Him; glory, glory, glory to God!"

After several minutes of this wonderful manifestation of God's great power, the speaking ceased and there reigned a heavenly peace—such peace as I had never known.

At that time, as if to superprove the experience and have it fit exactly into the Acts account, a remarkable thing occurred.

Still in a fixed position on the floor, still controlled by the blessed Spirit and powerless to move, I heard the door open and, bending my head, I saw two policemen enter. One of them, a sergeant, said, "What's going on here? It's quarter past two and you're disturbing the peace." Brother R. replied, "This is a Christian meeting." "Christian," said the officer, "I'm a Christian, but I never saw anything like this."

You remember how some of the people explained the strange demonstration that followed the descent of the Holy Ghost in the Acts account. They said, "They are filled with new wine." Listen to the record two thousand years after Pentecost.

The sergeant turned to me and said to Brother R., "What's the matter with this man?" Brother answered with quiet impressiveness, "He is filled with the Holy Ghost." "Filled with jakey," was the sergeant's quick reply!!! Hallelujah, Glory to God! How I laughed and how the saints laughed when we heard that A.D. 33, the ignorant ascribe the demonstration to new wine, A.D. 1921, the ignorant claim it is "jakey" (drink based upon the alcoholic contents of Jamaica ginger). Praise God, the power is just the same today. He brings the experience down to date with a current term. Well, glory to God! There were no arrests that night. The policemen could not stand the power and very shortly they went out into the night.

This account is given in considerable detail because it reveals with unusual clarity the nature of the experience on which these sects place such high value and the presuppositions which underlie that evaluation. Mr. T. was convinced that the fat woman who danced must be in the grip of an *outside* power, that the woman who spoke with tongues was actually speaking correctly a language which she did not know and was, therefore, possessed by a superior intelligence, and that he himself had been *entirely controlled* by the power of God because he found himself doing things he could not otherwise account for. The experience "fills him with rapture." He finds it "wonderful past describing."

Although this happened to be a Negro group, their service, as Mr. T. describes it, is typical of the white Pentecostal meetings I have visited. There is action from beginning to end, and it is in large part a musical performance. The Negroes have perhaps a better sense of harmony and rhythm than the whites, but they are all musical. Even the sermon is a musical performance. It does not matter so much *what* is said as *how* it is said. The singing voice is used, and while the preacher is holding forth the congregation maintains a musical accompaniment of "Amens" and "Yes, Lords."

The general prayer is said by all, each person praying, or singing, after his own fashion. Sometimes the effect is that of a discordant babel, but sometimes the voices blend and harmonize. The testimonies, which constitute an important part of the service, are interspersed with spontaneous singing. Throughout there is much singing, and when these people sing they sing not only with their voices but also with their hands and their feet and their bodies. The general effect of the singing, when it is done well, gives the individual the sense of being caught up and fused with the group. The fact that Mr. T. was a musically sensitive person may help to explain what happened to him.

It is worth noting that whereas the conventional Negro churches in the city were much concerned with the problem of white supe- riority and were endeavoring to solve that problem by imitating the whites, these little missions were so convinced that they had found the greatest of all blessings that they gave little thought to the matter of racial status. And other white persons besides Mr. T. were joining their circle. Rather generally in these radical sects there is a tendency to disregard the lines of color and race. In the country at large there are several of the Pentecostal sects which are composed of both white and black. One of these is known locally as the "Holstein Church." These people have found a new basis of fellowship which means so much to them that it cuts right through caste lines as fixed as those between white and black. Most of the sects, however, like the House of Prayer, began as Negro groups.

4. WHY THEY GREW

The explanation of the growth of these new sects may be sought first of all in considerations of culture and of taste. They have been recruited from those who, rightly or wrongly, have felt that they were not welcomed in the older churches. In any case they have not felt at home in the atmosphere of the dignified service and have found the informality and spontaneity of the small believers' groups much more to their liking. And just as these people prefer "St. Louis Blues" to a Beethoven sonata or the Chicago American to the New Republic, so also they prefer "When the roll is called up yonder" to "Our God, our help in ages past." They therefore gravitate toward the culturally like-minded.

It may be added that even those who make pretensions to "culture" can perhaps feel the pull of a service in which the entire congregation is taking part all the time in song and prayer and action as compared with a service which they sit through with folded hands and sometimes nodding heads while the choir and the preacher perform for their benefit.

Another factor is the reaction against the liberalizing and secularizing tendencies in the older churches. This is indicated by the fact that the most striking development of the Holiness sects was found in a university community. Not only were the cultural differences accentuated by the introduction into the older churches of a type of service which appealed to college people, but old beliefs and practices were being abandoned too rapidly for the rank and file, especially for those who came in from the more conservative churches of the countryside.

More than that, there are certain needs which the older churches are not meeting. On a recent visit to a Pentecostal church in this college town I heard the following testimony given by a manly-looking fellow in the early prime of life: "I know what it means to be under sin. I know what it means to have your conscience gnawing at your heart. I know what it means to be wretched and miserable. I know what it means to be delivered and to have the burden lifted and your heart flooded with joy and hope. I know what it means to have God talk to you just as He talked to the old prophets. I know you can be led of God and that He can guide you in every little bit of thing. Yes, my friends, I can testify that God lives and works today just as much as ever He did."

It was easy to see that this man was speaking straight out of his heart to the hearts of many who were present. They were people who knew what struggle meant, people who felt themselves beset with dangers both within and without. The testimony which this man gave is the message of the Pentecostal churches. They proclaim individual salvation from sin. They deal with a problem which for multitudes of men and women is still a matter of life and death. Their message may be something in the nature of a ready-made formula which is applied to all alike. It is certainly treatment without diagnosis. But at least it is treatment. The Pentecostal churches have some message for the soul that is sick, whereas the older churches all too often attempt neither treatment nor diagnosis.

Most important is the sense of reality which pervades the religion of these newer groups. They share the conviction that they have found God. They feel themselves able to bear witness to His presence in their own lives, as evidenced by their sense of release from the burden of guilt and by certain unusual experiences. Like Mr. T. they find themselves doing things they cannot account for, or uttering words that do not seem to come from themselves. These experiences they interpret as possession by a power beyond themselves. We may question the correctness of their interpretation, but that does not alter the fact that to many of them it gives a power to reorganize their lives and kindles in them a faith that is contagious.

Many factors thus have contributed to the rapid growth of the Pentecostal sects, but the one which most interests us in this chapter is its relation to economic distress. Their rapid expansion has been associated with the great depression which began in 1929. The constituency of the Pentecostal sects has been drawn from the underprivileged classes, upon whom the strains have fallen most heavily. And the growth has been most marked in those communities in which there has been a considerable population displacement, particularly in the Protestant South.

In an illuminating study of the distribution of the Pentecostal churches in the Southeastern states, Dr. John B. Holt has shown that they are concentrated in those counties in which there has been a marked increase in population.[5] They are least in evidence in those counties in which the population has remained stationary or has decreased. This may be explained in large part by the fact that uproot-

[5] "Holiness Religion, Cultural Shock and Social Re-organization," *Sociological Review*, October, 1946. See also Walter R. Goldschmidt, "Class Denominationalism in Rural California Churches," *American Journal of Sociology*, January, 1944.

ing brings with it the severing of old ties and makes the individual or the family responsive to new appeals. But it is also true that the population displacements in the South have been largely determined by economic distress. They are the modern counterpart of the driving out of the small white freeholders and white laborers by the disastrous competition with slave labor and the cotton gin in the early nineteenth century. It was among these emigrees from the South who settled in Kentucky and in southern Ohio and Indiana and Illinois that the revivalist movement took hold and swept the country.

The same process is being repeated today under a somewhat different form. Slavery as such is gone. But the Negroes are still in the South and the Negroes are desperately poor. They are forced to work for what they can get. In the South Carolina county which I surveyed in 1940 I found them working on the farms for fifty cents a day and furnishing their own food besides. The existence of this supply of cheap labor in the South determines the standard of living of the white worker also. To add to the difficulty, new labor-saving machinery is being introduced on Southern farms. In consequence large numbers of workers have been forced to move. They have moved into the Southern mill towns. They have also moved out to the west coast. It is among these people that the Pentecostals are chiefly to be found.

The history of the Christian Church contains not a few other instances of religious movements which started among the underprivileged in times of social stress. The early Christians themselves were such a group. So also were the Anabaptists, the Quakers, and the Methodists.

Why should periods of economic distress be marked so frequently by religious quickening? And what was the reason for the absence of demonstrable increase in mental illness during the recent economic depression?

The explanation may be found in our hypothesis that human nature is basically social; that the essence of religious experience is the sense of union with the internalized fellowship of the best; and that the essence of mental illness is the sense of isolation and estrangement from this same fellowship.

Economic distress draws attention away from the intrapsychic tensions and problems which are the primary factors in nonorganic mental illness. It may even lessen their tensions by satisfying the need for punishment. More important still, attention is drawn to the needs and sufferings of others. The sense of fellowship is increased. During the initial stages of the depression, it is said, most of the relief came from friends and neighbors. The strain was being shared and the sense of isolation thus tended to decrease. A state of mind favorable to religious experience rather than to mental illness was induced.

The fact that people suffer together through no particular fault of their own leads them in many cases to think and feel together intensely about the things that matter most. Through their suffering they are brought, like the acutely disturbed mental patient, face to face with the ultimate issues of life; the great verities with which religion deals come alive. But because the strain is shared and social support afforded, their mysticism is generally steadying and constructive.

It is thus to be noted that Mr. T.'s assumption was precisely that of Oscar in Chapter IV and of other acutely disturbed mental patients—the assumption that one is controlled, or possessed, by a power not himself. Because a prompting comes without our seeming to have anything to do with it, it is assumed that therefore it must come from a superhuman source. So striking was this common factor that when I first read Mr. T.'s story I at once thought he must surely be mentally unbalanced. When I called his pastor to inquire, he denied it. Mr. T. had indeed his peculiarities. He was a "cruel man"— cruel to all those who disagreed with him. But mentally ill? No. He had at no time been unable to carry on his work and there had been no evidence of any breakdown in personality organization.

Among those who join the Pentecostal cults and pass through such experiences there are, as we might suppose, some who become mentally disordered. I myself have dealt with a number of these. However, the amount of actual disturbance which is attributed to them is much exaggerated. In my recent study of the Holy Rollers, I took the occasion to examine the new admissions in the mental hospital which was serving in a region in which these groups were especially active. I was surprised at the relatively small number of cases in which the influence of these sects had been clearly a causal factor. Out of 249 new admissions in a six months 'period there were only 15 which could be considered at all. Closer study indicated that in these cases the disturbance was due to an accumulation of un-solved personal problems, and the influence of these sects, where it did appear, was never more than an upsetting factor.

Here also our hypothesis regarding the social basis of human na-ture is helpful. We do not say that a person is mentally ill merely because his beliefs are false. A hospital staff will look rather at the group relationships. "Delusions" would not be defined as "untrue beliefs." Delusions are rather beliefs, rooted generally in personal maladjustment and pertaining to one's role in life, which others do not share, and which thereby serve to isolate the person who holds them. If there are those who share the beliefs, no matter how bizarre they seem, the psychiatrists may shrug their shoulders but they will give the patient the benefit of the doubt.[6] Our Father Divines are not committable insofar as they have their followers. Only those are committed who become so disturbed that they cannot be handled by

[6] The first case assigned to me as a social worker at the Boston Psychopathic Hospital was that of a Portuguese cook who had been observed by a policeman thrusting up his hands in a peculiar manner on a crowded street corner in Boston. When he explained, in answer to the policeman's questions, that he had been baptized by the Holy Spirit and that the Holy Spirit was responsible for his peculiar behavior, he was promptly sent to the hospital. My task was to find out something about the group to which he belonged and about their opinion of him. When I reported that they all valued and cultivated such manifestations and that he was in good standing with them, he was at once released.

I have seen hundreds of cases brought before psychiatric staffs but I have yet to see any one committed because of peculiar beliefs wherever these beliefs were shared by even two or three others. This statement, however, must be qualified in several instances where the peculiar beliefs had resulted in violent or antisocial behavior.

their families or friends, or who have become problems by reason of beliefs which have caused them to be regarded as "queer" or different by their own group.

More important from the standpoint of this study is the steadying influence of the group. Mystical experiences come always with an emotional impact so strong that disturbance is likely to follow. But when these experiences are induced under group control, when they follow an accepted pattern, the danger of disturbance is reduced to a minimum and the constructive elements inherent in them are more in evidence. They may then bring new life and hope and tap new sources of power. This principle is important in any consideration of the interrelationship of general calamities and religious experience.

5. HISTORICAL COUNTERPARTS

In comparing themselves with the early Christians these Pentecostal people are not without justification. Not only were the early Christians an underprivileged group, but they also went in for emotional excesses. The Pentecostals are probably right in believing that their own "speaking with tongues" is similar to the "glossolalia" described in the New Testament. In both cases we undoubtedly have to do with ecstatic utterances significant because they seem to come from a superhuman source. But along with emotional excesses the early Christians had insights that went far in advance of their time. They had also wise leadership which was able to direct their enthusiasm into ethical and practical channels. And out of it came the great Christian Church.

The history of the Christian Church, as Richard Niebuhr has pointed out,[7] furnishes many instances in which the same process has been repeated. Little groups of like-minded persons, nearly always of the struggling, underprivileged classes, have come together on the basis of some new vision, some vivid sense of the presence of the

[7] The Social Sources of Denominationalism (New York: Henry Holt & Co., 1929); also Ernst Troeltsch, The Social Teaching of the Christian Churches, 2 vols. (New York: The Macmillan Company, 1931), I, 162 ff.

divine. Others have been drawn in on the basis of shared experience. Then gradually the voluntary society becomes a church. The original believers are replaced by their children and institutionalization follows. The sacraments become means of grace rather than symbols of faith. The creeds become standards of doctrine rather than statements of belief. Even religious experience itself tends to become standardized in the form of patterns which have to be induced by all sorts of meretricious devices. In general the process is one of leveling. The great prophetic, forward movements are leveled down and conventionalized. The eccentric and regressive manifestations are leveled up and become respectable.

6. Assets and Liabilities

The Pentecostal sects undoubtedly belong in the group of the eccentric and even of the regressive. Some of their fundamental assumptions are fallacious and dangerous. They believe that the divine manifests itself in the unusual and that the prompting which seems to come from without is thereby authoritative. Even though no personality disorganization may result, and even though there be no commitment to a mental hospital, these false premises are likely to produce all sorts of difficulties in groups as well as in individuals. The tendency to ascribe to a superhuman source the idea which flashes into the mind is as old as the human race and has some justification. Certainly new creative ideas do come in just this way. So also do ideas that are valueless and ideas that are false and disturbing. The error lies in the assumption that the process is the important thing. It is the same fallacy as that of the psychiatrist who is concerned because his patient "hears voices" and disregards what the voices say.

The old Christian mystics had to learn the lesson that some of the ideas which came darting into their minds could hardly come from God. They assumed that they must come from the devil. Some of us today may need to learn the converse principle that not every hallucination is necessarily of the devil. In any case we are beginning to learn that the way an idea comes is determined by the way the mind works and that the origin of our ideas is to be found in our desires and wishes. The important question is therefore not *how* an idea comes but *what* it is. To ascribe an idea to the Holy Spirit is properly to express a judgment as to its value. If, after grappling earnestly with some difficult and important life problem, one perceives the solution in a sudden flash of insight, he may be justified in believing that it comes from God. To recognize the psychological process is not to pass judgment on the ultimate origin. The latter will be determined by the individual philosophy of life with a consideration of value as the safest criterion.

But the Pentecostals go one step further. Their emphasis is so far removed from content and value that it relates to motor phenomena. To find themselves *doing* things they can't account for is for them the all-sufficient evidence of control by the Holy Spirit. More than that, they resort to very questionable devices for inducing these phenomena.

Another striking fact is that, even though the Pentecostal sects arise among the underprivileged, their religion does not concern itself with improving social and economic conditions. There is nothing in their message which goes to the heart of the problems of this sick and suffering world. They are content to let it get worse and worse. They have no social vision, no promise of salvation beyond that which is to come miraculously when the Lord returns in glory.

A further weakness is the diminutive size of the universe which their message depicts. It is only a little larger than the private world in which the psychotic lives. It has no room for all that we have been finding out about stars and atoms and plants and men. It is merely a tiny world into which to withdraw and feel secure. Such a religion may be a comfortable one for the older people. Like the delusional system of the paranoic it may give them stability. But it is not a satisfactory answer to the great problems with which religion undertakes to deal. It is not conducive to the attitude of reverence nor to the attainment of true perspective. And it is woefully hard on their children.

Yet with all their weaknesses these sects have constructive features which far outweigh the destructive and the regressive. They are manifestations of nature's power to heal. They are spontaneous attempts on the part of the common people to deal constructively with the stresses and trials which fall with peculiar severity upon them. Their unconcern with economic and social conditions which they are powerless to change and their concentration upon problems for which they are directly responsible is not an entirely unwholesome reaction. Certainly leaders of reform movements have abundant opportunity to become acquainted with other types, such as those who seek in attempts to reform the system an escape from the necessity of reforming themselves and those whose reforming zeal is an expression of their repressed hostilities.

These Pentecostal sects are bringing to many distressed individuals release from the burden of guilt. They are giving them hope and courage and strength to keep going in the face of difficulties. Insofar as the sects succeed in this, their economic and social status is likely to be raised. Insofar as they succeed in holding their young people, they are likely in time to become comfortable middle-class churches. Some of the newer sects are already on their way toward respectability. Their sincerity and earnestness are then likely to find their reward in the improvement of the individual and group status.[8]

[8] The process by which this economic advance takes place is by no means a simple one. Weber (*Gesammelte Aufsätze zur Religionssoziologie*, 3 vols. [Tuebingen: J. C. B. Mohr, 1922], I, 163 ff.), and with him Richard Niebuhr (*op. cit.*), has stressed the strengthening of morale and the effects of their asceticism in increasing productivity and limiting expenditure. The entire group would thus advance together in the economic and social scale. Pope in his study of the mill-village churches of the South (*Mill-hands and Preachers* [New Haven: Yale University Press, 1941], pp. 119 ff.) is impressed with the desire for status on the part of the under-privileged sect which leads to a cultivation of the well-to-do. According to Pope the entire group does not advance together, but the constituency itself is changed in the process. Walter Goldschmidt's careful study of class denominationalism in rural California (*op. cit.*) gives support to Pope's contention. This study leads to the conclusion that both factors are operative.

The Pentecostal sects are an expression of the same zeal and enthusiasm out of which some of the great religious movements have sprung. That these sects represent a movement which is likely to be recognized as of great importance in the history of the Christian Church seems hardly probable. They are too far removed from the best intelligence of the day. There is no evidence of a Paul or a Wesley to guide their zeal into the more constructive channels. They are nonetheless of great significance from the standpoint of this inquiry. They exemplify religious movements, arising largely under the influence of economic crisis, which are still in their creative phase. In the development of these sects we can see the creative forces of religion in the process of passing over into custom and habit.

RECONSIDERATION

The general conclusion at which we have arrived is that any genuine crisis experience is likely to result in religious quickening, and that this principle applies to social as well as to personal crises. The rapid growth of mystical sects during the depression may be explained by the fact that a considerable number of people, facing serious hardship, reacted in accordance with the Christian principles in which they had been reared. Instead of blaming others and seeking to reform the social order, they took stock of their own shortcomings. Thinking and feeling together intensely regarding the ultimate issues of life, they found their sense of fellowship deepened. Religion came alive for them. The reaction was a benign one and the appearance of mystical sects among the classes upon whom the strains fell most heavily was a manifestation of nature's power to heal. Such sects represent the creative phase of organized religion.

The psychological phenomena may be explained by the fact that periods of deep emotional stirring are fertile in ideas which come surging into the mind. The process is the same as that which we see in acutely disturbed mental patients. But when the process is induced within a social matrix and follows accepted patterns, the danger of personality disorder is at a minimum. In many cases the group itself may go off on a tangent. When, however, the intense emotion generated in such experiences comes under wise leadership, then an important and vital religious movement is likely to result. In either case a leveling process takes place. The eccentric and regressive movements are leveled up and become respectable, while the forward-looking prophetic movements are leveled down and become conventionalized.

VI. *War as Social Crisis*

AMONG the social crises which the human race is called upon to undergo there is none of greater magnitude than that of a great war. The question therefore arises, Is religious quickening likely to occur in time of war just as it does occur in time of economic distress? And if it does not appear, what is the explanation?

1. WAR'S BENEFICIAL EFFECTS

It may be recognized at once that war does produce effects which have religious value. It forces men out of old ruts and compels them to give up many stereotyped ways of thinking and acting. Now that World War II is over, the world is not going to return to what it was in 1938. For one thing, a new China is emerging. After sleeping for many centuries, Chinese civilization with its unchanging ways is being forced through the toil and agony of these terrible years to adopt the ways of modern machine civilization. Our own isolationism is also being broken up. We are being forced to recognize that we cannot live unto ourselves alone. We are being compelled to rethink our economic theories, and our entire educational and religious setup may have to be recast. All this may be for the better. Like acute types of mental illness, war tends to make or break.

In time of war the sense of fellowship is greatly increased. It may be increased to the point where the individual is carried along upon a great tidal wave of emotion. He may feel himself one with something bigger than himself and be keyed up to the point where he is able to perform deeds of heroism and self-sacrifice such as rarely occur in

95

time of peace. During a war the individual is expected to be ready to give his life and all that he has for the sake of the group, and most people respond to this expectation. This approaches religion. Over and over again in time of war religion and patriotism merge, and warring nations seek the sanction of religion for their cause. The First World War was fought to make the world safe for democracy. In the Second World War Japan claimed to be fighting a holy war to establish a new order in Asia. Many are the wars which have been fought in the name of the Church and of religion. This devotion is of the very essence of religion. Its spirit is beautifully expressed in the prayer of Ignatius Loyola: "Teach us, Lord, to serve thee in the spirit of the soldier, to give and not to count the cost, to fight and not to heed the wounds, to toil and not to seek for rest, to labor and not to ask for any reward, save that of knowing that we do thy will." [1]

War does increase the sense of fellowship; it calls forth heroic devotion; and it compels men to do fresh and earnest thinking. But

---

[1] According to all reports, this spirit was not greatly in evidence in the American army in the recent war. The great majority of the men had been drafted. They had been taken forcibly from their homes and jobs and placed under rigid army discipline to fight for objectives which were far from clear. The prevailing attitude among them was that the war was a dirty job to be finished as soon as possible. There was little of the sense that they were giving themselves for a great cause. This fact may help to explain the large number of neuropsychiatric breakdowns, most of which came not from the fighting fronts but from the camps. In spite of the attempt to screen out the psychopathic, which resulted in 1,750,000 neuropsychiatric rejections, there were in the period from January 1, 1942, to June 30, 1945, approximately 1,000,000 admissions to hospitals on the basis of neuropsychiatric disorder and 457,000 discharges from the army. Of those discharged for neuropsychiatric reasons, 49 per cent were classed as *psychoneurotic*, 10.5 per cent were *psychotic*, and 4 per cent were *epileptic*. It is to be noted that about 78 per cent of the neuropsychiatric medical discharges had seen no combat service. (John W. Appel, "Incidence of Neuro-psychiatric Disorders in the U.S. Army in World War II," *American Journal of Psychiatry*, January, 1946.)

On the other hand, at the time of the air raids in London, with all the terrific suffering which these involved, there seems to have been far less mental suffering than might have been expected.

The large number of neuropsychiatric casualties in our army is then to be explained not so much in terms of the conflict between danger and duty as in terms of difficulty, particularly in the absence of the sense of a great cause, in accepting the loss of personal identity required by the goose-stepping, heel-clicking rigidity which characterizes every military organization.

World War I was not followed by any great religious quickening. Many wars have been fought in the name of religion, but it is difficult to find any important religious movement which has resulted from war.

2. WHY NO RELIGIOUS QUICKENING THROUGH WAR?

How are we to explain this failure to carry over the deepened sense of fellowship into constructive religious movement? Does it invalidate the conclusion that social crises tend to result in religious quickening?

The following considerations should be taken into account:

a. HATRED OF OUT-GROUP

The sense of fellowship and the spirit of devotion and self-sacrifice which war engenders are limited to the in-group. For the out-group there is hatred. The army chaplain in World War I who proclaimed in my hearing that he was glad there was nothing in his religion which forbade him to hate the "Boches" was voicing a general attitude. So was the commanding general who after the Armistice called me on the carpet for daring to teach German forestry in the little school we had started in the Rhineland. I could teach as much French forestry as I chose, but no German forestry!

b. FAULTY DIAGNOSIS

This unreasoning hatred of the enemy brings with it loss of perspective and faulty diagnosis. Thinking is in terms of black and white. Everything is blamed on the enemy. No account is taken of the real evils, of the complex forces common to us all which are actually responsible for the terrible holocaust. We lose sight of our true objectives.

c. TRANSFER OF BLAME

War is a social crisis, but the prevailing reaction patterns are of the malignant rather than of the benign type. They are similar to those of the Armenian minister whom we considered in a previous chapter. This man had been the victim of a war situation. He had seen both his parents massacred. Then as a man he had been the victim of a domestic tragedy. His wife had been unfaithful. We can easily understand the bitterness within him and the sudden outburst of violence, but his reaction was nonetheless malignant. There was in his case no prospect of recovery. It is important to recognize that the bitterness which took possession of his heart drove out his religion. The same principle applies to social crises. The strong emotion of hatred may serve to maintain the integrity of the personality and the solidarity of the group, but it prevents the solution of the real problems and the attainment of the broader perspectives and enduring relationships which true religion requires.

d. FALSE ALIGNMENT

War involves a false alignment. The spirit and philosophy of life in which Christians believe is well represented among those against whom we were fighting. And the spirit and philosophy of life against which we were supposed to be fighting is abundantly represented among our own people. Here, for example, is a distinguished scholar, supposed to be an authority on modern European history, who contended that only one solution was open to us with the ending of the war: the complete destruction of the German people. His proposal was to destroy them by enslaving them and sterilizing them. It seems clear that between such an attitude and that of the Nazis there is nothing to choose. The policy he advocated was their policy and the spirit which he expressed was their spirit. He himself was thus a representative of the real enemy and far more dangerous to our future welfare because he was one of us and was giving authoritative expression to an attitude and a philosophy of life which inevitably sows the dragon's teeth. Christian is thus arrayed against Christian and the intense feeling and earnest thinking which war produces are not likely to center in principles and interests which are in keeping with the spirit of enlightened religion.

e. MILITARY VS. CIVILIAN STANDARDS

War brings with it an alteration of ethical standards. The army is in the saddle, and the army is a continuing body with a culture of its own which is quite at variance with democracy and with Christianity. For this reason the Christian principles which become operative in time of economic stress have little chance in time of war. The differing standards of war and peace, of army and civilian life, together with their religious significance, may be seen in the experience of a certain patient.[2]

At the time I dealt with him, this man was twenty-eight years of age. He had been raised in Georgia, the son of a Baptist minister. As a boy he had been a well-meaning and conscientious chap, but he had had serious difficulty in learning to manage the troublesome sex drive. At the age of sixteen he left home and went to work in a mill village. After two years he enlisted in the army, and with the uniform he adopted the army code. In accordance with that code he found a solution for his unsolved sex conflict. He had recourse to prostitutes, being careful always to report and get his prophylactic treatment afterwards. Many of his mates were doing the same thing, so he felt comfortable about it.

After nine years in the army, during which period he rose to the rank of sergeant, he married and went back into civilian life. In due course a child arrived. According to his account, there seemed to be something odd about the way his child was born. As soon as he got the news, his mind began running and jumping. A million things passed through his head. He was under a spell of fear. He felt that he had a lot of responsibility, but he was not thinking so much about the baby. He was thinking about human nature and its mechanisms. He was trying to understand the cause of all emotion, and he wrote an article expounding his theories on that subject. He sent it to a local newspaper and took great pride in the fact that it was published.

[2] This case is reported in somewhat more detail in my *Exploration of the Inner World* (New York: Harper & Brothers, 1936), Chap. VI.

The disturbance which brought him to the hospital did not follow immediately. It came a little later when things went wrong with his business; but it was essentially a continuation of the emotional turmoil which had seized upon him when he received word of the birth of his baby. In that disturbance he had a vision in which it seemed to him that he could see back to the beginning of all creation. It came to him that from the beginning of the world there had been two rulers over the peoples of the earth, God and Satan. One was just as powerful as the other. Between the two there had been a constant battle for supremacy. It came to him that there was no earthly reason why such a conflict should be kept up. He was sure that the Lord did not intend that people should be always and forever fighting each other. Then it came to him that he had a great mission in life. It was to be his task to go and see Satan and persuade him to come and meet God and to bring about a reconciliation between them. Satan would then bring all his following into the light and with this happy event the millennium would be at hand.

The meaning of this apparently preposterous idea may become clear if we bear in mind that this man's inner conflict had been a conflict between two sets of standards and that the disturbance began at the time his first child was born. He had, as he put it, two consciences. As a boy he had accepted the standards of his parents and of the church, but he had been unable to bring himself into conformity with the way of life thus required. With his enlistment in the army, he had accepted its easier sex code. Supported by this group and its attitudes, he was able to give expression to the forbidden cravings and be frank and untroubled about it. He seemed to have made a real adjustment. But with his marriage, and then with the birth of a child, the situation changed. Now he had a new role in life. He was no longer just a soldier. He was a father, and the responsibilities of parenthood identified him once more with his own father. He began therefore to think of his father's God, the symbol of that which was supreme in his system of loyalties, whose authority he had never questioned but from whom he had run away. It is clear that measured by the standards of his father and of his father's God, he would be weighed and found wanting.

But this man had identified himself with the army group and he believed in that group. Of course their standards were easier standards. They represented for him a concession to his frailties. This being the case, it is obvious that for him Satan was the symbol of the army and of its moral code. But his mates were after all good fellows. Hence his proposal. He would try to bring about an understanding between the symbolic representatives of the two groups with which he had been identified.

This man's primary loyalty had been to his parents and to other early guides upon whom he had been dependent for love and protection and whose generalized impress had determined his idea of God. Failing to measure up to the standards which he had thus accepted, he had made a temporary adjustment by identifying himself with a group in whose plan of life race perpetuation was of secondary importance. The conflict was precipitated by the experience of fatherhood, which brought the matter of race perpetuation to the fore and therefore required reconciliation with what in his social experience represented the abiding and the universal.

War brings with it an alteration of ethical standards through the ascendancy of the military way of life and the different goals which are in the forefront of attention. In time of peace our standards are determined by the ideal of family integrity and by the requirements of living and working together in friendly relationships. Emphasis is placed upon the virtues of honesty, truthfulness, tolerance, kindliness, sobriety, self-control. In time of war the paramount objective is that of winning the war by inflicting the greatest possible damage upon the enemy, while at the same time maintaining the organization and strength of the in-group. Emphasis is placed upon the virtues of courage, obedience, self-sacrifice, and efficiency, and the virtues of civilian life take a back seat.

War always means the cheapening of human life and giving free

rein to cruel and vengeful tendencies.[3] Here, for example, is an incident which came under my observation in World War I. The scene is close to the Toul sector. One brigade of the First Division has just come back from the front. A little group is gathered in the Y hut while Sergeant Niemann, himself of German blood, is telling about their memorable experience. Mrs. F., the Y hostess, is drawing him out. In racy and picturesque language he tells how "those blamed frogs" led them to the front-line trenches and left them there before they knew which end they were standing on; how one of the army mules insisted on braying at a most inopportune moment; and how in the resulting excitement some one kicked over the bean pot from which they were expecting to be fed. He comes then to the first German prisoner, a nice-looking fellow who couldn't speak English. Our sergeant, however, was equal to the occasion. He was able to act as interpreter and they got some real dope. After that they tickled their prisoner with the bayonet until he died. Mrs. F.'s comment was, "You did exactly right."

Or consider a story which went the rounds in the Forty-Second Division about a batch of twenty-four German prisoners taken by the "Alabams." They were sent to the rear. When they reached their destination, only four of them were left. The guards had drawn cards on the way back to decide which one they would shoot next.

Such stories could be multiplied. It is not to be assumed that they were true. Many soldiers like to masquerade as hard-boiled heroes. Nevertheless they represented a widespread attitude, a bloodthirstiness which was perhaps more pronounced among the women—at least it seemed so to hear them talk—than among the fighting men. Human life is cheap in wartime and the Germans were not alone in the committing of atrocities. Neither were the Japanese.

It is not pleasant to remember what happened to our standards of truthfulness. In the regiment I was with, it was the custom for the captain to regale his men at review with the latest batch of

[3] For a penetrating analysis of the military way of life see Meyer H. Maskin and Leon L. Altman, "Military Psychodynamics," *Psychiatry*, August, 1943.

atrocity stories, most of them manufactured out of whole cloth by some Allied agency. The purpose of these stories was to incite the men to hate the enemy. Propaganda was developed into a fine art and recognized as an instrument of warfare. I recall a conversation at Brest, while we were waiting to go home. The question under consideration was what had happened to our President's Fourteen Points. There was general agreement that they had been completely ignored in the Treaty of Versailles. The question at issue was whether there had ever been any intention of observing them. Some of the officers present, including a West Point colonel, held that they had never been intended as anything else than propaganda designed to weaken the German morale. And propaganda is used not merely to deceive the enemy and to win over neutrals but, most of all, as a means of control over one's own people.

The conclusion is that war inevitably brings with it a limited outlook. The deepened sense of fellowship which it engenders is confined to the in-group. The serious thinking is directed to immediate objectives and is distorted by powerful emotions. There is a marked tendency to think in terms of black and white, to magnify the motes in the eyes of the enemy and to ignore the beams obscuring our own vision. War breeds hatred and hatred bars the door to love and truth. For this reason the social crisis which war represents increases the spirit of patriotism but does not give rise to vital religious movements.

3. HEBREW PROPHETIC RELIGION AN EXCEPTION

One important exception, however, must be made. This is to be found in the development of the Hebrew-Christian religion.

In the beginning the Hebrew religion was a tribal one and Jahweh, the Hebrew God, was a war god. He was supposed to have chosen the Hebrews from out of all the peoples of the world to be His people and to have made with them a covenant. According to that covenant they were to have no other gods but Him, and they were to obey His commandments. If they did this, all would be well with them. If they disobeyed they would perish.

But the Hebrews met with national reverses. They were defeated in war. Their leaders were taken captive. The burning question therefore arose, What is the reason for these misfortunes? It was this question which was laid upon the hearts of the great prophets. In seeking the answer they were carried down into the depths of despair and anguish. They seem to have passed through states which must have approached psychosis, in which they stood face to face with an approaching day of doom and felt themselves commissioned as spokesmen of the Lord. The answer which they found was this: It is because of our sins that we are suffering. Jahweh is angry with us, and the Assyrians and the Babylonians are merely instruments in His hands. But Jahweh is a God of love as well as of justice. If therefore we repent and turn from our evil ways, a remnant will be saved.

A question may be raised regarding this conclusion of the prophets. The Hebrews were a small nation and they had greedy and powerful neighbors. It is hardly probable that even perfect obedience to the commandments of Jahweh would have saved them from the neighboring war lords. The important consideration is that their answer represented a benign reaction. As a rule, the patient who blames himself has a good chance to recover. At least, he has a far better chance than the man who dwells on his grievances, blames others, and finds alibis for his mistakes. So also with nations. In so far as the difficulty is outside ourselves, there is little we can do about it. If it is within us, we can deal with it. And so the great Hebrew prophets, in directing attention to the evils within their own gates and seeking to correct those evils, were leading their people in the way of life.

In Second Isaiah a far more penetrating answer is found. It is not, says that prophet, because of our sins that we are being punished. There is a deeper meaning in it all. Our suffering is for the healing of the nations. Israel is the righteous servant of the Lord and upon him is laid the iniquity of all. Through his suffering all shall be saved. We must therefore patiently endure this suffering in order that the promise may be fulfilled that in Abraham all the nations of the world may be blessed.

The sense of special mission was thus forged by the great prophets in the furnace of suffering.[4] It was fixed by Ezra and Nehemiah and the priestly group through ritualistic regulations which set them apart from other peoples.

Through Jesus of Nazareth the profound insight of Second Isaiah was carried forward to its climax. He also, like the great prophets before him, was concerned over the destiny of his people and the suffering and humiliation to which they were being subjected. And he also, like Second Isaiah, interpreted this suffering in terms of a divine, redemptive purpose, coming thus to the conclusion that the long-cherished hope of a place in the sun must be given up. The recognition of this necessity may well have been for him as the experience of death, but he came through with a new hope and a new message. Through him, and through his sacrificial death, the religion of the Hebrews became world-wide in its scope.

The task was completed by the apostle Paul, whose great achievement it was to free the religion of Jesus from the ritualistic, racial fetters which would have kept it a small sect within the Hebrew religion. It is perhaps not without significance from the standpoint of the problem of war that the man through whom the religion of Jesus was made world-wide was a representative of Jesus' enemies. Paul thus may be regarded as the answer to the prayer on the cross.

If the objection should be raised that the Hebrew-Christian religion developed not out of a war situation but out of defeat, we may note that the tendency to hate and blame the enemy is far greater among a defeated people than among the victorious. It is therefore all the more remarkable that a defeated and humiliated people should cling so tenaciously to the faith in their divine destiny and should at the same time refuse to blame their enemies

---

[4] It is not to be assumed that the Jews were free from bitterness. The Psalms furnish abundant evidence that such was not the case. The great prophets were rather trail blazers who represented religious insight at its best and who succeeded in winning an important following.

for their sufferings, searching their own hearts instead and seeking to correct their own shortcomings. This is something which has happened all too seldom in history. We seem therefore justified in concluding that the Hebrew-Christian religion, as represented by its great prophets, has something to teach us in the matter of dealing with the problem of war, not only in defeat but also in victory.

The law exemplified in the development of the Hebrew prophetic religion is not necessarily that of nonresistance to evil. Experience tells us that force is sometimes necessary for the wrongdoer's own good. But we may learn of the peril, both to the individual and to the group, of hating our enemies, of blaming our difficulties upon them and failing to recognize the evils which we alone can correct. We may also learn of the religious quickening which is likely to develop in any shared suffering when there is freedom from the spirit of hatred and blind self-deception.

RECONSIDERATION

In the case of war we have an apparent exception to the principle that crisis situations tend to be associated with religious quickening. Even though war is a social crisis of the greatest magnitude, it is difficult to find any important religious movement which has arisen out of a war situation.

The explanation may be found in the consideration that in time of war the reaction pattern is of the malignant rather than of the benign variety. The tendency is to hate and blame the enemy. There is therefore faulty diagnosis, and the real evils remain uncorrected. The comprehensive loyalty and the broad perspective essential to true religion are not achieved. A further consideration is the dominance of the military. In time of economic distress there is a tendency to react in accordance with the principles of the Christian religion in which most of our people have been reared. Not so in time of war. Not only are the attitudes of bitterness and suspicion everywhere prevalent, but the organized attitudes and virtues of the army take precedence over those of Christianity and democracy.

That the crisis of war may result in religious quickening when there is freedom from the tendency to hate and blame the enemy is shown in the history of the Hebrew prophetic religion. The great prophets explained the misfortunes of their people in terms of their own national sins and sought to correct those sins. This attitude represented a benign reaction and led to the deeper insight into the redemptive value of suffering which culminated in the life and teaching of Jesus of Nazareth.

VII. *Social Crisis and Religious Leadership*

FROM our study of the Holiness sects we concluded that they were spontaneous expressions of the religious fervor of the common people, attempts to deal constructively with the stresses and trials which fell with peculiar severity upon them during periods of economic distress and social displacement. This conclusion needs to be elaborated. It must also be recognized that the group experience must first be focalized in some individual and voiced by him before it can find expression in the form of a social movement.

This principle is strikingly exemplified in Blankton, the community considered in our second chapter. We explained the remarkable development of the Holiness sects in that community by the existence of a large number of economically distressed folk and by the presence of a large university, which accentuated the cultural differences and speeded up the process of liberalization and secularization among the old-line churches. But the picture would not be complete if we failed to take into account the factor of leadership. The influence of one man had much to do with this development.

1. THE CASE OF JOE CAMPBELL

Joe Campbell was a native of the town. As a boy he was known as a "tough." Although bright enough, he did indifferent work in school, played truant often, and ran with an outlaw gang. Fairly early in his adolescent years he began to drink and his manner of life was hardly to the liking of his pious parents. After finishing the eighth grade in his fourteenth year, he left school. His great desire at this time was to be free. He was therefore away from home much of the time, stealing rides on freight trains and getting involved in many wild escapades. He was not a bad worker, but he worked intermittently, drifting from one job to another and from one place to another.[1]

At the age of eighteen he had a conversion experience, but after three or four months he relapsed into the old ways, going from bad to worse. The drinking increased. Epileptic seizures, which had begun in his sixteenth year, became more frequent and more severe. The doctors gave him no hope. After nine very unsatisfactory years he was again converted. This time he staid put, and with his conversion he was cured of his epilepsy. He had promised the Lord to give Him all he had, and for five years he struggled with the feeling that he ought to preach, as some of his friends began urging him to do. Finally he made the venture. He took a small mission and was quite successful. The Methodists took note and offered him a conference appointment. However, it came to him that as a boy he had been an "awful rotter" and that he ought to go back home and show the people there what the Lord had done for him. He thereupon returned to Blankton and it was through his efforts that the first of the new Holiness sects was started. During his twenty-odd years of service in this town he officiated at more than eight hundred funerals and received more than two thousand persons into church membership. Always of an adventurous and fighting disposition, he busied himself with starting new organizations. He built several new churches in the country, and two in the city. After getting a new organization under way, he would turn it over to someone else and then start another.

As a preacher he had no claim to distinction, but one felt in him

[1] This story was obtained from several personal interviews with Joe, from my own early acquaintance with him, and from the president of the university, a stanch friend of his.

something of radiance and strength. Certainly there was now a sharp contrast between his present appearance and the ugly look and forbidding disposition of his earlier years. The chief factors in his influence were the dramatic change in his personal life, which has spoken louder than his words, the untiring energy with which he threw himself into his work, and the support of some of the city's leaders, including that of the university's beloved president. He ministered to the working people of the city, meeting them on their own ground, sharing their experiences, using their language. They accepted him at his own valuation as an instrument of a Power greater than himself. They listened to him and believed in him because he gave expression to vague longings of their own and called upon them to go in a direction in which they were prepared to go.[2]

Joe Campbell returned to Blankton just at a time when social conditions were ripe for change. The Methodists, the Baptists, and the Disciples had just built imposing new churches and had introduced a more formal type of service. The university was growing rapidly and was exerting an increasing influence upon the churches of the town. And the industries were expanding rapidly. This meant that people from the surrounding countryside were coming in large numbers to work in mill and factory. These people for some years fared reasonably well economically, but they were uprooted from their old associations. They did not take to the formal worship services of the old-line churches and they were ready to do something about it. Their

[2] Joe Campbell thus exemplifies Max Weber's concept of "charismatic" leadership. His influence was not due to expert training or to official position, but to the fact that in time of psychic and economic distress he spoke in the name of the superhuman and many persons accepted him in that role.

Weber contrasts this type of leadership with the "patriarchal" and with the "bureaucratic," both of which are rooted in the provisioning of the recurrent and normal needs of the workaday life.

For demands which go beyond the everyday routine, in times of distress and danger, men turn to the charismatic leader. But "charisma" as a creative power recedes in the face of the demands of routine and the compulsion of tradition and custom. H. H. Gerth and C. Wright Mills, *From Max Weber: Essays in Sociology* (New York: Oxford University Press, 1946), pp. 255–62.

readiness to act was greatly increased with the advent of the economic depression.

So it is always in social and religious movements. The ground must be prepared. Men of force, of vision, of singleness of purpose do not always get a following. Without a readiness on the part of the people to hear their particular message, they will exert little influence upon the course of human affairs. And without leadership social movements can hardly get under way.

What might have happened if Joe Campbell had not come back to Blankton at this time is something about which we can only guess. The chances are that since conditions were favorable some such movement would have been started anyway, but it might not have taken the same direction and it might not have gathered so much momentum. In a neighboring county where, except for the influence of the university, the social and economic conditions were much the same there was a similar development; but the sects which took the lead were Holiness groups of a more sedate variety and they did not gather the same strength.

2. TRADITION AND INNOVATION

It is not to be assumed that Joe Campbell brought any new social or religious message. It was rather the reverse. His was the old-time religion. His conversion experience had been induced under the influence of a Free Methodist mission in a Western city. It had followed patterns and had been based on beliefs which were accepted not only in that mission but in hundreds of others. It had been in line with the orthodox beliefs of several centuries of evangelical Protestantism. What was distinctive was his profound conviction that he had tapped anew the sources of spiritual power and had found the way of salvation, not only for himself but for others also. The problem with which he had been struggling was an intolerable sense of personal failure and danger. His message therefore had to do with his own role and that of others in peril similar to his own.

The extent to which mystical experience brings something new into the stream of tradition is a much debated question. The prevailing view among students of the psychology of religion denies the mystic's claim to new knowledge or to original ideas. Professor Coe speaks for most of them [3] when he says that the mystic brings his religious beliefs to the mystical experience; he does not derive them from it. And these religious convictions he acquires just as his non-mystical neighbor does, namely, through tradition and instruction grown habitual and through reflective analysis.

This study leads to a different conclusion. Arising out of crisis experiences and characterized by intense concentration and strong emotion, mystical experiences are most favorable to the creative processes. Their most pronounced characteristic is the abeyance of the logical faculties in favor of the intuitive.[4] In the acute disturbances this is carried to the point where the patient no longer accepts the culture patterns of his particular time and race.[5] Instead he gives undue credence to the new and strange ideas which come thronging in upon him.

Even in the less extreme forms mystical experiences are fertile in new ideas and new insights, but it is important to take into account the social conditions under which the experience occurs and the problem which is uppermost in the mind of the subject. It makes a world of difference whether the experience is a solitary one or occurs under the influence of some group which believes in these experiences, which seeks by every known device to induce them, and which accords high honor to anyone in whom they are successfully induced. It also makes an enormous difference whether the problem uppermost is that of personal salvation in the face of threatening disaster

[3] *Psychology of Religion* (Chicago: University of Chicago Press, 1916), p. 282. See also James Bisset Pratt, *The Religious Consciousness* (New York: The Macmillan Company, 1924), pp. 449 ff.

[4] Cf. Delacroix, *Études d'Histoire et de Psychologie du Mysticisme* (Paris: Felix Alcan, 1908), pp. 376 ff.

[5] Cf. John Dollard, "The Psychotic Person Seen Culturally," *American Journal of Sociology*, March, 1934. See also Boisen, "The Form and Content of Schizophenic Thinking," *Psychiatry*, May, 1942, and "Onset in Acute Schizophrenia," *Psychiatry*, May, 1947.

or whether, as in the case of the great Hebrew prophets, it is the fate of one's people or some other non-self-regarding them.

Joe Campbell's problem was one of personal salvation and the experience was induced under group influence. What it gave him was an answer to his own problem. He found a new role, a new mission in life. He saw himself now as a child of God and an heir of the ages. For this reason old religious beliefs which before had been stale and profitless took on new life and meaning because they had become associated with his concept of himself. In his case, therefore, the mystical experience gave emotional validation to beliefs which had been familiar since childhood but had never before become part of his own personality structure. Inasmuch as most mystical experiences are likewise primarily concerned with the problem of personal salvation, persons who have such experiences tend to be orthodox in their theological viewpoint.

This principle throws no little light upon the problem of historical determinism. It suggests that the limiting factors are to be found far less in the ideas which may come to a particular individual than in the organized experience of himself and his group. Especially in searching experiences of the mystical type, the ideas may be infinite in number and marvelously varied. But not all of them are accepted A new idea must first of all run the gantlet of the individual's own critical judgment, and judgment is selective rather than creative. Its function is to determine, from among the multitude of inchoate ideas which present themselves, what shall and what shall not be included in the structure of the personality.[6] In mystical experience logical thought may be in abeyance as compared with intuition, but it is still present, and before a person can function it must be in control. And then, after the individual himself has accepted the new idea or insight, it must be accepted also by others. He and his beliefs must meet the critical judgment of his friends and neighbors.

[6] For an illuminating discussion of creative as contrasted with logical thinking see William McDougall, Abnormal Psychology (N.Y. Scribner's, 1925), pp. 208 ff.

3. TRUE AND FALSE PROPHETS

What an individual accepts from among the ideas which come to him in periods of profound emotional stirring will depend in large measure upon his own desires and prejudices and needs. This principle applies also to the group. The mere fact that a man feels himself called to be a prophet, that he has reorganized his life on that basis, and that he has gathered unto himself a considerable following does not guarantee the validity of his ideas. The support of followers, even a few, will probably save him from commitment to a mental hospital, but the multitudes have been known to hear gladly other prophets besides the true ones.

False prophets are ever with us, and false prophets generally begin by deceiving themselves. Only the pure in heart can see God. Only those who are free from biasing interests are able to form sound judgments and arrive at true insights. The message of a particular prophet will be directly dependent upon his motives and his character. The yardstick by which his stature can best be measured will be the value of his message or of his cause and also the degree of achievement he has attained.

Here, for example, is a minister of religion who had been unfaithful to his wife and as a result had had a nervous breakdown. It was one of those acute disturbances which have a constructive outcome, but there was reason to suspect that in this case some of the problems had remained unsolved. When, therefore, I visited his church some months after his recovery, I asked myself what sort of message he would have for his people. His theme that morning was "Sabbath Observance." Clearly his deficiency in the weightier matters of the law was forcing him to be very particular regarding the tithing of mint and anise and cumin.

Here is another man, an aggressive, domineering, ambitious fellow who at the age of forty-five found himself working as a hired man with a wife and two children to support. For a man of his make-up and background it was an intolerable situation. What was he to do?

What he actually did was to throw himself zealously into the task of reforming the New England town in which he lived. Unfortunately the self-regarding motives and the unsolved problems in this man's life influenced his choice of causes. He had the boys arrested for playing baseball on Sunday; he made regular visits to all the stores in the town to make sure that printed copies of the tobacco laws were properly displayed; he organized anti-cigarette and anti-profanity clubs among the boys and girls in school; he watched the schoolhouse with all the zeal of a Daughter of the American Revolution to see that the American flag was hung out at the proper time and in the proper position—if it was not, the selectmen were sure to hear from him. On one memorable occasion when the village minister gave him a lift in his automobile, he swore out a warrant for the arrest of this minister because he had driven faster than twenty miles an hour, which at that time was the speed limit.

It may be guessed that this man's efforts at reform did not find much support among the people of his community. In fact, when designing men in that town wished to defeat some worthy measure, they sometimes did so by persuading this reformer to advocate it. This is an extreme example, but there are many cases in which self-regarding motives distort the sense of values, and they are quickly detected by one's neighbors to the detriment of one's influence.

Our village reformer had no clear religious motivation. He did devote much time and energy to the organizing of Sunday schools, but at no time did he identify himself with any church. He explained that the church had too many hypocrites in its membership. It seems clear that his interest in Sunday schools was due to the fact that they provided an arena for his activities.

Among those who stand high in the prophetic hall of fame there is no more instructive case than that of George Fox, the founder of the Society of Friends. We shall consider him in a later chapter in trying to show how one man with a significant message and a profound sense of mission can become the nucleus of a new social formation and how within the social process discriminations are

constantly being made which tend to distinguish between the true
prophet and the false.

4. Mystical Types

From the standpoint of this inquiry we may stress the fact that
the important religious movements of history have originated in the
searching religious or "mystical" experience of some individual
leader, and that mystical experiences usually carry with them a
compelling sense of mission. This does not mean that religion, in
either its individual or its collective manifestations, originates necessarily in experiences which are psychopathic. The dramatic type of
religious experience, as Starbuck has pointed out,[7] is to be regarded
as a phase of growth which occurs when for any reason normal
development has been blocked. Any new insight into the deeper
meaning of life, any significant widening of the horizon, any deepen-
ing of the sense of fellowship is sure to induce feelings of the type
we call "religious." However, since men seldom think intently until
they are compelled to do so, the great creative experiences are likely
to be associated with those periods when destiny is hanging in the
balance and the individual feels himself face to face with ultimate
Reality. With the intense feeling and narrowed attention which
characterize such periods, abnormal and pathological phenomena
generally accompany those that are creative and constructive. Since
such experiences carry with them a strong missionary drive, a sympathetic social milieu develops. As followers assemble there is likely to
be an effort to reproduce by artificial means the profound emotion
and the abnormal mental state which may have been incidental to
the new insight or vision. Such attempts are much in evidence in
the various forms of Holiness religion. They are also prominent
among Hindu and Buddhist holy men, who place great value upon
the trance condition.

The accompanying chart attempts to bring out points of likeness

[7] *Psychology of Religion* (New York: Charles Scribner's Sons, 1899), Chaps.
12 and 13.

MYSTICAL TYPES

	The Buddhist Mystic	The Holiness Devotee	The Hebrew Prophet	The Acute Schizophrenic
The common root:	An experience interpreted as possession by or identification with the superhuman			
Psychological process	Autohypnosis deliberately induced by narrowing of attention and ascetic practices	Group suggestions reinforced by music and following an accepted pattern	Narrowing of attention induced by intense anxiety over danger to people through war situation	Narrowing of attention induced by intense anxiety over sense of personal failure
Dominant mood	Sense of peace	Enthusiasm and joy often preceded by anxiety	Anxiety, earnestness	Panic, despair, sometimes exaltation
Tradition and innovation	Emotional validation of traditional beliefs under which experience was induced	Emotional validation of traditional beliefs which before had been dry and meaningless	Reorientation–new insights, often of great significance	Temporary or permanent break with accepted beliefs and culture patterns
Characteristic ideation	Cosmic identification	Auditory and motor automatisms, ideas of mission	Auditory automatisms, cosmic catastrophe, sense of mission	Auditory automatisms, ideas of death, of rebirth, cosmic catastrophe, mission
Concept of the superhuman	Supposedly impersonal but commonly accompanied by ideas of gods and demons	Trinitarian, personal; some belief in evil spirits	Personal, ethical, monotheistic	Personal, chaotic; commonly ideas of good and evil spirits

and difference among four such types, including the acutely disturbed schizophrenic. This chart makes no pretense of being exhaustive. It seeks merely to clarify certain relationships and the dynamic factors which are involved. We see that all four types are alike in the basic conviction that they are in touch with the superhuman and that as a result their concept of themselves has been radically altered. They are also alike in that their experience was induced by the narrowing of attention. But here the likenesses cease. Among the four types, the Hebrew prophets are distinguished by the fact that, in contrast to the Buddhist mystic and the Holiness devotee, their experience of the divine was not induced artificially, either through group suggestion or ascetic practices; rather it grew out of desperate concern with a genuine and pressing problem. In contrast with the schizophrenic, who also struggles with a genuine and pressing problem, they were concerned not about personal salvation but about the fate of the Hebrew people. The great Hebrew prophets, further, experienced no mere emotional validation of traditional beliefs, as do Buddhist and Holiness devotees, and no uncritical break with accepted beliefs and culture patterns, as occurs in the case of the schizophrenic, but achieved insights of profound significance and lasting value.

RECONSIDERATION

A striking feature of the dramatic type of religious experience is to be found in the compelling sense of mission which it carries with it. The man who after a period of struggle and darkness suddenly sees the light, who feels himself at one with a Greater-than-self and gets some new insight into the nature and destiny of man, commonly will feel that he has a message to impart to others. He is given a new role in life, that of a prophet, and he may become the nucleus of a new social formation.

Whether or not anything new is introduced into the stream of tradition by such a prophet will depend upon the problem which has been uppermost in his mind. The great Hebrew prophets, who were preoccupied with the fate of their people, achieved new insights regarding the mission of their people and the meaning of their sufferings. So also the man who is preoccupied with an overwhelming sense of personal failure is likely to get a new insight, but that insight will have to do with the problem on his mind—his own role. If he now conceives of himself as a redeemed child of God, traditional beliefs which before were dry and profitless take on new meaning because they are associated with his own role. Inasmuch as most cases of dramatic religious experience are rooted in the sense of personal failure, most radical mystics are orthodox in their religious beliefs. Their controlling belief is that they have tapped anew the sources of spiritual power.

The response which the prophet or leader receives depends largely upon popular readiness to accept his particular message. Men of vision, of force, of singleness of purpose do not always get a following. Unless the ground has been prepared, they will exert little influence upon the course of human affairs. Conversely, no matter how favorable the conditions may be, the development of a religious movement will depend upon the coming of some leader or leaders to give it form and direction.

The fact that a man feels himself called to be a prophet and gathers a considerable following does not guarantee the validity of his message. The ability to win a following is indeed not without significance. It will at least save him from commitment to a mental institution, no matter how eccentric his beliefs. When considered in conjunction with the value of his message, or cause, the degree of achievement provides a good yardstick by which to measure his stature as a prophet. Biasing interests are sure to impair judgment and insight, and the presence of self-regarding motives are damaging to one's influence as a leader.

VIII. *From Sect to Church: A Case Study*

FOR an example of the interrelationship of crisis and custom in the development of organized religion the Methodist Church and the revivalist movement out of which it sprang will serve as an exceptionally instructive instance. The story of Methodism is a classic example of the life cycle of organized religion which we encountered in Blankton. It shows a pattern which is recurrent amid the bewildering number of churches and sects stemming from the American plan of freedom of worship. Methodism furnishes also a striking example of the development of the social conscience of an American church and of the interrelationship of religion with economic and cultural factors. The development of religion in its American setting may be epitomized in the story of the Methodist Church.

1. THE PERIOD OF BEGINNINGS

Methodism began as a movement within the established Church of England. Its three outstanding leaders, John Wesley, his brother Charles, and George Whitefield, were faithful members of the Anglican Church and remained so until their death. Whitefield, in fact, died before the Methodist Church began its separate career, and the separation, although clearly necessary, was bitterly opposed by Charles Wesley and was permitted only reluctantly by John.[1]

[1] W. W. Sweet, *Methodism in American History* (Cincinnati: Methodist Book Concern, 1933), pp. 103–108.

The Wesleyan movement at the time of its beginning was only one of a number of religious awakenings. The work of Jonathan Edwards in New England antedated it by ten years. There had also been a great revival in Wales, and the Moravian revival had just got under way in Germany, starting influences which were felt also in England.[2] These movements may be regarded as manifestations of the same spirit which led a little group of serious-minded students at Oxford to meet together for meditation and prayer and the study of the classics. John Wesley, an ordained priest in the Anglican Church who had just returned to Oxford as an instructor in Greek, helped to organize this group in 1729.[3] His younger brother Charles was also a member, so also was George Whitefield. This little group was called sometimes "The Godly Club," sometimes "The Enthusiasts," and sometimes "The Methodists." It seems to have had a decisive influence upon Wesley's career.

In 1735 John Wesley went to America as minister to a group of settlers in Georgia and missionary to the Indians. His brother Charles accompanied him in the capacity of secertary to General Oglethorpe, the leader of the colony.

At the time he landed in Georgia Wesley was a rigid High-Churchman and a strict sacramentarian. For more than two years he labored as best he knew how among the settlers, seeking to enforce the High-Church regulations, but with meager results. He was then returned to England at the instance of his people, thoroughly discouraged and sick at heart.[4]

On his way to Georgia Wesley had made the acquaintance of a group of Moravians and had become much interested in them and in their religion. Back once more in England, he met another Moravian, Peter Boehler, who urged upon him the need of purging away his intellectualism and accepting a simple faith. Meanwhile Charles

[2] Halford E. Luccock and Paul Hutchinson, *The Story of Methodism* (Cincinnati: Methodist Book Concern, 1926), p. 73.
[3] *Journal of the Rev. John Wesley*, 4 vols. (London: J. M. Dent), I, 4.
[4] Sweet, *op. cit.*, pp. 33–34.

Wesley and George Whitefield had found a deep and satisfying religious experience. John Wesley's conversion took place three days after that of his brother. He had gone, he tells us,[5] very unwillingly to a meeting in Aldersgate Street. Someone there read Luther's *Preface to the Epistle to the Romans,* describing the change which God works in the heart through faith in Christ. During this reading he felt his heart strangely warmed. He felt that he did trust in Christ, Christ alone, for salvation, and an assurance was given him that his sins had been taken away and that he was saved from the law of sin and death.

Not long after this experience he went to Germany and spent some time at Herrnhut with the Moravians, becoming more and more impressed with them and their way of salvation.

Early in 1739 he returned to England and began preaching the new gospel which had been taking shape within him. He got a remarkable response. Many persons fell to the ground, some of them with violent seizures, passing through great agony of mind but emerging into a state of peace and joy.[6]

George Whitefield at this time was also making a considerable stir as a preacher. He had hit upon the idea of preaching in the open air, for which, with his powerful voice, he was particularly suited. He invited John Wesley to join him. The plan seemed to Wesley quite irregular and it was only with many misgivings that he accepted. He soon found himself preaching to crowds which ran from one thousand to twenty thousand in number, not only on Sundays but also throughout the week.[7]

These meetings attracted wide attention. They also evoked much opposition. It was charged that it was unethical to go into another minister's parish and preach to his people. Objections were also made because of the frequent abnormal manifestations among Wesley's hearers. Even Whitefield had grave questions about these. It seems

[5] *Journal,* I, 102.
[6] *Ibid.,* I, 169 ff.
[7] *Ibid.,* I, 184.

that they were peculiar to John Wesley's preaching. Wesley himself, although much perplexed over them, was convinced that they were the work of the Lord because of the excellent results which followed in terms of changed lives.[8]

An important feature of Wesley's work lay in his capacity for organization. Whitefield was content to deliver his message and let results take care of themselves. Wesley gathered people together into societies, and within different societies he organized "classes." These classes were small groups of persons, a dozen or so in number, who met regularly to confess their sins and to share their religious experiences one with the other under the guidance of some local leader. They were something in the nature of spiritual clinics, which under wise leadership had great possibilities for usefulness.[9]

The use of lay preachers developed in a natural manner. One of the converts began preaching. Wesley was about to stop him but became persuaded that he was called of God.[10]

And so the movement spread not only throughout England and Ireland and Scotland but across the ocean to America, carried there by George Whitefield, where it met with its greatest response, and where it became a separate organization.

George Whitefield's first visit to America was in 1737, when he took up the work from which John Wesley had withdrawn. He returned to England in time to have a part in the beginnings of the new movement, which he brought to America in 1739. From that time on much of his time was spent here. He traveled through the colonies, preaching to large numbers of people and meeting with

[8] *Ibid.*, I, 210 ff. The abnormal manifestations seem to have been especially frequent in the first year of the new movement, and Wesley devotes considerable space in his *Journal* to describing them and discussing their significance. Again in 1744 he records a number of such instances and institutes a sharp inquiry as to what had happened to his earlier converts. He concludes that these symptoms can no more be imputed to natural causes than to the Spirit of God and that it was undoubtedly Satan tearing them as they were coming to Christ (*Journal*, I, 417). Elsewhere in the *Journal* he does not record many such instances. We may infer that he comes to regard them with disfavor (*Journal*, II, 489).

[9] Luccock and Hutchinson, *op. cit.*, pp. 187 ff.; also Sweet, *op. cit.*, p. 42.

[10] Sweet, *op. cit.*, p. 43.

warm response from persons of all classes and all denominations. He did not, however, do much in the way of organizing societies. This task was left for workers who first appeared in 1766. By the end of the colonial period there were twelve circuits, twenty-four preachers, and five thousand members, most of them in the South.[11] During the War of the Revolution the movement continued to grow in spite of Wesley's bitter condemnation of the rebellious colonists. By 1784 the membership had increased to fifteen thousand.

2. THE METHODIST CHURCH BEGINS ITS SEPARATE CAREER

In 1784 an important step was taken. Wesley agreed to have preachers ordained in America and he commissioned two "superintendents" with authority to perform the ordinations. He took this step only because of the insistent demand for it on the part of his American followers. They wanted ministers who were authorized to administer the sacraments. Wesley's plan of having the sacraments performed by clergymen ordained in the Church of England did not fit American conditions. Such clergymen were not available, and most of the American converts had never been identified with the Church of England and felt no loyalty toward it, especially after the victorious termination of the war with England. The new step, once taken, meant that the movement had become an independent organization for which the name "Methodist Episcopal" was adopted.

3. METHODISM ADAPTS ITSELF TO PIONEER CONDITIONS

The new organization adapted itself readily to pioneer conditions. Its lay preachers were for the most part young and vigorous men who spoke the language of the people. By means of the circuit-rider system they were able to care for large, thinly settled districts, and by means of the "class" system local leadership was developed. The open-air meetings employed by Whitefield and Wesley in England were beautifully adapted to conditions in the new country. They became "camp meetings." The fact that the Wesleys had made ex-

[11] *Ibid.*, chap. V.

tensive use of congregational singing was another important factor. Above all was their concern with the moral problems of ordinary men, their profound belief in the validity of their own religious experience, and the methods they worked out for inducing such experiences in others.

Methodism followed the frontier. Unlike the Presbyterians, who established churches only where they found Presbyterians, the Methodists established churches wherever they found frontiersmen. They came in the persons of their circuit riders and of their zealous converts, and they recruited members from among the new settlers. The Methodist Church was made up of the common people, those upon whom the strains of poverty and hardship fell most heavily. By the year 1844 the number of its members had increased to a million.

4. Associated Churches

Closely associated with the Methodist Church in its revivalistic campaign were the Baptists, the Disciples of Christ, and the Cumberland Presbyterians. All of these were churches of the common people, and they held in common the policy of ordaining ministers who had not had professional training. All of them placed emphasis upon the saving of individual souls.

The Disciples of Christ, the largest of America's indigenous churches, offers some interesting contrasts to the other three. This church traces its origin to the work of a Presbyterian minister named Barton W. Stone in Kentucky early in the nineteenth century. It began in a series of revival meetings characterized by many abnormal phenomena. Stone's forces eventually joined with the followers of Alexander Campbell, under whose leadership the movement was considerably changed. Campbell's interest was more intellectualistic and practical. As against the radical mysticism of the Methodists he stressed reason and the good life with the Bible as the only authoritative rule of life and conduct. As against the divisiveness of the Presbyterians and of the Baptists he stressed church unity. As against the centralization of the Methodists he stressed local autonomy. In these views he had talking points which he and his followers used with telling effect in their many disputations.

5. The Slavery Issue [12]

The revivalist movement focused attention upon the salvation of the individual soul just at a time when some harassing and difficult social problems were coming to the fore. Chief among these was the slavery issue.

The importation of Negro slaves had begun in the seventeenth century in response to the demand for cheap labor. Started under the direction of English colonial companies, the slave trade became immensely lucrative to English shipping interests. It is estimated that at the time of the Revolution there were more than half a million Negro slaves in America, nearly all of them on the landed estates of the Southern seaboard.[13]

The growth of slavery did not take place without considerable opposition from the thinking people of America. Both Washington and Jefferson, although slaveowners themselves, regarded it as an evil wholly inconsistent with the American ideal and looked forward to the time when it might be abolished. Many churches, both Northern and Southern, deplored it and passed resolutions against it. Some church groups, among them the Quakers and the Covenanters, definitely forebade slaveholding by their members. For this reason large numbers of them left the South in order to get away from slavery.[14]

While Southerners at the beginning of the nineteenth century thus deplored the institution of slavery and sought some way to reduce its evils, their attitude had greatly changed before the end of

[12] This section and the next are taken from unpublished lectures by Arthur E. Holt.

[13] Charles A. and Mary Beard, *The Rise of American Civilization* (New York: The Macmillan Company, 1930), I, 107.

[14] See Chap. II, p. 9. It may be noted that there are now more Quakers in Indiana than in any other state in the Union, a fact which is explained by the migration from the Carolinas in the early nineteenth century.

the third decade. This change may have been due to economic pressures, but the decisive factor seems to have been the rise of the abolition movement in the North. As Wendell Phillips and William Lloyd Garrison and other Northerners began to voice their indignation about the evils of slavery in the South, the Southerners rose to its defense, and Southern preachers of all denominations began to find scriptural authority for the institution.

The changing attitude of the churches with reference to slavery is strikingly exemplified in the case of the Methodist Church. In 1796 its General Conference went on record as strongly opposed to the institution of slavery. It demanded that no slaveholders be appointed to official positions in the church except as they took such steps as the laws permitted for the emancipation of their slaves. It demanded further the dismissal of church members who were engaged in selling slaves.

In 1800 the regulation was passed that no Methodist preacher should own slaves and that any preacher who by any means came into the possession of slaves should forfeit his ministerial standing until he had executed legal emancipation.

In 1816 the General Conference concurred in a committee report which took the position that, while the practice of slavery was contrary to the principles of moral justice, the evil seemed to be past remedy. The regulations against slaveholding were altered to permit the appointment of slaveholders to official positions in those states which did not permit legal emancipation.

In 1824 the Committee on Slavery devoted itself to the problem of religious ministry to the slaves.

In 1828 and in 1832 resolutions regarding the evils of slavery were tabled.

In 1836 the General Conference sent a pastoral letter to its preachers, members, and friends stating that it was opposed to agitation on the subject of abolition and would use all prudent means to put it down.

In 1844 it was found impossible to reconcile the views of the

Northern and Southern conferences, and in 1846 the church was divided.

In 1856 the Northern Church took the position that the buying, selling, and holding of a human being as property is a sin against God and man.

6. REVIVALISM AND THE SOCIAL GOSPEL

A review of the various resolutions and ordinances of the Methodist General Conference on the subject of slavery indicates that the public order was taken for granted. The church disclaimed any intention or any right to interfere in civil and political affairs and concerned itself wholly with the conduct of its members and officeholders.

It seems fair to say that the revivalist movement brought into being a new kind of church, one which is separate from and independent of the social order and lives by evangelism. This new departure in religion did not bring about any change in attitude with reference to personal morality, but it did greatly affect the attitude toward social problems. The new type of church was so much interested in saving souls that it lost sight of the relationship of these souls to a public order.

7. CAPITALISM AND IDEALISM

The Civil War resulted in the overthrow of the slaveholding aristocracy of the South and the triumph of the trader class of the North. It ushered in a period of both hardheaded materialism and soaring idealism. On the one hand there was the rapid growth of business enterprise. Northern leaders in banking and industry had reaped tremendous profits through financing the federal government and furnishing supplies to its armies. They now entered upon a period of amazing expansion.

Negro slavery in the South was legally abolished, but the North had its own form of slavery. A premium was placed upon the importation of cheap labor from Europe by means of a high protective tariff. Each year hundreds of thousands of people poured into this country, not merely from the West and North of Europe, but now from the South and East. Once here, they were mercilessly exploited. So also were the natural resources of the country. It was the period of capitalism's complete triumph. Individualism was in the saddle. The free play of individual self-interest was supposed to bring about the welfare of all.

Along with this development there was also a high degree of idealism. The virtues of industry, frugality, and honesty were exalted to the skies. Many leading capitalists were devout church members. The rules of the game in which they were engaged might not be above criticism, but they were personally well-meaning and honest and ready to contribute to the public good. They gave liberally to the founding of colleges and hospitals and libraries and to the promotion of religious enterprises.

Among the churches it was an era of hope. A new and better world was just around the corner. Socially-minded men and women threw themselves into settlement work in city slums. The temperance movement got under way. The Young Men's and the Young Women's Christian Associations had an extraordinary growth. Missionary work was greatly expanded under the slogan "The evangelization of the world in this generation."

During this period great changes were taking place in the field of religion. The old belief in the infallible authority of the Holy Bible was overthrown through the findings of higher criticism. The old ideas of the world and of man's place therein were radically altered by the Darwinian theory of evolution. Among many of the churches the new ideas were vigorously resisted, but a growing body of thinking people in all the major churches were adopting the "liberal" point of view.

The Methodist Church was not at once affected by the new beliefs and attitudes. Its clergy were still deficient in college and seminary training and its constituency was still largely rural. It still relied to a considerable extent upon the revival meeting for the recruiting of its membership. It still looked upon the dramatic type of conversion experience as essential to salvation, even though disturbing questions were being raised in the minds of some of its leaders. But it was increasing rapidly in wealth and power and in the educational level of its constituency.

8. FORTY YEARS OF WAR

In 1914 came the great world holocaust. America entered the war upon a wave of idealism. The world was to be made safe for democracy. America helped to win a smashing victory. But the outcome was an armistice, not a peace. Following the First World War there was great economic and industrial achievement. There was hope and idealism, but at the same time much disillusionment and confusion and uncertainty. Perhaps the outstanding feature of the period from the standpoint of this study was the tremendous advance of higher education and the increasing prestige of science. This was accompanied by a marked tendency toward the secularization of religious work and a growing uncertainty regarding its aims and its techniques.

9. THE GROWTH OF CITIES AND THE PROCESS OF DEPERSONALIZATION

No review of the religious development of America can afford to ignore the growth of cities and the changes which this has brought in our way of life.

The United States of America began its career as an agricultural nation. At the outbreak of the Revolution there were in the colonies only five cities with more than seven thousand inhabitants. The great majority of America's four million people were living in face-to-face communities of the type we studied in our third chapter. With the passing of the years this nation has become heavily urbanized.. Nearly three-fifths of its people live in towns of more than twenty-five hundred and almost a third in cities of more than a hundred thousand inhabitants.

The change which this has wrought in the life and outlook of our people is enormous. In the country community everybody knows everybody else; in a city people frequently do not know their next-door neighbor. Herded close together, they are yet far apart. In the midst of the crowd the individual feels himself alone. The chances are that he will be employed not by men whom he knows but by some impersonal corporation. There is association, but of a different kind. In the country association is based upon propinquity, and people of all types have to learn to live and work together; in the city like is drawn to like. The processes of differentiation and stratification are active in the city. Similarities of belief, of class, of race, of taste become the basis of association to a degree which is impossible in the country. It is easy in the city to find social support for widely different beliefs and interests, and rapid changes in social attitude thus become possible.

This makes a profound difference in the composition and function of the church. Different needs must be met, different types of people must be ministered to, and the shifting population of a big city leaves many a one-time wealthy and influential Protestant church stranded in the midst of a Roman Catholic or Hebrew territory.

Most important of all is the depersonalization which has taken place in thinking. Horizons have been widened, and that is good; but all too commonly there is failure to carry over into the problems of the enlarged world the values which are so much more readily discernible in a face-to-face community. Many social evils are tolerated because their implications in terms of concrete human suffering go unnoticed. Our culture has thus become mechanized and depersonalized.

RECONSIDERATION

Methodism began as a *movement* at a time when the common people of England and America were suffering under adverse social and economic conditions. It began under the leadership of highly trained and able men who were convinced that they had tapped anew the sources of religious power. Under Whitefield it remained unorganized, but under Wesley's leadership it assumed more definite form and became a sect. It became thus a body of believers banded firmly together on the basis of a shared experience and a common faith which they accepted as absolute. It has now become a church [15] with a fairly prosperous membership made up chiefly of those who have been born in Methodist homes. And in the process vision and enthusiasm have been converted into habit and custom.

The early Methodists believed that a person had to be converted in order to be saved and they made a more or less dramatic type of religious experience a prerequisite to church membership. Probably no religious organization has striven more earnestly to keep alive the divine fire in accordance with the original faith. There is, however, a growing recognition of the fact that this effort has not been wholly successful and that in all too many cases the result has been a standardized pattern of religious experience induced by artificial devices.[16]

[15] A "sect," according to Sutherland and Woodward (*Introductory Sociology* [Philadelphia: J. B. Lippincott Co., 1940], pp. 528 ff.), is a religious organization which is at war with existing norms; its unity rests not merely upon inner loyalty to a common cause but upon conflict with out-groups which hold different beliefs. A "church," on the other hand, is at peace, not only with other religions, but with other phases of the social organization as well. Troeltsch (*The Social Teachings of the Christian Churches*, 2 vols. [New York: The Macmillan Company, 1931], I, 39–69) takes exception to the negative emphasis in such a definition as involving a value judgment from the point of view of the established churches and the existing social order. As such it obscures the social processes which are involved. Troeltsch therefore looks upon the *sect* as a voluntary organization made up of those who are morally and religiously qualified, while a *church* is an institution into which one is born. The sect stands rigidly and uncompromisingly for what it conceives to be the enduring Christian principles. The church, on the other hand, is not absolutist in its position but is ready to listen, to compromise, and to recognize other values. According to this view, which is held also by Weber (*From Max Weber* [New York: Oxford University Press, 1946], pp. 305–306) and Richard Niebuhr (*The Social Sources of Denominationalism* [New York: Henry Holt & Co., 1929), organized religious bodies begin as sects and under normal conditions develop into churches or their sociological equivalents. Under this definition rigid "come-outer" bodies, such as the Psalm-singing Presbyterians whom we encountered in Middle County, would be churches rather than sects, but churches in their terminal stages.

[16] Illuminating studies of suggestion and suggestibility in the production of this type of religious experience have been made by George A. Coe. See especially his *Spiritual Life* (New York: Fleming H. Revell Co., 1900), Chap. 3; also his *Psychology of Religion* (Chicago: University of Chicago Press, 1916), Chaps. 8, 10, and 16.

Many Methodist churches today report no clear-cut cases of dramatic conversion experience of the type formerly regarded as essential to salvation.

Meantime the social conscienec of the Methodist Church has been very much on the alert. However, individualistic the church may have been in years gone by, it is now aggressively concerned about the social problems of the modern world.

In the course of time the educational standards of the clergy have been raised. The old emotionalism has largely disappeared and the services of worship are becoming more and more dignified. The growing liberalization of the Methodists and their development into a true church is evidenced by the recent union of the three largest branches, the Methodist Episcopal, the Methodist Episcopal, South, and the Methodist Protestant. With its eight million members it is now the largest of our Protestant bodies.

IX. Creativity and Conservation in the History of Religion[1]

BOTH as sect and as church, organized religion has conservative and creative functions. Churches therefore lay themselves open to the well-known Marxist charge that religion is the opiate of the people and the upholder of the *status quo*. This charge is especially justified in the case of the great Asiatic religion. If we can accept Max Weber's conclusions, Confucianism, Hinduism, and Buddhism have all been associated with the special privileges of some dominant class and have served to keep the common people quiescent under conditions which were manifestly evil. The extent to which they have been able to do this bears witness to the stabilizing power of religion and its influence upon the attitudes, values, and customs by which men do business and carry on from generation to generation.

But this charge seems less justified in the case of the Hebrew-Christian religion. Our Western culture has been a changing and

[1] This chapter is a summary of three lengthy chapters in the original manuscript which were worked out in collaboration with Professor Arthur E. Holt and had the benefit of his firsthand studies of the religions of India. In them we relied much upon Max Weber's at-that-time-untranslated *Gesammelte Aufsätze zur Religionssoziologie*, 3 vols. (Tuebingen: J. C. B. Mohr, 1922); upon James Bisset Pratt's *India and Its Faiths* (Boston: Houghton Mifflin Co., 1916) and his *Pilgrimage of Buddhism* (New York: The Macmillan Company, 1928); and upon Ernst Troeltsch's *Social Teachings of the Christian Churches*, 2 vols. (New York: The Macmillan Company, 1931). The general conclusions are given without specific citation of authorities.

dynamic one and its religion has had no small part in its development. There are many kinds of men and many kinds of social organization; so also there are different kinds of religion, some good, some not so good. The question therefore arises: Why do some religions favor and some retard social change?

The interrelationship of religion and culture is of course no simple problem. The rapid changes now going on in the Far East remind us of that. Even before World War II began China was in process of transformation and Japan had been largely transformed. It was not religion which was bringing about that transformation, but contact with Western culture and its products. The missionaries whom we sent to these countries found their chief function far less as teachers of the Christian way of life than as exponents of Western science.

Yet according to the hypothesis which underlies this book, religion does have an important part in social organization. It has to do with those interpersonal relationships which are nuclear and those which are ultimate. It originates in the relationships to parents and early guides and it represents an attempt at orientation with reference to that which is supreme in the system of loyalties.

1. Relative Conservatism of Asiatic Religions

The contrast between the Hebrew-Christian religion on the one hand and the Asiatic religions on the other in the matter of social change may be explained in large part by the varying emphases upon these relationships.

In the Asiatic religions, particularly those of India and China, there is a magnification of the nuclear, or primary, relationships. In both these countries the family is all-powerful. In China the authority of parents and ancestors has been supreme—even after they were dead. There has been no transcending it. In consequence, Chinese culture has been extreme in its traditionalism. The same is true in Hinduism and Buddhism. The chief sources of authority have been the finite ancestors.

In Christianity, on the other hand, there has been the concept of a universal Father whose authority transcends that of the finite parents and of all earthly rulers; and the Church's Founder taught that the subordination of all finite loyalties to the infinite was a condition of entrance into the kingdom of heaven by the individual believer. Christian teaching thus centered in a higher loyalty and cultivated a broader vision. It thereby fostered religious experience of the more creative type through emancipation from the customary and the traditional induced commonly under the stress of crisis situations.

A second factor in the relative conservatism of the Asiatic religions may be found in the fact that they have had no church. That is, they have not practiced religious assemblage for the purpose of instruction and common worship. There has been thus little opportunity for the rethinking of religious beliefs in the light of changing conditions. Custom and tradition have been given full sway. In Judaism and Christianity, on the other hand, we find synagogue and church. The religious assemblage thus provided for the purpose of instruction and common worship has been the focal point of all religious activities. The existence of the church with its pulpit and its class meetings has been an important factor in Christianity's success in adapting itself to different social orders such as Roman imperialism, medieval feudalism, and modern industrial democracy. In addition, it may help to explain why the cultures with which Christianity has been associated have been dynamic in type.

There are other factors—e.g., the vested interests of some dominant class such as the scholars in China, the Brahmins in India, and the Buddhist monks—which had a part in blocking social change in Asia, but we seem justified in holding that the existence of a church and the emancipation from family domination in the Hebrew-Christian culture have been factors of enormous sociological significance which go far toward explaining the ability of their people to resist the encroachment of privileged classes and the dominance of tradition.

2. Interaction of Creative and Conservative Forces Within Christian Religion

History shows that the development of the Hebrew-Christian religion has been marked by periods of stagnation far more extensive than the periods of religious quickening and growth. There have been not a few periods in our Western culture when the forces of religion have been marshaled for the support of an existing social order. But there have been other periods when new insights won the day and forward movements resulted.

Periods of stagnation and sterility are found whenever organized religion becomes involved in a struggle for power or for position. The recognition of the Church by the Roman Emperor was thus no unmixed blessing. It drew into the fold many whose dominant motive was desire for status. It was attended by compromise and sacrifice of principle to the detriment of spiritual health. So also the worldly power which the Church exercised in the Middle Ages was not conducive to prophetic vision. Under such conditions the ruling classes were deferred to and the Church itself became bogged down with vested interests. Those who threatened the established order were sternly dealt with by the Church of the Middle Ages.

Periods of stagnation and sterility are also found where religion has been dominated by the desire of some group to maintain its integrity against the onslaughts of a surrounding culture or against the privations of pioneer life. Thus in the Psalm-singing churches of Middle County and commonly among colonist groups attention is fixed upon the past. The emphasis is upon the beliefs and practices of the elders. Conformity to custom and ritual becomes a paramount requirement. New insights and new practices are then likely to be suppressed as evidences of disloyalty.

An outstanding example of the conservative function of religion is to be found in Post-exilic Judaism. The conservative emphasis did indeed tend to stifle the prophetic voice which had been such a marked feature of the early history of the Jews. It was with this conservatism that Jesus of Nazareth clashed and so met his death. Judaism's achievement has nonetheless been remarkable. It has succeeded in maintaining the cultural integrity of the Jews throughout all these centuries, even though they have been scattered all over the world among people of other races and other cultures.[2]

The creative manifestations of organized religion seem to have been associated chiefly with periods of social crisis. The economic distress which we found in Middle County as a factor in the rapid development of the Holiness sects is no isolated phenomenon. Early Christianity also made a special appeal to the poor and the oppressed. So did the Anabaptist movement of the Reformation period and the Wesleyan movement of the eighteenth and nineteenth centuries. The spontaneous manifestation of religious experience in these periods seems to be an expression of a tendency present throughout the history of the Christian Church. In every century, according to Troeltsch, groups of people have taken their religion in earnest, and the health of organized religion is in large measure dependent upon the extent to which they have been permitted to express themselves and have been linked with the best thought of their time.

National danger and disaster have been the occasion of religion's supreme manifestation, as in the case of the Hebrew people. The distinctive feature of this reaction lay in the Hebrew prophetic message, which clung to the faith in the divine destiny of the people without hating or blaming the enemy. Instead the Hebrews searched their own hearts and sought to mend their own ways. Out of this essentially wholesome reaction came the deeper insight which determined the role of Jesus of Nazareth—the hope of a world redeemed through the suffering of the righteous.

The Protestant Reformation was another great crisis. But it was of a different type, comparable perhaps to the coming of age of a

[2] Klausner points out that the Jews have been able to maintain themselves only in Christian and Mohammedan cultures, where the Old Testament has been accepted as a basis of religious authority. (From *Jesus to Paul* [New York: The Macmillan Company, 1943], pp. 605–609.)

vigorous individual. Although Protestantism was an expression of many forces, some of them social and political rather than religious, it was nevertheless attended by marked religious quickening and brought with it far-reaching changes in social and religious organization. There seems to be ample support for Weber's view that Luther and his fellow reformers made a contribution of vast importance toward the building of modern civilization. They swept away the accumulated impedimenta of the centuries and returned to the essentials of the Hebrew religion. They opened the doors of the monasteries and directed religious zeal into the work of the world. They opened the pages of the Bible and placed the responsibility for interpreting it upon the enlightened conscience of the individual. They sanctified marriage and found their ideal of the holy life in the Christian home. They still sought salvation in a future life, but they so interpreted the doctrine of immortality as to enable them to defy the present order and seek to remake it. Even the sublimated magic of the sacraments was in large measure dispensed with. Certain sacraments were still observed but they were regarded rather as outward symbols of an inward grace.

It is not necessary to oversimplify the forces involved in the development of the modern age to recognize the importance of these accomplishments. Without them that development might not have taken place. At the very least, the Reformation gave the green light to the forces which have built the present civilization. It may even be claimed that it laid the foundations of a culture in which popular education, thrift, honesty, and personal initiative have made possible the vast industrial and scientific structure of the Western world.

3. THE AMERICAN EXPERIMENT

The practical working out of the system of organized religion which Protestantism introduced is best represented in the United States of America. Nowhere else do we find more strikingly exemplified the interplay of the creative and conservative forces in organized religion.

The American plan of freedom of religion came into being largely as a result of early immigration policies, particularly the encouragement given to nonconformist Protestant groups to make their home in the New World.

It so happened that the portion of America in which England had staked its claim seemed relatively barren. It held no promise of the gold and jewels for which Spanish and Portuguese adventurers crossed the sea. Its chief output was cotton and tobacco; and cotton and tobacco could be raised only by the sweat of the brow. Laborers were therefore needed and the colonial companies quickly discovered that oppressed religious groups made excellent settlers. Thus when other European nations were engaged in exterminating their heretics, the English were encouraging not only their own dissenters but also those from the Continent to settle in their colonies. In time the idea arose of making the English possessions solidly Protestant to offset the Roman Catholic domination of South and Central America and Canada.

These colonists came over in groups and formed settlements of their own. They were radicals in religion in the sense that they took their religion in earnest, but their emphasis was practical and intellectual rather than mystical and it centered in the purpose of preserving the group identity and its associated culture. Their aim was to establish like-minded, church-centered communities. The logical outcome of this original schema would have been a regimentation according to race and religion. The New England Congregationalists, the Scotch-Irish Presbyterians, the French Huguenots, the German Lutherans, Mennonites, and Dunkers would have had their own separate settlements and would have pushed westward by groups.

But this colonial policy was by no means consistently carried out. The chief departure lay in the importation of Negro slaves, people of a primitive culture who in their helplessness were ready to adopt the religion of their masters.[3]

[3] It is to be noted that our immigration policy has never permitted the importation of non-Christian peoples whose religion and culture would be capable

The economic suffering which this importation of slave labor inflicted upon the small Southern freeholders and laborers brought with it a new development of great significance. With the introduction of the cotton gin and the rapid increase of slave labor, these impoverished people were forced westward. Among them there arose a new type of religion, characterized by emotional fervor and evangelistic zeal and great concern for the moral problems of the common people. This new religion, represented chiefly by the Methodists, the Baptists, and the Disciples, swept through the Middle West, disregarding lines of class and clan. It helped to lay the foundations of a culture which was little concerned about tradition and precedent and much concerned about the requirements of the immediate situation.

Following the abolition of Negro slavery the policy of "America for Protestants" was disregarded and the labor supply was drawn chiefly from the Roman Catholic countries of southern and eastern Europe. These immigrants were also exploited, but they had the right to vote and the protection of a powerful and resourceful church which helped to maintain their morale and to unite them for political action. This meant the strengthening of the very conservative Roman Catholic religion.

With World War I European immigration was greatly curtailed. The chief source of supply for labor became our own South with its relatively high birth rate and its economic disadvantages. Owing to the competition with cheap Negro labor and to the introduction of improved farm machinery, the white laborers of the South found themselves in dire straits. In consequence they began emigrating to the cities and to the Far West. Among these uprooted and economically distressed people a revivalistic religion similar to that of the early nineteenth century again arose. It was characterized by deep emotion and the sense of direct identification with the divine and it

---

of withstanding those of the dominant group. The bars have been up against Chinese, Japanese, Hindus, and Moslems.

tends to break through the barriers of caste and class. This is the type of religion we encountered in Blankton.

RECONSIDERATION

This brief survey of the interplay of the creative and conservative forces in the great world religions offers the following explanation of the relative conservatism of the Asiatic religions:

1. The all-powerful family, whose authority in China, and to a less extent in India, has continued even after the parents were dead, as contrasted with the Hebrew-Christian belief in the supreme authority of a personal God.

2. The absence in the Asiatic religions of assemblages for the purpose of religious instruction and common worship, a need which in the Hebrew-Christian religion has been supplied by synagogue and church.

In the Hebrew-Christian cultures the presence of church and synagogue and the emancipation from family domination have been factors of enormous sociological significance in enabling their people in varying degree to resist the dominance of tradition and the encroachments of privileged classes.

Their success in doing so has been least in periods in which the church has become involved in the struggle for power, or where the dominant interest has lain in the maintenance of group integrity against the onslaughts of some surrounding culture. The periods of creativity have been for the most part associated with social crisis. The Protestant Reformation may be compared with the coming of age of a vigorous individual. The practical working out of the system which Protestantism has introduced seems best represented in Protestant America.

X. Creativity and Conservation
in American Protestantism

From the standpoint of this study the salient feature of the religious situation in America is the degree to which the creative forces have been allowed to develop. The absence of an established church and the right to worship in accordance with the dictates of the individual conscience have given rise to a multiplicity of churches and sects. Various racial groups have brought with them their own churches, and new sects have appeared in considerable number. To a remarkable degree the religious propensities of our people have been free to express themselves and run their own course, no matter how unusual or bizarre the form they might assume. The result has been an experiment in variation and selection of great interest to the student of religion.

This chapter considers the present situation in American Protestantism with special reference to the characteristics of our churches, their social significance, and the direction in which they are moving.

We may begin by recognizing that there are certain characteristics which American Protestant churches hold in common in contradistinction to the institutions of other religions. These characteristics may be summarized as follows:

1. All Christian churches, Catholic as well as Protestant, make a practice of religious assemblage for the purpose of instruction and of common worship.

2. All Christian churches, Catholic as well as Protestant, may be

said to constitute a super-social fellowship. They are in the world but not of it. They are critical of the present order and yet participate in the social process.

3. All Protestant churches believe in the sanctity of the family and support a married clergy. Control of the sex drive is insisted upon, not for its own sake, but for the sake of the marriage relationship. In this they contrast sharply with Catholicism and with Buddhism, which find the holy life in celibacy and monasticism.

4. All Protestant churches expect the individual to think for himself and have great faith in popular education. In this they differ from the Roman Catholic Church, which forbids independent thinking in religion; its schools and colleges are conducted largely for the purpose of religious indoctrination. There is also a marked contrast with the indifference toward popular education which has characterized other ethical religions.

5. All Protestant churches find an expression of religious zeal in the daily work. The virtues of industry and thrift are stressed and the individual is encouraged to develop whatever creative power he may possess. In this there is a contrast with Roman Catholicism and Buddhism, in which the zeal is directed into the monasteries. Under Confucianism industry is controlled by the tradition-minded family. Under Hinduism it is completely controlled by the caste system and innovations are discouraged.

We are here concerned with socially significant characteristics in which American Protestant churches diverge one from another and from their parent church, the Roman Catholic.

Our churches are too numerous to consider individually. We shall therefore endeavor to discover among them groupings and dynamic action patterns which constitute types.[1] With reference to these the

[1] Cf. Heinrich Kluever, "The Typological Method," in Stuart A. Rice (ed.), *Methods in Social Science* (Chicago: University of Chicago Press, 1931).

This study of American churches differs from E. E. Clark's *Small Sects in America* (Nashville: Abingdon-Cokesbury Press, 1939) in seeking to distinguish different components according to which a particular church may be classified.

The basis of this study is found chiefly in observations of my own made in

CHARACTERISTICS OF TYPICAL AMERICAN CHURCHES,

	INTERNATIONAL	TRANSPLANTED NATIONAL CHURCHES		TRANSPLANTED FREE CHURCHES				INDIGENOUS CHURCHES			
		STATUS UNCHANGED	STATUS ALTERED	INTELLECTUALIST	DOGMATIST	EVANGELISTIC	COMMUNAL	REFORMIST	MYSTICAL	ADVENTIST	THERAPEUTIC
BEST REPRESENTATIVE	Roman Catholic	Protestant Episcopal	Missouri Synod Lutheran	Congregational	Reformed Presbyterian	Methodist	Mennonite	Disciples of Christ	Assemblies of God	Jehovah's Witnesses	Christian Science
HISTORICAL ANTECEDENTS	A world-wide organization centered in Rome. Members from many races.	The established Church of England.	The established church of Germany.	An English body which became the established church of early New England.	A Scotch-Irish Psalm-singing body of the "come-outer" type.	An English body which recruited most of its members in America.	A German branch of the Anabaptists, semi-communal, strongly non-resistant.	An adaptation to frontier conditions in Middle West. The largest indigenous group.	The largest and fastest-growing Holiness sect. Organized in 1914.	The most active and distinctive of the adventist sects.	The largest of the healing sects.
ATTITUDE TOWARD PRESENT ORDER	Institutional interests paramount. Inclined to support *status quo.*	Discriminating acceptance. Inclined to support *status quo.*	Noninterference. Piety *within* established order. Intent on preserving cultural heritage.	Discriminating acceptance-favorable to social change.	A tradition of defiance. Intent on preserving group integrity.	Increasing concern with social betterment.	Noninterference and nonresistance. Withdrawal into communities of its own.	Discriminating acceptance-favorable to social change.	Absorbed with personal salvation in face of imminent return of the Lord.	Evil beyond repair. Parousia imminent. Refusal to fight or to salute flag.	Absorbed with personal, indifferent to social problems.
REPRESENTATIVE CLASS	Priests and monks. Membership from all classes. Underprivileged urban classes well represented.	Laymen and clergy on equal footing. Members from middle and upper urban strata. Monied aristocracy prominent.	Members from later German immigration of rural artisan and tradesman classes.	Laymen ascendant. Members from middle and upper urban classes. Intellectualist aristocracy prominent.	Membership largely rural.	All classes well represented. Strong in country as well as city.	Chiefly farmers and small tradesmen of German descent.	All classes well represented. Strong in country and city.	Recruited chiefly from underprivileged classes	Recruited chiefly from underprivileged classes	A white-collar, middle-class constituency.
SOURCES OF RELIGIOUS AUTHORITY	The Bible as interpreted by the hierarchy.	Widely divergent views — held together by loyalty to organization.	A literally inspired Bible. Little stress on present-day inspiration.	Tested experience. Scientific efforts supported and findings welcomed.	A literally inspired Bible. Its authority demanded for all church procedures.	Stress on personal religious experience and guidance. Open-minded toward science.	A literally inspired Bible and the leading of the Holy Spirit.	Somewhat divided.	A literally inspired Bible and promptings of Holy Spirit.	A literally inspired Bible and present-day revelation.	The Bible as interpreted by Mrs. Eddy.
CONCEPT OF THE SUPERHUMAN	Deity of Jesus; worship of Virgin and of saints. Some belief in demons.	Liberal.	Rigidly orthodox.	Liberal.	Rigidly orthodox.	Liberal.	Orthodox.	Liberal.	Orthodox beliefs with special stress on Holy Spirit.	Orthodox beliefs with special stress on deity of Jesus and his return	Omnipotent Mind.
CHIEF END OF LIFE	Salvation in future life. Holy life in present through escape from world.	Personal and social regeneration. Magnification of beauty.	Personal piety and future salvation.	Personal and social regeneration.	Future salvation through right living in present.	Personal and social regeneration.	Future salvation. Personal piety and brotherhood within Christian community.	Personal and social regeneration.	Personal salvation through dramatic transformation of character.	Escape from a perishing world.	Peace of mind.
MEANS OF GRACE	Sacraments working *ex opere operato.* Penance. Holy life through celibacy and monasticism.	Much stress on sacraments. Religious assemblage stressing common worship.	Faith and right living in present. Belief in sacraments retained.	Education, discipline, industry, co-operation. Instruction stressed in religious meeting.	Obedience, industry, austerity, neighborliness, education.	Old charismatic emphasis giving way to educational.	Faith, industry, obedience to church discipline.	Baptism by immersion still required. Emphasis otherwise educational.	Charismatic and ascetic. Speaking with tongues required. Ban on worldly amusements.	Faith, spreading of gospel. Little stress on common worship.	Faith, meditation.
METHODS OF RECRUITING	High immigration and birth rates. Training in parochial schools.	Birth rate low. Many members drawn from other bodies through social interests.	High birth rate. Training in parochial schools.	Birth rate low. Somewhat dependent upon transfers from other churches.	Birth rate high. No other sources. Losing ground.	High birth rate. Evangelistic campaigns.	High birth rate. No other source.	Birth rate fairly high. Protracted meetings much used in past.	Chiefly through evangelistic campaigns.	Through personal visiting and distributing of literature.	Personal evangelism.
TRAINING OF CLERGY	Highly trained.	College and seminary.	College and seminary.	College and seminary.	College and seminary.	Untrained men formerly ordained. Standard now higher.	Mostly a self-supporting lay ministry.	Untrained men *were* used. College training now the rule.	Special calls and group endorsement.	No regular ministers.	Mostly lay readers and healers.
INTERCHURCH RELATIONS	Rigidly forbidden.	Limited by requirement of episcopal ordination.	Rigidly non-co-operative.	Eagerly co-operative.	Somewhat aloof.	Co-operative.	Aloof and self-sufficient.	Co-operative.	Sometimes ignored by established churches.	Aloof.	Aloof.

various religious bodies may be placed in the effort to determine their social and religious significance.

The accompanying chart is an attempt to show schematically the outstanding characteristics of certain churches which have been selected as typical in the sense that they represent related characteristics which are free, so far as possible, from complicating and divergent tendencies. Negro churches are not included here because they are a problem in and of themselves and because there is not among them sufficient diversity to require this method of treatment.

It will of course be understood that the characteristics here given cannot pretend to do justice to all the complexities involved. Only the central and distinctive traits and tendencies are indicated.

1. HISTORICAL SETTING AND DOMINANT INTEREST

According to the Religious Census of 1936 there are in the United States of America 218 white churches and sects, 30 Negro, a number of Jewish bodies, and a small number of other organizations—Buddhist, Theosophist, Spiritualist, etc. Of the white Christian bodies, 125 were brought here from across the ocean and 93 may be called indigenous. In the matter of membership the contrast is much greater. Of the indigenous bodies only two, the Disciples of Christ and the Churches of Christ, have more than a million members and the total for the 93 bodies is not more than 7,000,000 as against some 57,000,000 in the imported church bodies.[2] Even those bodies which

---

the course of survey work done during the past forty-three years. The territory covered includes 24 counties and 18 rural and urban communities distributed among 14 states—Missouri, Tennessee, Kansas, Iowa, North Dakota, New York, Maine, Massachusetts, Illinois, Indiana, South Carolina, Alabama, Ohio, and Michigan. While these observations do not lend themselves readily to quantitative treatment, they include careful records of interviews and observations regarding religious beliefs and practices which are of special value in interpreting census reports and church yearbooks.

[2] The figures used in this chapter are those given by the National Council of Churches in its Yearbook for 1955. They are for persons over 13 years of age. The Jews and the Negroes are not included. In the case of the Roman Catholic Church, which reports all baptized souls, the membership was reckoned at 75 per cent of the reported figures.

originated here are closely related to the imported churches, and all churches are motivated in some degree by an interest in preserving their group integrity. In this attempt to consider the characteristics of American churches I have therefore used as a base line the historical antecedents together with the dominant interests which they manifest. We thus get a category which corresponds somewhat to Malinowski's concept of the "institutional charter," or to an institution's concept of its purpose.[3] From this standpoint, the following types may be distinguished:

a. INTERNATIONALIST

The Roman Catholic Church with its membership of 24,000,000 is a world-wide organization with a single head, the Pope, who in accordance with the Roman Church's historic position claims authority over the sovereigns of the world by reason of his role as representative of the King of Heaven. This church was brought to America by various national groups, notably the Irish, the Austrians and southern Germans, the Poles, the Italians, the French Canadians, and the Mexicans. Although internationalist in its distribution and organization, its dominant interest seems to be ecclesiastical.

The Eastern Orthodox Church and the Lutherans are also represented by different national groups, but they have no one head. Their organizations are national rather than international and in most cases their American churches are independent of Old World authority.

b. TRANSPLANTED NATIONAL CHURCHES

Some 34 church bodies with an aggregate membership of about 8,500,000 have sprung from the established national churches of Europe. As tax-supported institutions, these churches in their original habitat were closely identified with the existing national order and with its ruling classes. In the process of getting transplanted two types have resulted:

[3] Bronislaw Malinowski, A Scientific Study of Culture (Chapel Hill: University of North Carolina Press, 1944), pp. 52 ff.

i. Those Whose Status Is Unaltered

The Protestant Episcopal Church with a membership of 1,900,000 is the best representative. While no longer tax-supported, as it was originally in six of the thirteen colonies, it has been transplanted into a kindred culture. The moneyed aristocracy is well represented in its membership and it gets many new members through the drawing power of social prestige. It is also strongly entrenched in the army and navy. The Presbyterian Church is the established church of Scotland, but so much of its membership has come from the north of Ireland, where it is not an established church, that it belongs rather among the free churches.

ii. Those Whose Status Has Been Changed

The Lutheran Church with a membership of 4,500,000 is the best representative of this type. It was transplanted into an alien culture; it came in for the most part with a later stream of migration; and it has been made up largely of artisans, farmers, and small tradesmen. This is particularly true of the Missouri Synod and of the Scandinavian bodies. The Dutch Reformed Church, consisting of two bodies with some 250,000 members, bears a close affinity to the other Calvinistic bodies which had so much to do with the making of the nation but belongs in the changed-status group. The Eastern Orthodox churches have about 1,700,000 members.

These transplanted national churches, while loyal to their adopted country, have centered much of their interest upon maintenance of the group integrity and preservation of their national culture. For this reason they have been conservative in their outlook. Their attention has been fixed on the past rather than on the future. They have cherished the language and literature of their fathers and have clung to the customs and viewpoints of the old country. They have performed an important service, however, in the transmission of their cultural heritage and the prevention of a hasty and meretricious Americanization on the part of the second and third generations.

This service has not been confined to the imported national churches, but it has been strikingly characteristic of them.

c. TRANSPLANTED FREE CHURCHES

Eighty-seven of the churches listed in the 1936 census, with a total membership of about 25,000,000, belong in this group. These churches have sprung for the most part from Old World nonconformists. Under the English colonial policy these people were encouraged to settle in the New World, and they had an important part in launching this country upon its independent career and in shaping its policies and institutions. Among the transplanted free churches the following dominant interests and tendencies may be distinguished.

i. *Intellectualist*

The Congregational Church with about 1,200,000 members is perhaps the best representative of this type. In the old country it was a nonconformist body and was overshadowed by the Church of England. In this country it became the established church of early New England. As such it was able to give expression to a faith in education which is characteristic of Protestantism. This it has maintained to an unusual degree. It founded the first college in the New World and many others thereafter. It was also active in the establishment of the common school system.

The divisions of the Congregational Church have resulted in radically liberal bodies, such as the Unitarian and the Universalist churches, the one being an intellectualist and the other a popular form of the same movement. The Congregational Church today is rather solidly committed to the liberal point of view it has had for more than fifty years. Most other large bodies are still considerably divided. The Congregational Church has also throughout its history been committed to a fairly vigorous social action program.

ii. Dogmatist

The Presbyterian group, with an aggregate membership of about 3,500,000, may be taken in certain of its subdivisions as representative of this tendency. It has shared the Congregational Church's faith in education; it has been scarcely less active in the founding of schools and colleges; and it has been even more insistent upon an educated ministry. But it has been much more concerned about correctness of doctrine. Six of its nine subdivisions have grown out of the demand for scriptural authority for all church procedures and articles of faith. In general the church bodies which have emerged from the Presbyterian Church have been characterized by strong resistance to change and great concern for the letter of the law, while the main body is still divided between the orthodox and the liberal points of view.

This change-resisting, legalistic tendency, based upon the view that the Bible is the literally inspired Word of God, is widespread among our American churches. An extreme example is the Synod of the Reformed Presbyterian Church, the same body which we have already encountered in Blankton. We are taking it as an example of the dogmatist type. It is a small denomination which sings only the Psalms of David and permits no instrumental music in its services of worship. It is at the same time rigid in its requirement of college and seminary training for its ministers. Its refusal to allow its members to vote or to sit in juries or to swear to support the Constitution of the United States has been carried over from its "come-outer" attitude in the old country.

iii. Evangelistic

This emphasis has been best represented in the Methodist Church, with some 9,000,000 members, whose development has already been considered. This church, like the Congregational and Baptist churches, was an English nonconformist body. In America it adapted itself to pioneer conditions and met the needs of the common people.

Through its revival meetings it cultivated dramatic types of religious experience and most of its members were recruited in this country. Of its ten subtypes, not one was determined by doctrinal considerations, but by plan of organization, attitude toward slavery, and type of religious experience. The latter was the most frequent issue and most of the bodies which have emerged from the Methodist Church have been made up of persons who felt that the main body was getting too worldly and who sought more dramatic outlet for their religious feelings.

The powerful Baptist Church, with a membership of about 10,000,000, also adapted itself to pioneer conditions and made wide and vigorous use of the revival meeting. Its subdividing, however, has been mostly on the basis of doctrinal issues.

iv. Communal

This emphasis is best represented by the Mennonites, a pietistic German body which has believed profoundly in the leading of the Holy Spirit and has sought to work out the principles of Christian brotherhood in communities of its own. Stern discipline, requirement of distinctive dress, and other evidences of separateness have been the chief factors in causing its seventeen subdivisions. These factors also help to account for the fact that this group is now 83 per cent rural; the very rigid Amish sects are almost entirely so. The Society of Friends, the Dunkers, the Moravians, and the Plymouth Brethren are related groups. The aggregate membership is about 500,000.

d. INDIGENOUS BODIES

In classifying 125 denominations as importations from the Old World it is not to be assumed that each one has its counterpart in Europe. Such is far from the case. The number has been greatly increased in the process of transplantation. The German Lutheran Church, for example, is now divided into three major bodies, each representing a different generation of immigrants, with the most recent the most conservative.[4] Among these there is little co-operation. Two Scotch-Irish Psalm-singing Presbyterian churches became in America five bodies representing different streams of immigration and reflecting the difficulties incidental to getting adapted to the new situation. The story of their formation is instructive.[5] Two groups were brought from the old country before the Revolutionary War. In 1782 they made the highly sensible decision to unite. The Associate and the Reformed Presbyterian churches thus became the Associate-Reformed Presbyterian Church. This merger, however, did not meet with unanimous approval. Some of the Associate churches at once seceded, and sixteen years later a Reformed Presbytery was again organized with a membership composed chiefly of new arrivals from north Ireland who could not be reconciled to the non-existence of their own church. The attempt at union thus resulted in three churches where only two had been before.

In 1832 the newly organized Reformed Presbyterian divided on the issue of voting, a more prosperous and progressive urban following insisting upon the right to vote, a rural following opposing the innovation. An attempt by the progressives to force the issue completed the schism. The number of churches was increased to five when another merger, the United Presbyterian Church, was formed and small groups of "come-outers" in each of the constituent bodies refused to acquiesce. This process was greatly reinforced by subconscious factors such as the desire for leadership and the repressed hostilities arising out of the stern discipline characteristic of many of these churches.

A very important factor from the standpoint of this study is the fact, already noted, that in many of the imported churches a major concern has been the preservation of the group integrity against new

[4] H. Paul Douglass and Edmund de S. Brunner, *The Protestant Church as a Social Institution* (New York: Harper & Brothers, 1935), pp. 24 ff. See also Heinrich Maurer, "Studies in the Sociology of Religion," *American Journal of Sociology*, 1924–26.

[5] Boisen, "Divided Protestantism in a Midwestern County," *Journal of Religion* (October, 1940), XX, No. 4.

customs and attitudes. They were intent upon preserving their own culture and were not ready to give themselves wholeheartedly to the building of a new one. They resisted assimilation into the new culture as if it were equivalent to extinction. They were looking backward rather than forward. Hence the strong resistance to change which characterizes them.[6] New bodies formed on this basis will not be regarded as indigenous. We are concerned here with the new formations which represent attempts to meet new conditions. Among these we may distinguish the following types:

i. Reformist Movements

The Unitarians, the Universalists, and the Disciples of Christ have an aggregate membership of about 3,500,000. The Unitarians under the leadership of men like Channing, Parker, and others went too fast for the main body of the Congregationalists and were disowned. Their adaptation was to the frontiers of knowledge and their appeal was to a cultured group. The Universalists represented a popular rebellion against the old Calvinistic doctrine of predestination. But neither group ever had a large following. The Disciples, on the other hand, under the leadership of Alexander Campbell, won a large following on the basis of their appeal to common sense as against the emotionalism of the Methodists and to Christian unity as against the

[6] Heinrich Maurer in his study of the Missouri Synod Lutherans (op. cit.) offers an explanation of their conservatism. "The Lutheran," he says, "was a minority group. His very language was against him. If it preserved him, it also mummified him. In his American off-spring he faced daily the problem of identity and continuity. With every child he reared, he swelled the growing majority of those who knew him not. Because this hostile majority was identified with change and with the rationalism of Calvinistic creeds, our minority group became traditionalism personified. It did not merely stand pat. It went backward to the eighteenth and even to the seventeenth and sixteenth and fifteenth centuries to choose its foothold. The demand for assimilation was met with alienation and estrangement."

Elsewhere he says, "The dominating element in the situation of our immigrant culture group is fear of change, and the oldest rational medium for meeting change is religion. The particular creed under consideration entails sublimation of a static universe and conceives the process of soul conservation in terms of identity and continuity" (p. 485 ff.).

divisiveness of the Presbyterians and Baptists. This following was chiefly in the Middle West and the movement was essentially an adaptation to frontier conditions. It involved the policy of ordaining ministers who were not professionally trained. Today this group is divided about equally between the liberal Disciples and the very conservative Churches of Christ.

ii. Mystical Sects

While not large in the aggregate the mystical sects are today the fastest growing of our American religious bodies. There are more than forty sects with a total membership of perhaps 1,500,000. A number of these are offshoots of the Methodist Church and claim, not without reason, to be what the Methodist Church was a hundred years ago. Their rapid growth cannot be accounted for by any one factor. As has been pointed out,[7] it coincided more or less with the economic depression of the 1930's and apparently represents a spontaneous attempt to meet the strains of shared distress on the part of those strata of society among whom the strains were most acute. It is also a reaction against the liberalization and secularization of the established churches. The Pentecostal and Holiness groups take their religion in earnest. They are conservative in their theology but radical in their religious faith. The Nazarenes, with some 240,000 members, are the largest of the Holiness group, and the Assemblies of God with 370,000 members are the largest of the Pentecostal groups. An interesting phenomenon is the large number of "Free Pentecostals," churches which have sprung up spontaneously and have no national organization.

iii. Adventist Sects

Jehovah's Witnesses is today the most active of these groups. This is an organization of more than 300,000 adherents which lays little stress on common worship but engages in vigorous missionary ac-

---

[7] Cf. Chap. V. See also Boisen, "Economic Distress and Religious Experience," *Psychiatry*, May, 1939.

tivity. Its members regard the present order as evil beyond repair and their aim is to save souls from out of a perishing world. Their militant resistance to conscription during the war and their little interest in common worship is not characteristic of the Adventists as a group. The Seventh-Day Adventists, an older and larger organization with about 250,000 members, is now fairly well institutionalized. Expectation of the second coming of the Lord is prominent in many other bodies, particularly in the mystical sects, and it affects their attitude toward present-day social problems. It may discourage efforts at social reform. On the other hand, as Mannheim points out,[8] such vivid expectation of the future has a certain explosive power which may make the group ready for social change and action.

iv. Healing Sects

The practice of faith healing is found in many of the Holiness sects. The outstanding representative is, however, the Christian Science Church, wtih an estimated membership of more than 250,000. These are mostly middle-class, white-collar people. Their concern is chiefly with the solution of personal ills to the neglect of social ills. Unity, Divine Science, and New Science and New Thought are other small groups of kindred type.

2. ATTITUDE TOWARD THE PRESENT ORDER

The cultural influence of any religion will be both direct and indirect. By providing the individual with incentives to work, by determining his ethical standards, by encouraging him to think for himself, it may be preparing the way for social change even though its teaching is concerned primarily with the future life. In the case of a conscious attitude toward the established order the influence will be direct, and in any consideration of a church's social influence it has a first claim to attention. The conservatism of China and India may thus in large measure be explained by the attitude which the

[8] Karl Mannheim, *Ideology and Utopia* (New York: Harcourt, Brace & Co., 1936), pp. 190 ff.

religions of those countries took toward the present order. In China the social order was accepted as good. In India the social order is looked upon as eternal and unchangeable; the caste system is upheld and made tolerable by religious beliefs. Under Buddhism the social order is regarded as evil and unchangeable and salvation is found through escape into Nirvana. In Islam the attitude is one of stoic resignation. Such attitudes are certainly not conducive to social progress. Among American churches six different attitudes may be distinguished:

a. INSTITUTIONAL INTERESTS PARAMOUNT

It is not unfair to give this as the attitude of the Roman Catholic Church. There will be many exceptions, so far as individual priests and laymen are concerned, but the church as an organization, while vigilantly watchful of all that goes on in the social order, seldom interferes except as its own interests are affected. Its historic attitude has been that it is the one true ark of salvation. It is therefore unwilling to join hands with other churches and it has little faith in social change. On the other hand, it has done fine and effective work in support of the rights of minorities and oppressed groups, especially in times of industrial strife.

b. NONINTERFERENCE

This has been the characteristic of the Lutheran Church. Its motto has been "Piety within the established order." As a national church the Lutherans have long been accustomed to live at peace with the state under the doctrine that politics is none of their business. This attitude has been characteristic of American Lutherans, who as a body have never interfered in American politics.[9] It has made for

---

[9] "The proper attitude of the Christian toward political affairs is one of holy indifference. Let those cut each other's throats who have no treasure in heaven. The state is but a hostelry and the Christian but a guest to whom it cannot occur to overthrow the rules of the house." Quoted by Maurer as expressing the attitude of the Missouri Synod Lutherans (op. cit., pp. 485 ff.).

peaceable relations with their neighbors and has at the same time helped to maintain their cultural heritage in the new surroundings.

A similar attitude has characterized those communal groups whose aim has been to make Christian brotherhood effective within their own communities. With them it has taken the form of the doctrine of nonresistance and represents a lesson learned from futile attempts at resistance.[10]

c. INDIFFERENCE

This attitude differs from that of "noninterference" in that it arises not so much out of doctrinal rationalization of a delicate situation as out of special interests and emphasis. The Christian Science Church is a good example. In the effort to secure peace of mind it shows little concern over existing social evils. Similar indifference with reference to the social order is found commonly in groups which are intent on "saving souls" and therefore focus their attention upon the individual to the neglect of social salvation.

d. PESSIMISM

This attitude is best represented by the Adventist groups. They are much concerned about the present order, but they look upon it as bad and destined to get worse and worse until the Lord returns in glory. Efforts to improve it are therefore worthless. They seek only to save souls as brands from the burning. Their most vociferous representatives today are the Jehovah's Witnesses.

e. DEFIANCE

The older Calvinists also looked upon the present order as bad. Man was totally depraved and needed to be reborn; so also the present order. But they proposed to do something about it and they set out to make the world over. Among our present-day American churches there are no conspicuous representatives of this attitude

[10] Niebuhr, *The Social Sources of Denominationalism* (New York: Henry Holt & Co., 1929), p. 52.

except, perhaps, as it survives in such churches as the Reformed Presbyterian. The outstanding representatives of Calvinism today are the churches which contributed most toward the making of the nation. They are now well established and strong and their attitude is greatly altered.

f. DISCRIMINATING ACCEPTANCE

This is the attitude of an intelligent, well-meaning ruling class. It is also the attitude of any truly democratic society. It is characteristic of the great body of American Protestants, particularly the old-line churches.

3. REPRESENTATIVE CLASS

Far more than is generally recognized, beliefs and attitudes are determined by the desires and needs of the individual and of the group. The life situation of the believer and of his group will thus largely determine his attitude toward the social order. According to Mannheim,[11] the vested interests of some dominant class tend to determine the "orientation toward the transcendant" in such a way as to fortify their position.

This view of Mannheim's is in line with Weber's proposition [12] that each of the great religions is associated with some particular social class. Thus, in China Confucianism was the ethical system of a cultured, worldly bureaucracy. As perhaps in no other country, the common people respected learning and looked up to the educated class. And the scholars basked in their adulation. They were content to allow the common people to remain uneducated and unenlightened religiously, for popular superstition increased their own prestige. They were content also with a clumsy orthography which was suggestive of magic, for this likewise increased their prestige and made it more difficult for new aspirants to enter the circle of the elect.

[11] Op. cit., pp. 6 and 30 ff.
[12] Religionssoziologie, 3 vols. (Tuebingen: J. C. B. Mohr, 1922), I, 240 ff.

Similarly, in India a representative hereditary class of educated men, the Brahmins, functioned as priests for individuals and for the community. These men determined the caste system, in which they were the privileged group. It was the religious teaching for which they were responsible which upheld that system and made it tolerable for the lower castes. In Buddhism the monks alone were the Buddhist fellowship. Others were objects, not subjects, of religion. The monks were the sole interpreters of the ancient tradition.

In the case of the Hebrew-Christian religion, as a rule the middle classes have been dominant. In Roman Catholic Christianity the priests and monks have perhaps been ascendant, but the middle classes have throughout held great power; the Protestant Reformation was the result of a clash between them and the ecclesiastics.

In America, where Protestantism has dominated, there are no such ruling classes as the Chinese scholars or the Hindu Brahmins. The authority of priests and monks is at a minimum. Nevertheless the principle of a dominant class determining orientation still applies. In each of our church bodies there are certain classes which are likely to give their stamp to the organization. Four series of contrasts may thus be taken into account: (a) clergy—laity; (b) native—foreign; (c) ruling class—underprivileged; (d) urban—rural.

a. CLERGY—LAITY

At one end of the scale stands the Roman Catholic Church—an organized hierarchy with celibate priests and monks as the holy group and a Pope who rules by divine right. The interpretation of the sacred Book is left entirely to the hierarchy; so also is the means of grace. The laity are merely objects of their ministration and have nothing to say regarding religious belief or ecclesiastical policy. Even in their religious assemblages the Mass is performed by the priest for the people.

At the other end of the scale are the Mennonites, the Primitive Baptists, and the earlier Friends, who have refused to recognize any professional clergy.

In the great body of American churches ministers are not thought of as having any special power by virtue of their office but only because of special training and equipment. This is the case in the Congregational, Presbyterian, Methodist, Baptist, Lutheran, and other older Protestant churches.

In the Episcopal Church the belief in the Apostolic Succession is retained. Its clergy are priests, set apart and endued with power by virtue of their office, but laymen are given a voice in the affairs of the church more or less on an even footing with the clergy.

b. NATIVE—FOREIGN

The contrast here is between those who have set the patterns of American culture and later arrivals who are not ready to be assimilated into that culture. For the most part the unassimilated groups speak a foreign language and their churches have served as agencies for the perpetuation of the imported cultures. In general, however, such churches have served a useful function in preserving the real values of the cultures they represent and in preventing a spurious Americanization of the "allrightnick" type.

c. RULING CLASS—UNDERPRIVILEGED

There is much difference among our churches as regards the social strata from which their congregations are drawn. Many local churches have in fact somewhat the semblance of a social club. Weber holds that the club is an institution distinctive of American life. He explains it as an outgrowth of the Protestant sect.[13] However that may be, a considerable degree of social stratification is prevalent in the churches of an American community.[14] The Episcopal Church, for example, may be made up largely of middle- and upper-class folk with a generous sprinkling of the well-to-do. The Congregationalists and Presbyterians are composed largely of middle- and upper-class

[13] *Ibid.*, I, 207 ff.
[14] Cf. W. Lloyd Warner and Paul S. Lunt, *The Social Life of a Modern Community* (New Haven: Yale University Press, 1941), Chap. 17.

families with a good representation of the professional and business classes. The Methodists have all classes well represented, as do the Baptists and Disciples. The Holiness and Pentecostal sects draw chiefly from the underprivileged. The Roman Catholic Church, which is the .east democratic so far as control and organization are concerned, is probably the most democratic in the make-up of its congregation. In its membership there is a heavy representation of the more recent arrivals and of the underprivileged and in its churches people of all classes worship together.

d. RURAL—URBAN

This contrast may appear in local rather than in ecclesiastical organization. Country people may prefer a church of their own to a church of the same denomination in town. Here, for example, is a town of three thousand with a beautifully equipped Methodist church and an able minister, but many Methodist country families drive through that town to attend another Methodist church a mile and a half on the other side in the open country. This is not an uncommon occurrence.

There are, however, considerable differences among the denomina·tions in the matter of rural representation. The Episcopal Church has less than 15 per cent of its membership in towns of under 2,500 inhabitants. The Presbyterians have a rural representation of 29 per cent, the Congregationalists 35 per cent, the Methodists 45 per cent, the Baptists 53 per cent. Some religious bodies, such as the Christian Scientists and the Unitarians, are almost entirely urban. The largest rural representation is in the Mennonite bodies. The Brethren are next.

A denomination with a strong rural representation is in a far healthier state than one which is heavily urban. The middle and upper classes of the cities are not reproducing themselves; the surplus population comes from the country. The fact that 80 per cent of the Roman Catholic membership is urban is an indication that the

United States is likely to remain Protestant, even though the Catholic membership is drawn largely from the working classes.

4. SOURCES OF RELIGIOUS AUTHORITY

Five chief sources of authority may be recognized among religious bodies:

1. Custom and tradition.
2. Experiences and promptings interpreted as superhuman in origin in the person of the individual believer.
3. The pronouncements of leaders to whom supernormal faculties are attributed.
4. Sacred books.
5. A hierarchy.

These five sources of authority may all be operative in a single religion, but the relative emphasis placed upon them differs widely from one religion to another and from the early to the later stages in the development of a given religion.

First in order is the authority of custom and tradition. This is the authority of unthinking obedience. It is the authority exercised by most people over their children. Some children never transcend it. In China, as we have seen in Chapter IX, filial piety has dominated. Loyalty to finite parents has been binding even after the parents are dead—binding even to the seventieth generation. That the Chinese is not without his share of interest in the mystical is sufficiently indicated by the presence in China of magic and sorcery, but in Chinese religion of the upper classes the mystical tendencies have remained undeveloped. Superhuman authority is seldom claimed even for the great religious leaders. The deference for the past has been so great that little independent thinking has been done even by the educated. Chinese scholarship has been preoccupied with what the ancient sages have said.

Religious experience may be said to begin with the transcending of the authority of the finite parents through experiences and promptings interpreted as superhuman in origin. Such experiences, accord-

ing to our findings, are the fountainhead of religion. Religious
movements in their creative stages are not far removed from mystical
experience in the person either of the believer himself or of someone
he trusts absolutely. But the creative stage soon passes and even in
those religions which have believed in and cultivated mystical experiences, the tendency has been to ascribe authority to some inspired
leader and to require individual revelations to conform to his pre-
cepts. The Roman Catholic saints have had to conform to the traditional teachings; otherwise they were disowned.[15] Even in Protestantism Luther thundered against the Zwickau prophets for their
effrontery in pretending to revelations from on high. It is only here
and there that groups like the Society of Friends consistently place
reliance upon the "openings" of the individual believer.

What we do find in all world religions is a body of sacred writings
which are supposed to set forth the utterances and revelations of the
founder or founders.[16] The great difference has been in regard to the
authorized interpreters. In some cases the sacred books are written in
a language which differs from that of the common speech. The tendency then has been to endow them with magical properties and to
ascribe magical powers to those who were able to read the sacred
language. Such was the situation in the cases of the Brahmin priests
and the Confucian scholars, and also in large measure of the medieval
Catholic clergy, particularly in the period when translations of the
Bible were forbidden.

In Judaism the Old Testament was regarded as a sacred book and
there grew up around it a body of interpretation which was also
more or less binding. But two things were distinctive of Judaism. It
was characterized by diligent efforts to instruct its people. And it
contained a group of men of gigantic stature who felt themselves
charged with a divine message. In them the prophet reached heights

[15] Henri Delacroix, Études d'Histoire et de Psychologie du Mysticisme (Paris:
Felix Alcan, 1908), pp. 418 ff.
[16] For an interesting comment on this fact see Charles Horton Cooley, Social
Organization (New York: Charles Scribner's Sons, 1927), p. 73.

never attained among other peoples either before or since.[17] Jewish prophecy reached its climax in Jesus of Nazareth, who taught that while not one jot or tittle of the law should fail, the entire message of the prophets could be summed up in the simple principles of loyalty to God and love of neighbor. He thus cut through all legalism and all traditionalism to the very heart of the religious and ethical life.

In the Protestant Reformation the problem of religious authority was a primary issue. Both the Reformers and the Catholics agreed in regarding the Bible as the divinely inspired Word of God. They differed as to who was to do the interpreting. The hierarchy took the position that none but the Pope could claim that right. The Reformers placed the responsibility upon the enlightened conscience of the individual.

Striking features of the religious situation in Protestant America are the relatively little weight given to custom and tradition as compared with the Asiatic religions, the decreasing prestige of hierarchical and charismatic leadership, and the growing claims of science.

The great majority of our Protestant churches still accept the Bible as the divinely inspired revelation of God. Their insistence upon the right of the individual to interpret it for himself, however, has led to great emphasis upon popular education. Growing knowledge has produced a new understanding of how we got our Bible and of the processes involved in revelation or inspiration. There are in consequence an increasing number of persons in all our major churches who do not look upon the Book of Genesis as an authority regarding the age of the earth and the process of creation. These people, the *liberals*, regard the Bible as the record of the religious experience of the Hebrew people. They seek religious authority in the tested experience of today and they are ready to make use of the methods of science in the domain of religion itself.

But this group is still a minority. The great majority, perhaps as much as three-fourths of our American Protestants, hold to the

[17] Weber, *op. cit.*, III, 281 ff.

orthodox position. They still look upon the Bible as divinely inspired.

This orthodox group has recently been in some ways reinforced by a sophisticated movement which has sprung from the anguish of war-torn Europe. The "neo-orthodox" movement, as it is called, goes back to the historic revelation in Jesus of Nazareth for the basis of its religious thinking.

Among the Holiness sects, intuitive promptings arising out of mystical experience are accepted as authoritative. We have already considered the processes involved. What needs to be noted here is that among these groups attention is usually centered upon the individual's own role in life and that the dramatic experiences which they value and cultivate are induced under group influence. For this reason these experiences seldom result in new social and theological insights. They serve rather as emotional validation of the traditional beliefs and practices under which they were induced. Most of the sects which go in for radical mysticism are orthodox in their theology, and they tend to accept the authority of the Bible.

5. Concepts of the Superhuman

Among practically all our American churches the concepts of the superhuman are personal and ethical. There are of course many differences. In the Roman Catholic Church there is something of a pantheon. Not only do Catholics believe in God as a heavenly Father, but they also believe in the deity of Jesus and they worship the Virgin Mary and pray to the saints. There is often a belief in demons.

In orthodox Protestantism there is no worship of the Virgin or of the saints, but belief in the deity of Jesus is a cardinal doctrine. This includes belief in the virgin birth, in the vicarious atonement for sin, in Jesus' resurrection, and in his promised return in glory. Among liberal Protestants Jesus is accepted as the supreme revelation of a God of love, who is thought of as personal. According to the liberal view Jesus is divine, but that divinity consists in the full manifestation of potentialities present in all men.

A fourth view is that of the humanists, who take an agnostic position with reference to the personality of God. God, they say, is man-made. As a frank religious belief, this is confined to a small group, chiefly in the neighborhood of educational centers, but it is reflected in the increasing nebulousness of the beliefs of liberal Christians.

The beliefs of American Christians regarding the superhuman contrast sharply with those of the intellectualist religions of Asia, in which God is thought of as an impersonal cosmic spirit. But the religion of the common people, according to Weber, is characterized by the persistence of primitive nature gods and the prevalence of crude personalistic concepts. Apparently the intellectualist religions with their impersonal concepts of God might suffice for the fortunate few, but not for the common people. The nature gods would therefore represent an attempt on their part to meet an unsatisfied need; it will receive attention in a later chapter.

6. THE CHIEF END OF LIFE

The chief end of life with which we are here concerned is not that of official pronouncements but rather the motivations which seem to control the lives of most believers. Among these we may recognize three continua in accordance with which it is possible to rate the different church bodies:

1. This-worldly ....Other-worldly
2. Social ....Individualistic
3. Ethical ....Mystical

These traits are by no means mutually exclusive. A religion may be social and ethical and this-worldly and at the same time concerned with the problem of personal salvation in a future life and ready to value and foster experiences of the mystical type. These are not opposites of good and bad, but complementary requirements which must all be met in a well-balanced religion.

Confucianism is thus distinctly this-worldly and ethical, and it has a social goal, the survival and prosperity of the family. The lack of concern about a future life and the minimal interest in mystical experience mean not strength but weakness. Certain elements essential to a vital religion are lacking.

In Hinduism the goal of the intellectualist devotee is identification with the Cosmic Spirit. The goal of the common man has been improvement of his status in the next rebirth. The emphasis is thus individualistic, other-worldly and mystical. Herein are its sources of strength. Its weakness lies in the lack of social and ethical and this-worldly interests.

Among American churches the other-worldly emphasis is represented in extreme form in Roman Catholicism. There religious zeal is directed into the monasteries, and celibacy is regarded as essential to the holy life. The monastic discipline stresses prayer and contemplation. There are elaborate concepts of the future world which stress the idea of a "purgatory" as an intermediate state between heaven and hell and a place where souls are purified. The Catholic Church is also quick to recognize and channelize mystical experience. For those of its people who take their religion in earnest and wish to follow the heroic way of life, it has its monasteries and its convents and it provides social outlets for religious zeal in labors in behalf of the sick, in the training of the young, and in the championing of minority groups.

Another extreme of other-worldliness is to be found in Adventist bodies like Jehovah's Witnesses, which look upon the present order as wholly bad and are intent upon saving individual souls from the wrath to come. It should be recognized, however, that the other-worldly emphasis, especially when it is combined with the mystical, may enable the individual to feel himself independent of the trials and vicissitudes of the present life and set him free to struggle for the remaking of the present order.

The this-worldly tendency may be seen in those groups whose dominant interest lies in the preservation of group integrity against the onslaughts of an alien culture or in humanistic religions which concern themselves with social betterment and are skeptical regarding the superhuman.

The extreme of mysticism is to be found in the Holiness groups, with which we have been so much concerned. As we have seen, their mystical emphasis is combined with the ethical, and even though they are other-worldly and individualistic they are likely to make important contributions to social progress.

The old Puritans laid great stress on education for the good life and gave little recognition to the "twice-born" type of experience. This attitude is widespread today, especially among our liberal churches. The general trend seems to be away from the other-worldly and the mystical toward a this-worldly, social, ethical emphasis.

7. Means of Grace

By the term "means of grace" we have reference to those procedures and practices by which religious faith is perpetuated and re-created. These vary widely from crude practices of a magical variety to religious education, private prayer, and common worship. They will be considered in detail in a later chapter. Our present task is a survey of the various means of grace which characterize the different types of American churches. Six general types may be distinguished:

a. SACRAMENTAL

This type is seen in extreme form in the Roman Catholic Church. Catholics believe that the sacraments work *ex opere operato* and are effective only in the hands of a priest and by virtue of his office. The Episcopal Church retains a strong sacramental emphasis, particularly as regards the office of the priest. Insistence upon a particular form of baptism, as with the Baptists and Disciples, rests upon the assumption that these rites are something more than symbolic.

b. ASCETIC

Asceticism has long been practiced by religious devotees in all parts of the world and rests upon certain laws of the spiritual life. There are many persons who require some opportunity for dramatic commitment and self-sacrifice. This the Roman Catholic Church has provided in its monastic orders and in the discipline which they enforce. Abstention from worldly amusements is a requirement of the Holiness and Pentecostal sects. Their stern morality may be explained as a result of their acquaintanceship, out of the very poverty of their lives, with the temptations rising from elemental human drives not subliminated by an active life with many interests. Their self-denial also may be a means of inducing the mystical experiences which they value. In any case, according to Weber [18] and to Niebuhr,[19] the limitation of expenditure and the increase in productivity which result from such asceticism tend to explain why Quakers and Methodists so often become prosperous.

c. CHARISMATIC [20]

The charismatic emphasis is found in those bodies which insist upon some form of dramatic religious experience such as conversion, sanctification, and speaking with tongues. The Methodists and Baptists used to belong to this group. Charismatic emphasis is now characteristic of the Holiness sects.

d. LEGALISTIC

A considerable number of churches lay stress upon creedal conformity, obedience, and adherence to established customs. This is particularly the case with churches which are intent upon preserving their cultural heritage against the encroachments of the culture of their adopted country.[21]

e. EDUCATIONAL

Where the holy life is found in the vocation, and the virtues of discipline and industry are stressed, education comes to be recognized

[18] *Op. cit.*, I, 184 ff.

[19] *Op. cit.*, pp. 70 ff.

[20] This term is borrowed from Clarke's *Small Sects of America*. It is used in a somewhat different sense from Weber's concept of "charisma."

[21] Commenting on the Missouri Synod Lutherans, Maurer remarks (*op. cit.*, fourth article): "Where Americans 'got religion,' where it left them emotionally agitated, that for them was 'Schwaermerei.' One did not *get* religion, one had it. The Christian must stand on the true faith of the true church and believe and obey because it is *writ*. There and there alone did he partake of the assurance of grace."

as a means of grace. The placing of responsibility for the interpretation of the Bible upon the enlightened conscience of the individual has meant a demand for enlightenment. Hence the educational zeal of Protestantism, best represented in this country by the Congregational and Presbyterian churches.

f. DEVOTIONAL

Individual prayer and meditation is stressed in Hinduism, Buddhism and Islam. Common worship is something that is distinctive of the Hebrew-Christian religion and is found in no other except in embryonic form. The significance of this fact and the psychological and sociological importance of common worship will be considered in a following chapter. It may be noted here that during the past forty years there has been a marked decrease in the number of worship services among churches of the liberal persuasion, but with hardly an exception the Sunday morning worship service is still the focal point of the church's program.

8. METHODS OF RECRUITING

There is considerable difference among the various church bodies in regard to the means by which they are able to maintain or increase their membership. The chief factors to be taken into account are as follows:

a. POPULATION MOVEMENTS

i. Immigration from Europe

Changes in the rate of immigration from the various European countries explain the changes in the growth of certain religious bodies. The greatly increased immigration from southern and eastern Europe before the First World War accounts for the rapid growth of the Roman Catholic Church in that period. Before the Civil War and immediately afterward it was the Lutheran Church which was receiving the great increase.

ii. *Population Displacements Within This Country*

The westward trek and the movement from country to city have had a profound effect upon the churches, depleting some and greatly augmenting others. The same thing is true of the shifting currents of a large city. We have seen that the rapid growth of the mystical sects in the 1930's took place among uprooted underprivileged people in our industrial centers.

b. BIRTH RATE

Church bodies which are chiefly urban, such as the Episcopal, Unitarian, Presbyterian, and Congregational churches, are at a considerable disadvantage in the matter of growth in membership, because the population strata from which they draw their members have a low birth rate. Church bodies with strength in the rural districts, such as the Methodists, the Baptists, and the Lutherans, are in a much more favorable state.

c. RELIGIOUS EDUCATION

Two different plans are relied upon in the training of the young:

i. *Complete Control of Education Through the Establishment of Parochial Schools*

This is the Roman Catholic plan. The Catholic Church is today supporting 6,500 parochial schools with an enrollment of more than 2,000,000. The Missouri Synod Lutherans also make wide use of parochial schools. They report more than a thousand such schools and upwards of 70,000 pupils.

ii. *Secularized Common Schools Supplemented by Religious Instruction on Sundays in the Church School*

This is the plan followed by the vast majority of Protestant churches. In an increasing number of communities the churches are allowed one afternoon a week in the public schools for religious instruction.

d. TRANSFER FROM OTHER CHURCHES

i. Through Evangelistic Campaigns

The Holiness sects of today and the Methodists, Baptists, and Disciples of former years have won most of their members from the constituencies of other churches. This process has been favored by the fact that many of the children of the established churches do not identify themselves with the church of their parents, and that newcomers in a particular community are often neglected by the established churches. Furthermore, any vital religious message tends to disregard and transcend established lines and to appeal to all those who have ears to hear.

ii. Through Social Stratification

There is always a tendency to gravitate toward those of kindred tastes, especially when the factor of social prestige is involved. This tendency has more than made up for the low birth rate of Episcopal, Presbyterian, and Congregational churches.

9. THE EDUCATION OF THE CLERGY

During the settlement of the Middle West the education of the clergy became a burning issue. The Presbyterians, by insisting upon a professionally trained ministry, lost a constituency which was logically their own. The Methodists, the Baptists, and the Disciples, who made use of untrained ministers, took it over. The factors involved were not merely the practical requirements of serving a scattered population with an insufficient supply of trained men. The untrained men often had a better understanding of frontier people. They shared their experiences. They spoke their language. They were, moreover, exponents of an emotional type of religion and of a style of preaching which was repugnant to the educated but which found favor among the ranks and file of the people.

The Methodists and Baptists and Disciples today are raising their standards of theological training, but they have still many ministers who are without either college or seminary training.[22] The Holiness and Pentecostal groups have few trained men. Some bodies, such as the Mennonites and the Primitive Baptists, insist upon a self-supporting lay ministry.

10. INTERCHURCH RELATIONS

Of the white churches listed in the *Year Book of American Churches* for 1954, twenty-five bodies with a total membership of 26,000,000 are members of the National Council of Churches.[23] This means that nearly three-fifths of the white Protestant church membership is in the co-operating bodies. It also means that nearly nine-tenths of the Protestant bodies are not co-operating in this important interchurch organization. We are reminded that there are problems to solve in the matter of religious co-operation. As regards the small bodies, most of them are sects which are not ready to co-operate. And this unwillingness extends to certain large and important bodies such as the Southern Baptists and the Missouri Synod Lutherans.

RECONSIDERATION

A review of our findings indicates that the first effect of the commingling of religions has been an accentuation of differences. Each

[22] A study made by Douglass and Brunner (*op. cit.*, p. 113) gives the following figures on the education of ministers in 1926:

	Both College and Seminary	College Only	Seminary Only	Neither College nor Seminary
Lutheran (Mo. Synod)	85%	3%	7%	5%
Protestant Episcopal	62	7	20	11
Presbyterian, U.S.A.	69	7	11	13
Congregational	53	10	14	23
Disciples of Christ	18	37	4	42
Methodist Episcopal	26	20	9	45
Northern Baptist	36	10	22	32
Roman Catholic	68	4	20	8

[23] There are also five Negro bodies with an aggregate membership of more than 9,000,000.

group has found itself placed upon the defensive. Beliefs and practices dear to it are challenged. The natural reaction is to reaffirm these beliefs and practices. Thus at the beginning of the last century many forward-looking Southerners were strongly opposed to the institution of slavery. But when Northern abolitionists put in their appearance and began to find fault with a Southern institution, the Southerners united in its defense and Southern clergymen found scriptural support for what they had formerly regarded as an evil.

The competitive situation itself may stress the differences and bring about a certain degree of differentiation. The Southern Methodist may thus take pride in his liberalism because the Southern Baptist is conservative, and the Southern Baptist tends to stress his fidelity to the old-time religion in proportion as the Southern Methodist becomes liberal.[24] This tendency is furthered by the fact that rituals and creeds tend to become mere symbols. They lose their original significance and become battle flags and rallying slogans for unthinking adherents.

But the process does not stop here. The association as friends and neighbors of people of different faiths has also the effect of promoting mutual understanding and rapprochement among them. The number of churches and sects may be multiplying, but the major bodies are decreasing in number and increasing in size. A study reported by Douglass and Brunner,[25] based upon 14,000 cases, indicates that among Presbyterians, Congregationalists, Methodists, Episcopalians, Friends, Disciples, and Lutherans there are practically no prejudices against intermarriage and that membership in any one of these bodies would not constitute a bar to presidential availability in the minds of the members of the other bodies.

As to the small bodies which do not co-operate, the stanchly conservative "die-hard" groups may be regarded as milestones along the path of progress. They represent positions once held by the larger bodies but now abandoned by them. The mystical and Adventist

24 H. R. Niebuhr, op. cit., pp. 230–31.
25 Op. cit., pp. 259–64.

sects, on the other hand, are reminders of our unsolved problems. As reactions to the process of social stratification, they tell us of the existence of class and even caste lines in this professedly democratic country. As reactions to the problems of economic distress, they remind us that the free play of individual self-interest has resulted in the piling up of immense fortunes for the few rather than in the well-being of the many. As reactions to the growing nebulousness of religious belief, they tell us of the limitations of the gospel of enlightenment and of the sagging foundations of the faith on which this nation was built.

Among the larger co-operating bodies the main lines of advance may be summarized as follows:

1. There has been a lessening of the tendency toward social stratification. Each of the larger bodies tends to become more like the others in the distribution of wealth and culture.

2. A growing liberalization of religious belief has resulted from the spread of education and enlightenment in which the Protestant churches have believed so strongly. The old belief in a literally inspired Bible is giving way before the view that the Bible is the record of the religious experience and insights of the Hebrew people and that the divine revelation of which it bears record is a continuing process to be tested in terms of the human values stemming from it.

3. An immediate effect of this liberalization of religious belief is a certain nebulousness in the ideas of the superhuman and a consequent loss in conviction and zeal. The ideas of God, however, are overwhelmingly personalistic and, if the conception of religion developed in this book is correct, they are likely to remain so.

4. Increasing liberalization has meant increasing concern with the present life. Even among the conservative Protestant bodies faith in a future life serves as a stimulus to right living in the present. Among liberals there is a characteristic emphasis upon the problems pertaining to social betterment and a soft-pedaling of the immortality theme.

5. Magical features still appear among the means of grace, but the emphasis upon them is diminishing. Baptists and Disciples are becoming less insistent upon the rite of immersion. Episcopalians are more willing than they used to be to recognize nonepiscopal ordination.

6. While there is still much stratification among our Protestant churches, it is a matter of no slight significance that immigrant bodies such as the Lutherans, which have been free to worship in their own way and to preserve their own language and culture, are coming gradually of their own accord into closer fellowship with the other Protestant bodies.

Evidences of such an advance are appearing simultaneously in all our larger church bodies. The Congregational Church, which was selected as the best representative of the liberal tendency, has only a somewhat larger proportion of the liberally-minded than most of the others. Among all liberals there is a tendency toward a loyalty to the group which refuses to be greatly concerned by differences of doctrine and ritual.

According to Max Weber, the American experiment itself is an expression of the Protestant philosophy of life. Many different forces have of course been operative in that experiment, but among them the beliefs and attitudes of Calvinistic Presbyterians and Congregationalists were not least in importance. They had no little part in launching this country upon its independent course, in formulating the ideals of freedom and opportunity for all, and in setting the patterns of our competitive economy.

New conditions have today arisen, conditions due in part to the tremendous industrial development, in part to the inadequacy of the competitive economy on which it rests. Both of these Weber regards as fruits of the Calvinistic way of life. In the world of the future the solution of such problems will depend upon our readiness to do some fresh thinking and upon the possibility of working out some synthesis of the different religions and cultures. Perhaps American Protestantism will have a contribution to offer.

XI. The Development and Validation of Religious Faith

IN the preceding chapter we examined the beliefs and practices of different types of American churches with special reference to those which are common and those which are divergent and distinctive. Now confronting us is a consideration of religious belief in general, of the creative and conservative functions which it performs, of the way in which new beliefs get started, and of the means within the normal social process by which the superior beliefs are sifted out from the inferior. A critical evaluation of the common core of Protestant Christian belief will then be attempted in the light of our findings.

1. THE RELIGIOUS BELIEFS OF GEORGE FOX AND HIS FOLLOWERS

The significance of religious faith and the processes by which a deviating set of religious beliefs are translated into social organization can be seen nowhere more clearly than in the case of George Fox and his followers.

When George Fox in his early twenties was plunged into a profound disturbance, his recovery began with what he called an "opening." The Lord showed him that it was not necessary to be educated at Oxford or Cambridge in order to qualify as a minister of Christ. This opening gave him a new role in life and made clear his future course. It was followed by other openings, all of which he regarded as revelations from above. The insights thus brought him were organized into a philosophy of life and constituted a message which was in some respects a departure from the religious beliefs of his time and people. This message found acceptance among many of his contemporaries, and by the time of his death he had become the acknowledged leader of some forty thousand persons.

The psychological process involved in an "opening" has already been dealt with (Chapter IV, p. 66). An idea, or thought formation, takes shape in the regions of dim awareness and then darts into consciousness in so vivid a fashion that it is ascribed to a superhuman source. Inventors, poets, and others who do creative work frequently have such experiences. Among men of religious genius they are of crucial importance. They figure in what is called "inspiration," or "revelation."

Most religious movements are based upon faith in the divine authority of some such experience, either at first or at second hand. Fox was convinced that his experience was in no wise different from that of the old Hebrew prophets. Probably he was right. Others also of our great religious leaders have had their inspirations, their revelations, their messages from the Lord. But so have many mental patients. They, too, hear God talking to them and believe that they have been given a prophetic mission. How are the true prophets distinguished from the false? How is a deviating set of beliefs, like those of George Fox, organized and tested?

We have been proceeding on the assumption that personality is the internalization of the organized beliefs and attitudes of the group. Now come the questions as to how the beliefs and attitudes of an individual may bring about a new social organization, and how such an organization is able to perpetuate itself and fit into the general social setting.

What was original in Fox was not so great in proportion as we might suppose. Although he started forth entirely on his own and was never ordained by any existing group, he was greatly indebted to the Calvinistic Christianity of his time. We shall go far astray if we do not recognize this fact.

The Calvinism under whose influence Fox was reared was strongly intellectualistic and formalistic in its emphasis. It began as a reaction of the intelligent urban classes to the Roman Catholic efforts to control their thinking. By the time Fox came on the scene the scholastic tendencies had become quite pronounced. There was great emphasis upon correctness of doctrine. Theology was worked out into a fine-spun system in which the sovereignty of God, the total depravity of man, and the vicarious atonement of Jesus Christ were primary tenets. Although it had reacted against the magical concept of the sacraments held by the Roman Catholic Church, Calvinism still believed in the efficacy of the sacraments, and the keeping of the Sabbath and the holiness of the sanctuary were greatly stressed. The tendency in Calvinism was to think of Christianity as an authoritative revelation delivered once for all in the past.

This was George Fox's background. He reacted against Calvinism. His teaching emphasized the differences and passed over in silence those things which he held in common with it. He says little about man's sinfulness and need of salvation, but this omission does not mean that he took an optimistic view regarding the innate goodness of human nature; rather he assumed the Calvinistic view.

Except for his distinctive doctrines, Fox's theological beliefs were quite orthodox.[1] What Fox and his followers did constantly stress was the conviction that they had tapped anew the sources of spiritual power. They believed that they had found a new way of life, and they set out to follow it uncompromisingly and to invite all men to share it. This new source of power they called by various terms—"the Light," "the Light of Christ," "the Light within," "the Spirit of Christ," "the Seed," "the Root," "the Truth," and, later, "the Inner Light."

But this conviction was an all-important one, and it meant a thoroughgoing reorientation with reference to the central theological doctrines. Revelation for Fox and his Friends was a continuous

[1] Elbert Russell, The History of Quakerism (New York: Harper & Brothers, 1942), pp. 47 ff.

process, not something given once for all in the past. They accepted the Bible as the Word of God, just as the Calvinists did, but they held that the same Spirit who inspired the Scriptures and was supremely manifest in the historic Christ spoke also to their condition. This Spirit of God was present with all men in all ages as the guide, teacher, and redeemer of men, insofar as they were ready to receive Him.

Where the Calvinists conceived Christ's work of redemption as a transaction designed to appease the wrath of a just God because of man's sin, placing it thus in the judicial and metaphysical field, the emphasis of the Friends was upon the work of the inward Spirit of Christ in transforming the lives of men. Salvation for them was no isolated experience of conversion and no state of bliss, but a continuous living by the Spirit. Their constant aim was to awaken and develop this Inner Light, which they held to be something independent of forms and ceremonies and human learning.

The ministry among the Friends was not dependent upon academic preparation. Neither was it a matter of orders. It was a divine gift. And sacraments had no part in the Friends' services of worship. They sought rather to cultivate the capacity for knowing God by meditation, public worship, Bible study, waiting for the moving of the Spirit, and obedience to the truth. In fact the absence of forms and sacraments became for them the form around which the faithful rallied.

During the early period of Quakerism the voluminous writings of the faithful consisted chiefly of religious confessions and autobiographies, and of apologetic documents which sought to defend the Society from specific charges and justify their position in the eyes of the public. There was little attempt to systematize the theological beliefs. The early Friends did not regard any creed or theological formulation as an essential part of the Quaker religion.[2] The most important early systematic statement, that of Barclay in 1676, places in the forefront the Quaker belief in the Inner Light as the primary

[2] Ibid., p. 174.

source of religious authority and holds that the Scriptures are a secondary rule of faith, a source of instruction and comfort and the only outward judge in theological controversy between Christians. They are, he says, a test of pretended religious guidance, but since they themselves are the product of the inspiration of the Spirit of God, the Spirit of God rather than its product must be the ultimate authority.[3] All this was quite in accordance with Fox's views and this position prevailed for a considerable period.

Early in the nineteenth century a cultured and influential member of the Society, J. J. Gurney, became deeply interested in theology and wrote a number of essays and books which reflected a growing tendency within the Society and had considerable effect upon its development.[4] Gurney, like many of the better-educated Friends of his time, had been greatly influenced by Evangelical Protestantism, which, under the influence of the Wesleyan movement and of other movements for social and religious betterment, had been taking on new life and vigor. His doctrinal system shows Calvinistic features which are clearly at variance with the early Quaker position. The supreme outward authority of the Scriptures, the depravity of man as a result of the fall, and the vicarious atonement of Jesus Christ are all accepted and emphasized.

Meantime the Society was being torn asunder by a bitter controversy. The more influential and better-educated Friends of the large city meetings, who had felt the impact of the Evangelical movement most keenly, regarded themselves as the "orthodox" party and attempted to discipline some of the rural members who were upholding the final authority of the Inner Light. The result was the separation into the Orthodox and the Hicksite branches. The latter was in the beginning the larger numerically but is now much the smaller.[5]

Since 1827, according to Dean Russell,[6] there have been three pe-

[3] *Ibid.*, p. 178.
[4] *Ibid.*, Chap. 25.
[5] *Ibid.*, Chap. 23.
[6] *Ibid.*, p. 319.

riods in the development of Quaker doctrine and organization. The first period, which ended in 1861, resulted in the triumph of evangelical theology over quietism,[7] both in doctrine and in methods of religious work. The second period, which ended with the First World War, was marked by the triumph of evangelicalism over quietism in ministry and worship. The third period, which is not yet ended, is marked by the struggle between the old evangelicalism and modern liberalism. Russell thinks that the new authority of science and philosophy is providing new life for Quaker mysticism and its faith in the Inner Light.

We have then this significant development: A group starts out with a definite and radically mystical emphasis. It refuses to be bound by fixed doctrines, and it regards the promptings of the Spirit in the heart of the individual as the final authority in religion. But eventually it re-emphasizes the standardized doctrines and forms which it had originally rejected, and now it has been largely reabsorbed into the main body of Christian believers, retaining only as emblems of its historic position the avoidance of all sacramentarian practices and, in some branches, the practice of waiting upon the promptings of the Spirit.

Nevertheless the Society of Friends is still very much alive; it retains certain distinctive features; and never were the Quakers held in greater respect than they are today. Their numbers are not large, but they have remained true to the principle of religious inwardness and good will among men, and their fine record during the two world wars was such as to commend them to thoughtful people. The followers of George Fox in many respects have been reabsorbed into the larger Christian group, and some of his distinctive beliefs have been given up, but his message as a whole has been amply validated by the quickening which it brought and by the creative forces which it set in motion.

[7] This term denotes the practice of waiting for the prompting of the Spirit in public worship and the philosophy of life associated therewith.

2. ANALOGOUS DEVELOPMENT OF CHRISTIAN THEOLOGY

The development of Christian theology parallels to a considerable extent that of the religious beliefs of the Society of Friends.

Jesus, like Fox, was convinced that he had tapped anew the sources of spiritual power. He believed that he had found the true way of life and he followed it with singlehearted devotion, inviting others to take up their cross and follow him. He was not uninterested in theology, but his concern lay chiefly in simplifying the elaborate structure of belief and practice which the Judaism of that time had built up. He reduced all the law and the prophets to the simple principles of love of God and neighbor. In so doing he clashed with the religious leaders of his time, but throughout he felt himself at one with the great Hebrew prophets; he was no innovator but the champion of the Hebrew prophetic religion.

Following the death of Jesus there arose the belief in Jesus as the risen Lord. This was something new and distinctive, and for many generations the theologically-minded centered their attention upon the doctrine of the Trinity in which the belief was incorporated. In dealing with this problem the keen intellect of Paul of Tarsus had an important part. Not the least of his accomplishments was his contribution to the beliefs in the divinity of Christ.[8] But Paul, like Jesus and like Fox, was interested primarily in the vitalizing life of the Spirit, and theological dogmas were to him of secondary importance. His other great contribution lay in freeing the religion of Jesus from the ritualistic fetters which would have kept it a minor part of the Jewish religion, while at the same time retaining the Old Testament as a basic part of the Christian Bible. Christianity was thus at the outset cut loose organically from its parent religion, while at the same time keeping the basic beliefs of that religion, and it was never reabsorbed.

With the passing of the years, as the Christians increased in num-

[8] This deeply rooted belief, supported as it is by the beauty of the figure which the Gospels reveal, may explain the fact that religious leaders such as Fox, even though revered by their followers, were kept in a subordinate place.

ber and in power, their interest in theology increased—and for the same reasons that apologetic and theological writings appeared in Quakerism. It was important for the early Christians to gain recognition from the ruling classes and from the intellectually elite. It was also important for the purposes of religious education that the basic beliefs should be clarified and systematized.

Elaborate systems therefore were worked out. In all of them the aim was to harmonize the Christian beliefs with those of the intelligent people of the time and to bring out the points of likeness and difference, not merely to make them intelligible to others, but to support the faith of the believers. For the Christians themselves it was essential that their beliefs should be integrated with the best in their social organization. These attempts are represented at their best in the work of St. Augustine, who brought together the finest elements of the Hebrew, Greek, and Roman cultures [9] and made them available for the religious thinking of the Western world throughout the succeeding millennium.

Here and there throughout the history of the Christian religion new groups would spring up. People who, like George Fox and his followers, felt that they had tapped anew the sources of spiritual power would seek to bring the elaborated system of beliefs and practices back to first principles. Until the time of the Reformation these various new beginnings were for the most part reabsorbed or kept within a single dominant body. For the most part their mystical experiences merely gave emotional validation to certain features of the main tradition, though in some cases they introduced new insights and made new contributions. Those groups which diverged too widely in belief and practice were successfully suppressed.

With the Reformation the main current of the Christian tradition was divided. The basis of that cleavage, as we have seen, lay in the concept of authority. Both the Roman Catholics and the Reformers agreed in accepting the Bible as the divinely inspired Word of God.

[9] Adolph Harnack, "Augustin's Konfessionen," in *Reden und Aufsätze* (Giessen: J. Rickersche Verlagsbuchhandlung, 1904), I, 51 ff.

They differed on the question of who was to do the interpreting. The Catholics held that the Church was the final authority. The various Protestant bodies have been at one in claiming final authority for the enlightened conscience of the individual.

Since the Reformation the religious beliefs of Christendom have become increasingly complex, and that complexity is nowhere greater than in the United States of America. It is hardly possible today to speak of any main current of Christian tradition. Yet certain common elements among the Christian churches which have been dominant in American culture go far toward explaining the strength and the weakness of that culture. These elements include faith in the common man, belief in the right to follow the dictates of one's own conscience, belief in the right to interpret the Bible for oneself, and consequent emphasis upon popular education.

3. THE SIGNIFICANCE OF RELIGIOUS FAITH

This brief review of the development of a particular set of religious beliefs and of the larger development out of which they came throws light upon the significance of religious faith and upon its place in the social process.

Both Quakerism and Christianity originated in the experience of individuals. In both cases they were men who were convinced that they had tapped anew the sources of spiritual power and were commissioned as spokesmen of a Greater-than-themselves. Setting forth with deep emotion to proclaim their message to others, they became nuclei of new social formations. Other men were won by their earnestness and enthusiasm, accepted their leadership, shared in their mystical experience.

Thus new groups were born. They were organized not around abstract values but around what was regarded as a living and eternal relationship. From the beginning the aim of the group was to make that relationship dominant in all departments of life and to extend it into an unending future. The distinctive beliefs were so stated as to bring out the points of likeness and contrast with prevailing beliefs and practices in order to support their own faith, to appeal to the best contemporary intelligence, and to facilitate transmission to the rising generation. In this process vision and emotion inevitably waned, but not without being translated into habit and custom. Although the new beliefs were sometimes altered in the process, reverting to the old type, the social and personal structures were profoundly modified.

Religion and culture are in this way closely interrelated. Cultures are of course profoundly affected by new inventions such as steam engines and telephones and by new discoveries such as the Copernican system and the theories of evolution and atomic energy, but changes in religious belief have to do with the more intimate, nuclear relationships of life. They center in the dynamic source of all values, and they are likely to have great influence upon those organized beliefs and attitudes regarding the ways of living and working together which constitute a particular culture. And every culture tends to be associated with some distinctive orientation toward that which is regarded as universal and abiding in the social relationships.

This inquiry has shown that new beginnings in religion occur spontaneously under the stress of life's crisis experiences, both personal and social. New prophets are constantly appearing upon the scene, some true, some false; some giving expression to religious beliefs which are superior and forward-looking, others to beliefs and practices which are inferior and regressive; some worthy of devotion and admiration, others rightly consigned to institutions for the mentally ill. It is necessary, therefore, to consider carefully how the true prophets are distinguished from the false and the superior beliefs from the inferior.

4. Criteria of Validity

a. OPERATIONS OF COMMON SENSE

Within the normal social process discriminations between superior and inferior religious beliefs are constantly being made. The following criteria may be distinguished:

i. Consistency

The fact that a well-organized philosophy of life, regardless of its truth or falsity, has value to the person who holds it is an important consideration. Thus as soon as George Fox began to think of himself as a minister of Christ, and a new set of beliefs took shape around that role, his personality was reorganized. He emerged from confusion and uncertainty and despair to become a stable, self-assured, and socially effective man who was able to sway others with his deep convictions. So also in the case of many mental patients, whenever a disordered state is followed by a systematization of their beliefs, the disordered condition ceases. Although others may not believe in their ideas, insofar as they believe in themselves and have some settled philosophy of life they become stabilized persons.

The tragic plight of the paranoic, however, points to the insufficiency of this single criterion. There is always danger in seeking consistency with certain preconceived ends and concepts without taking into account the complex and changing factors which actually enter into the situation. This is a danger from which philosophers and theologians have not always escaped. Among the religious there is a common tendency to accept certain traditional beliefs as authoritative and to base their reasoning upon them. Even many who call themselves liberals make judgments on the basis of preconceived values. This, as Dewey points out,[10] excludes from the field of inquiry all consideration of ends and consequences and reduces inquiry to a consideration of the means of realizing objectives already agreed upon. Such a tendency leads inevitably to the danger of a self-consistent system built up after the fashion of the paranoic without regard to the complex and often contradictory facts.

But consistency in the sense of increasing harmony in the internal organization, together with increasing adjustment to the external world, is an important criterion in the validation of any belief or system of beliefs. Fox's place as a prophet rests upon the facts that

10 *Logic* (New York: Henry Holt & Co., 1938), p. 495.

he had a well-integrated system of beliefs which he exemplified in his personal life, that those beliefs found response among other religious people of his time, and that his central insights have stood the test of time, even in the face of our rapidly increasing knowledge of the universe.

ii. Continuity

To a peculiar degree George Fox was a solitary figure. His primary experience grew out of the sense of loneliness in a serious-minded boy who found himself the butt of many cruel jokes. It began with the command to forsake all and be as a stranger unto all. Apparently he had come to the place where he had to choose between an attempt to be a good fellow and fidelity to the faith of his fathers. He chose the latter, and never afterward did he ally himself to any existing group. Instead, he himself founded a new group. Yet Fox, like most middle-class Englishmen of his time, was very much under the influence of the Calvinistic interpretation of Christianity. He reacted against it, and in his teachings he emphasized those things in which he differed. Those things he held in common with Calvinism he took for granted. In his reaction against Calvinism, he appealed constantly to the authority of the Gospels and of the letters of Paul. Although a solitary figure, a prophet with a new message, he belongs definitely within the stream of Christian tradition.

So it is with other prophets and mystics. They may be innovators who bring some new message and have some important new insight, but there is always a stream of tradition by which they test their beliefs and by which they in turn are tested. To get outside such a stream of tradition is to be placed inevitably in the category of the insane.

Among different cultures and among different religions there is much variation in the degree of tolerance shown toward those who diverge from the traditional and generally held beliefs. The greatest degree of tolerance is probably to be found in Protestant America.

iii. Social Acceptance

The existence of a group of followers is another criterion by which a prophet is judged. At least in democratic America, under its principle of religious freedom, the Father Divines are not committed as insane; neither are they stoned or placed in jail. No matter how peculiar the beliefs, we give them the benefit of the doubt if they have succeeded in gathering together even two or three in the name of religion. The same principle operates to some extent even under autocratic rule and among tradition-minded peoples. Certainly the existence of some who believe in him will give inward support to any would-be prophet in any culture, and the presence of even a few disciples will greatly increase his chances of getting a respectful hearing. And with the increase in the number of adherents there is a corresponding increase in the drawing power of a new faith. The crowd tends to follow the crowd.

iv. Social Consequences

The chief yardstick by which the claims of any prophet and the validity of any set of religious beliefs are measured is to be found in the social consequences. The fruits which a religion brings forth will more or less automatically determine its power of survival. Blind leaders of the blind may attract large numbers of followers, but they are likely to fall into the ditch. In the end they will be measured by the extent to which their beliefs and practices have enabled their followers to survive in the stern struggle for survival and to achieve a more abundant life as measured by quality and breadth and complexity.

b. CONTROLLED OBSERVATION

The criteria which we have considered are used both consciously and unconsciously within the social process. Common sense requires that our beliefs should be reasonably consistent with each other and that they should not depart too far from what is generally accepted.

It also takes account of consequences and is swayed all too easily by the opinions of the crowd. But such procedures are slow and often wasteful. It is therefore necessary to discover more satisfactory means for testing the validity of our religious beliefs in order that we may avoid expensive errors and that religious faith may be directed into the more creative channels. Herein lies the task of that discipline which is known as "theology." [11]

Thus far, however, Protestant theology has shown a strange lag. There exists today a wide gap between that co-operative enterprise to which we give the name of "science" and the efforts of those whose task it is to organize and test the religious experience of our people.

The Protestant churches of America have been greatly interested in higher education. They have founded many colleges and universities, including some of the largest and most influential. They have also lent their support to a system of popular education which culminates in tax-supported universities. To those institutions they have entrusted the task of exploring human nature. No little progress has been made, but so far their inquiry has very seldom extended to the level of the religious. The tendency during the last fifty years has been toward a narrow specialization which ignores the larger perspectives. Seeking to be exact and "scientific," our psychologists have busied themselves with what they can see and measure in the laboratory. Our sociologists have been cumbered about with statistics. And both have generally disclaimed responsibility for the study of motives and values, issues which are of central importance in personal and social organization.

Theologians, on the other hand, have made little use of the methods of co-operative inquiry as developed by the scientific worker. They have indeed done some fine and careful work in the field of biblical criticism and of church history, but the realm of religious

[11] This term is here used in its more inclusive sense, to embrace the disciplines which have or should have to do with the organizing and testing of religious belief.

experience is rarely touched before its records have gathered much dust on library shelves.[12]

There exists today a great need for carrying forward the empirical study of human nature in its various aspects to the higher reaches and broader perspectives with which religion is concerned. In full accordance with the methods of scientific inquiry, it ought to be possible to bring together the findings and insights of the different specialized fields and to use them to guide our thinking on matters in the realm of faith.

RECONSIDERATION

The conclusion at which we have arrived is that the development and validation of religious faith is a vital part of the social process. Religious beliefs have to do with the nuclear and with the ultimate relationships of life, with its origins and with its ends. They are fundamental to the ways of living and working together which constitute what we call a "culture," and new social formations or modifications in the existing social order are likely to be linked to some deviating philosophy of life. For this reason we find within the social process

[12] This situation is reflected in the paucity of the journals in the field of religion which can lay claim to scientific standing. In spite of the size of the professional group concerned, there are today hardly more than ten such journals published in this country, an interesting contrast with the psychiatric profession with its less than four thousand members and its twenty journals. In the journals we do have, empirical studies of human nature and of religious experience are conspicuous by their absence. In the *Journal of Religion* for the fourteen years from 1931 to 1944 there were 283 articles, of which only eight were empirical studies of religious experience and only five others made use of empirical studies by other workers. Many of them represented careful documentary research, but most of them reported merely unchecked observation and reflection. In the *Review of Religion* for its first nine years there were 102 articles and none was empirical in the sense that it made use of the methods of science to study living religious experience. *Religious Education* for the seven years from 1936 to 1943 contained two hundred articles, most of which dealt with contemporary Christianity, but only twenty of them were quantitative studies or attempts to give an exact account of the present status or historical development of some clearly defined and limited situation, group, or institution.

In the current books on theology very little attempt is made to begin with the study of actual religious beliefs and of their origin and significance. Anton T. Boisen: "Co-operative Inquiry in Religion," *Religious Education*, September, 1945.

various means for sifting out the superior religious beliefs from the inferior and the more trustworthy prophets from the less trustworthy.

A new belief must not deviate too widely from beliefs already held or it will upset the balance of the personality and subject its advocate to the suspicion of insanity. It must be capable of assimilation into a more or less coherent system. It must command a certain modicum of social support; and always it will be judged by its consequences in terms of the well-being of its adherents.

The history of the Christian Church reveals many instances of the process by which new religious beliefs are adopted and old ones modified. The new belief is first voiced by an individual, then accepted by an increasing number of believers. A new sect may thus be formed, which develops its particular system of tenets and practices, and makes its distinctive contribution. It is then likely to become indistinguishable from the parent body, except, perhaps, for certain forms and slogans which serve as rallying insignia for faithful, though un-understanding, adherents.

In Christianity, as an offshoot of Judaism, we have a division of major importance, a body of beliefs of peculiar value incarnated in a luminous personality, which was not recombined with the parent stream. Instead it has maintained its own identity, incorporating within itself certain features from the dominant Graeco-Roman culture and exerting a determining influence upon Western civilization. The question demanding attention next is how far the religious beliefs which are central in American Protestantism can stand inspection in the light of our criteria of validity.

XII. Central Tenets
of American Protestantism

OUR survey of the characteristics of typical American churches has led us to the conclusion that despite the wide diversity among them there are still certain common elements which have been important factors in our culture, certain central tenets to which the Luthers and the Foxes and the Wesleys tend ever to return. These may be briefly summarized as follows:

1. That man is a child of God and that the present life is continuous with a life after death in which reward and punishment are meted out to the individual.
2. That human destiny is under a control that is intelligent and friendly and can best be represented by the idea of God as a heavenly Father.
3. That God makes known His will to men through the promptings of conscience and the inspirations of the creative mind, and that the great historical revelation is to be found in the books of the Old and New Testaments.
4. That the life and teachings of Jesus of Nazareth are the supreme revelation of the character and will of God, and that salvation is to be found through faith in him and the acceptance of the way of life which he exemplified.
5. That the way of salvation is expressed supremely in Jesus' sacrificial death and that it involves three steps: (a) conviction of sin, (b) regeneration, and (c) sanctification.

6. That the perpetuation and re-creation of religious faith is conditioned upon religious assemblage for the purpose of common worship and instruction.

We shall now attempt to apply our criteria of validity to the examination of these tenets, taking account of our brief excursions into
the field of history and of our observations of those searching experiences which afford us the nearest approach to controlled experi-
mentation in the realm of religious experience.

1. THE NATURE AND DESTINY OF MAN

Our survey of the beliefs of the Christian churches of America has
shown us that they all agree in regarding man as very important. He
is, they say, the child of God. Although born in sin and subject to
human frailties and perversities, he has an immortal soul, and the
present life is merely a period of training for a life hereafter. In that
future life each man will stand revealed as he really is, and those who
are worthy will be received into the Kingdom of God. Those who
are not worthy will be banished into outer darkness. Is this just wishful thinking? Have we found any evidence to justify such a high es-
timate of human nature? And what are the social effects of such a
belief?

It seems to be quite in accord with our working hypothesis that
human nature is fundamentally social. The view that the personality
is the internalization within the individual of the social organization
to which he belongs has implications which are of tremendous significance theologically. The individual human being in this view is
one with Something above and beyond himself. He exists for a few
short years as the temporal embodiment of an eternal process.
Within him are incorporated the results of millions and millions of
years of development. Within him lie potentialities which look forward into an unending future. In the light of what science is telling
us regarding the evolutionary process, atomic energy, and the in-

finite complexity of the human organism, the psychotic patient whose eyes are opened so that he can see back to the beginning of all creation, who finds that he has lived before in previous incarnations, who feels that he is one with God, may not be wholly mistaken. It is perhaps no accident that these ideas crop out again and again in individuals who are struggling desperately for personal salvation and that they appear in many religions. In the case of the mental patient the difficulty lies not so much in the fallacy of the ideas as in the fact that he has not been able to assimilate them. Either his universe is thrown into terrific disorganization, or else he builds it again too small and with too little regard for the organized experience of his time and group.

In the matter of inherited sinfulness and the danger of "damnation," the Christian beliefs find much support in our observations in the mental hospital.

We see, for one thing, the perversity of human nature—the stubborn clinging to inherited tendencies which make for distress and woe and prevent the realization of the personal and social potentialities of mankind.

We see also the importance of the thoughts of the heart. Nonorganic mental illness, as is being increasingly recognized, is to be explained in terms of the struggle of conscience with unruly desires rather than with actual misbehavior.[1] So delicate and potent is the human conscience in its operations that, according to some authorities,[2] the "superego" can never really be deceived.

We have discovered, furthermore, that the sense of guilt, which is being more and more generally recognized as the major factor in nonorganic mental illness, consists essentially in the sense of being banished from the inwardly conceived fellowship of those whom one counts most worthy of love and honor. Guilt is due, according to

[1] Karl Menninger, *Love Against Hate* (New York: Harcourt, Brace & Co., 1942), p. 205.
[2] Karen Horney, *The Neurotic Personality of Our Time* (New York: W. W. Norton & Co., 1937), p. 221, also Chap. 13.

Franz Alexander,[3] to the presence of desires and tendencies which can be neither controlled nor acknowledged for fear of condemnation.

Any mental hospital can furnish abundant evidence of the remarkable lengths to which men will go in the effort to protect themselves against unfavorable self-judgment, which, according to our view, is also social judgment. In the hospital we see in exaggerated form the many devices employed. We are all familiar with the device of withdrawal into a world of wishful thinking, with the plan of taking refuge in fancied illness, with the tendency to transfer blame upon other persons, and with the many other distortions of belief which are resorted to, outside the hospital as well as within, in order to escape self-blame.

Most instructive also is what happens when an individual loses faith in himself and gives up the struggle. Examples crowd the back wards of our mental hospitals. The incoherent thinking of these patients, their disjointed speech, and their incongruous ideas tell us that they are living in a private world of their own. These symptoms also indicate fragmentation which has taken place in their personalities. They tell us that the experience of being "damned" is an ever-present reality. Damnation, however, according to our observations in the hospital, is not a matter of eternal torment. Suffering seems to be remedial. It indicates usually that the healing forces are at work. When hope goes, pain and suffering are likely to go with it.

We are led to the conclusions that the sense of being cut off from the fellowship of the best is something supremely intolerable; that the deepest need of the human heart is the need for love; and that the Christian view of salvation as a matter of fellowship with God and membership in the kingdom of heaven seems a true insight.

The belief that the personality survives in some form after death is a deep-seated one. According to observations of mental sufferers, ideas

[3] *Psychoanalysis of the Total Personality*, Nervous and Mental Disease Publishing Company, New York, 1930, Lecture V.

of death tend to be associated with ideas of rebirth.[4] There is considerable evidence that many suicidal attempts have behind them some inchoate hope of a new start. The idea of cosmic identification, so common in the acute disturbances, suggests the possibility that after death the consciousness of the individual, without losing the memories which determine personal identity, may be merged with some Larger-than-self. As the cell is to the personality as a whole, so, it may be, is the personality to some more inclusive consciousness.[5]

For this belief in the survival of the personality there is indeed no convincing evidence. Neither is there any evidence of man's perfectibility, either individually or socially. At the same time there is no evidence which conflicts with the hope of immortality or with the dreams of a better order of society. And there is abundant evidence that faith in a future life and in a redeemed society may serve as a powerful incentive to courageous living in the present.

Not least in importance are the social consequences of the Christian doctrine of man, especially the beliefs of the Calvinistic churches which have had so much influence in America. As contrasted with the complacency of Confucianism, which took an optimistic view of the world and looked upon man as innately good and capable of becoming better, American Christians have emphasized the world's imperfection and man's innate depravity. As contrasted with the Buddhists, whose world view is pessimistic, they have emphasized man's infinite potentialities. Unlike the Hindus, who have accepted the world as unchangeable, American Christians generally believe that they have never-dying souls to save and that fitness for the skies is dependent upon a life of service to one's fellows here below.

Christian beliefs have thus thrown into sharpest possible relief the opposition between human frailty and the moral law, between consciousness of sin and the need of salvation, and between the respon-

[4] August Hoch, *Benign Stupors* (New York: The Macmillan Company, 1921), Chap. V.
[5] Cf. William McDougall, *Abnormal Psychology* (New York: Charles Scribner's Sons, 1926), pp. 546 ff.; also Gustav Theodor Fechner, *Zend Avesta* (Leipzig: Im Insel Verlag, 1922).

sibilities of this present life and punishment in a life hereafter. Christian beliefs, particularly those of Puritanism, says Max Weber,[6] have made for commitment to the never-ending task of making over the existing world. Where the Confucianist sought to adapt himself to the world and the Buddhist to escape from it, the Christian has sought to overcome it.

2. THE FATHERHOOD OF GOD

The Christian churches of America are agreed in believing that human destiny is under an intelligent and friendly control that can best be represented by the idea of a heavenly Father.

That the idea of God as a Father is a true insight is supported by psychoanalytic experience. Psychoanalysts are convinced, on the basis of their intimate studies of human nature, that each individual's religion and his idea of God are derived from his relationship to his parents or parent substitutes. To think of God as a father therefore represents accurately the genesis of the concept of God. It also carries with it the idea of authority and of kindliness.

Belief in the fatherhood of God is belief in a supreme object of loyalty, and it corresponds to certain fundamental requirements of human nature which have been revealed by this study. First of all, it represents the need of love. To define religion, as some do, as the "pursuit of the highest moral values" [7] seems in the light of our findings somewhat questionable. Values, we have concluded, do not exist in and of themselves. They are rather functions of the social relationships, and the idea of God makes those relationships supreme and living and real. Religions in which the idea of a personal God does not appear are religions of an intellectualist aristocracy. They do not meet the needs of the common man. Thus in China and also in India, where the better-educated think of an impersonal Cosmic

---

[6] *Religionssoziologie*, 3 vols. (Tuebingen: J. C. B. Mohr, 1922), I, 534.

[7] See the Symposium on "The Definition of Religion" in the *Journal of Religion* for March and May, 1927, particularly the article by Eustace Haydon and Edward Scribner Ames. See also Chapter 2 in *A Psychological Study of Religion* by James H. Leuba (New York: The Macmillan Company, 1912).

Spirit, the masses have believed in all sorts of spirits, some friendly, some mischievous, some cruel. The popular religion was little influenced by the best intelligence of the time. The idea of God stands for the fellowship of the best, without which the individual cannot live. It represents something which is operative in the lives of all men whether they recognize it or not. It is a condition of religious vitality that this internalized sense of fellowship should be strong and active.

Belief in God is an assertion of the integrity of the universe as contrasted with the disorganized or disturbed universe of the mental patient or with the bewildering pantheon of nature deities such as we find in Hinduism and among the Chinese masses. Belief in God can hardly fail to have a unifying effect upon the individual and upon the group. By providing a common object of loyalty it tends to develop those common standards and ways of living and working together which constitute a "culture." It is related particularly to the ethical system.

In China the absence of any universal, personal God seems to explain the lack of any general system of ethics.[8] The fact that there has been no transcending of the loyalty to the finite ancestors has meant that each Chinese family has had its own Ten Commandments and the Chinese Empire has remained a loosely organized system of kinship groups. The same situation has obtained in India, where each caste had its own code and no universal ethical system had been worked out. The acceptance of some loyalty conceived of as supreme and universal is thus seen to be a great aid in social and personal integration.

Belief in a sovereign heavenly Father represents furthermore the requirements of reverence and humility. The importance of these requirements is signalized in the experience of the religious crank or zealot who ignores the views and attitudes of his fellows and brings the divine down to his own level, so that his universe becomes little larger than himself. The man without reverence and without hu-

[8] Weber, op. cit., I, 523.

mility, be he crank or scientist, is out of right relationship with the universe and with the society of which he is a part. To the lack of reverence and of perspective we may attribute religious wars and perhaps also wars which make no claim to religious sanction.

Finally, belief in a sovereign heavenly Father represents the requirement that the lesser loyalties be transcended. This requirement is the religious equivalent of the principle of autonomy and maturity in the educational and therapeutic field, but it carries with it an additional value. The fact that maturity is thought of in terms of the transfer of loyalty from the finite parents and teachers to a heavenly Father provides for social support at the very center of the organization of the self. For the truly religious man humility before God becomes a source of strength and comfort and makes him independent of the opinions of men and of the trials and vicissitudes of his temporal existence.

Belief in the fatherhood of God thus seems in accord with what can be observed in the laboratory of life. It appears spontaneously in those who are passing through searching crisis experiences and it represents something of supreme importance in the lives of all men, whether they recognize it or not. It is rooted in the love which is the deepest need of the human. It stands for the integrity of the universe and makes for the unification of personal and social life. It demands the achievement of spiritual maturity and calls for reverence and humility. In all these particulars belief in God accords with the conditions of personal and social well-being. Its social consequences are of incalculable value.

3. DIVINE REVELATION

Among the Christian churches of America there is full agreement in the belief that God makes known His will to men and that the great historic revelation is to be found in the Bible. Among the Protestant churches there is also agreement that the individual has the right to interpret the Bible in accordance with the dictates of his own conscience.

The belief in the authority of the Bible has had important social consequences. It is of no little importance that the Old Testament has been included as part of the sacred book. The Christian culture thus has been built upon the Hebrew culture, and from it have come norms and standards which have had great influence in Western civilization. From the New Testament has come the ideal toward which the finer spirits have sought to move.

Of enormous importance in American culture has been the Protestant insistence upon the right of the individual to interpret the sacred book for himself. This emphasis has provided an incentive to the development of popular education. It has encouraged men to think for themselves. It has undergirded the democratic movement and the institutions associated therewith. It has had much to do with the development of science and industry. One result has been an enlightened study of the Bible itself, which has modified our concepts of religion and of the processes by which the creative manifests itself in human life.

With this problem of revelation or inspiration we have been much concerned in this inquiry. In one particular our findings have been negative. We have found no evidence that there is in religious experience any special way of knowing.[9] George Fox's assumption that ideas which came flashing into his mind with peculiar vividness were of divine origin is no longer tenable. We have found the same assumption in many psychotic patients. They also believe that God talks to them, and this belief is the basis of their disturbance.

The possibility of revelation is not ruled out for this reason. But to accept an idea as authoritative because of the way in which it comes is extremely dangerous. We must not base our discriminations upon the psychological process involved. The real distinction is to be found in the realm of value. More than that, it must be recognized that there is no difference between the creative insight of the

[9] For a divergent view, if I understood him aright, see Douglas C. MacIntosh, *The Problem of Religious Knowledge* (New York: The Macmillan Company, 1927).

scientist and that of the seer or prophet, except as regards subject matter. Both seer and scientist are pathfinders.Their significance lies in the fact that they depart from the beaten paths and arrive at new insights and new sources of power. Both break out of the closed universe of traditionalism and authoritarianism.[10]

It is quite true that the mystic is likely to be conservative in his theology, especially when the problem at the center of his attention has been his own role in life. In finding a new role, he discovers that traditional beliefs once dry and profitless take on new life and meaning because they are now associated with that role. In addition, the very strangeness of the experience may cause him to lean more heavily upon the support of tradition. Nevertheless many mystics have been pathfinders. George Fox, for example, broke with the view that the source of authority in religion is to be found chiefly in a sacred book and that the means of grace is entrusted to some special group.

The great difference between the scientist and the seer lies in the fact that the scientist has developed certain methods of testing his insights and that such methods have been little used as yet in the field of religious experience. Scientific claims are based upon objective evidence which can be verified or disproved by others, whereas the prophet's claim is based upon his deep but subjective conviction that he is the spokesman of the Lord, and his followers accept his word as authoritative because they believe in *him*.

The question arises as to how far the methods of science can be applied to religious truth as well as to other fields of human experience. The answer must be partly negative. Religious experience is and must remain private and personal. In all mystical experience the emotions are deeply involved and co-operative inquiry is not easily possible. Nevertheless certain principles can be established and certain errors can be recognized.

Thus, we see, the old naïve faith that ideas and promptings

[10] John Dewey, *Reconstruction in Philosophy* (New York: Henry Holt & Co., 1920), p. 54.

which flash into the mind are to be attributed to a superhuman source because of the way they come is not tenable. False and misleading and diabolical ideas come the same way, and for every true prophet there are scores of blind leaders of the blind. But the human mind does operate creatively, and religious faith is not without justification in believing that in times of deep emotional stirring and intellectual quickening ideas of great value do come. What is needed is the attitude of humility which is willing to put religious insight to the test. The attitude of faith must be combined with the readiness to be corrected wherever error lurks. In this there should be no difference between the attitude of the religious man and that of the scientist.

Scientific method can give no certain answers to questions of faith. Proof of the existence of God there will never be. Neither, perhaps, are we likely to find proof of immortality. But we can guard against certain common errors. We can find help in building upon foundations which are relatively sure. The advent of science need not still the prophetic voice. It should help it rather to speak with greater authority. It should also help in distinguishing between the true prophets and the false and in rebuilding religious faith upon a body of tested and ordered experience in which personal authority and prestige and tradition give ground before a growing knowledge of spiritual law.

4. THE PERSON AND WORK OF CHRIST

The acceptance of Jesus of Nazareth as the supreme revelation of the divine is the bond of union among American Christian churches. This acceptance varies in viewpoint. The orthodox view believes in Jesus as the personal savior who through his death upon the cross atoned for the sins of men and thus, as the risen Christ, received power to give salvation to those who believed in him. The liberal view emphasizes the faith of Jesus and the way of life which he exemplified. Common to all is the acknowledgment of him as the object of loyalty and the determiner of the ideals and standards by which the Christian judges himself.

The origin of this belief in Jesus as Savior dates back to the early years of the Christian religion and is related to a question upon which observations in a mental hospital may throw some light. Did or did not Jesus think of himself as the Messiah of the Jews? The tendency among present-day New Testament scholars is to hold that he did not. They ascribe this idea to his followers rather than to Jesus himself.

This question has been discussed elsewhere.[11] It is only necessary here to recall the fact that in those searching experiences which are to be regarded as manifestations of nature's power to heal, and as such are closely related to the more dramatic types of religious experience, we find a certain characteristic constellation of ideas. There are ideas of death, of world disaster or world change, of some important role which the individual himself is to have in the impending change, of rebirth or previous incarnation, and of mission. These ideas crop out spontaneously. Where we find one, we are likely to find the others also. Now according to the Gospels' account, Jesus had all of these ideas. They are deeply embedded in the Gospel sources. It is impossible to deny that he proclaimed the imminent coming of the Kingdom of God which was to follow some catastrophic change; that he thought of himself as having an important role in this Kingdom of God; and that he looked upon his own death as a condition of the fulfillment of his mission. It seems probable too that he expected to be raised from the dead, an idea which would correspond to that of rebirth.

Observations in the hospital therefore answer the question which one eminent New Testament scholar has asked:[12] How could Jesus possibly have arrived at the conviction that he was the official apoca-

[11] Boisen, *Exploration of the Inner World* (New York: Harper & Brothers, 1936), Chap. 4. See also "What Did Jesus Think of Himself?" *Journal of Bible and Religion*, January, 1952.
[12] S. J. Case, "The Alleged Messianic Consciousness of Jesus," *Journal of Biblical Literature*, December, 1926.

lyptic Messiah of the Jews? The hospital laboratory furnishes abundant evidence that this idea, together with the idea of world catastrophe and the ideas of death and rebirth, appears spontaneously in certain types of experience.

This inquiry has led to a further pertinent conclusion: There may be some elements of truth in these notions which appear with such surprising frequency in experiences of this type. They may represent a true insight. Man *is* infinitely great. Even the most insignificant and commonplace person, science tells us, is composed of an infinite number of solar systems; he is a galaxy in himself. The significance of Jesus may well lie precisely in the fact that he was able to see in true perspective that which hospital patients see as in a glass darkly. And he was able to rebuild his life on the basis of the new role which was given him and to make it strong and true and in full accord with the finest spirits of the ages.

But regardless of whether Jesus did or did not think of himself as the Messiah of the Jews, there can be no question that his followers so considered him. Jesus the inspired teacher became for the early Christians the risen Lord. Our recognition of the social nature of man enables us to understand the significance of that fact. A teaching, a philosophy, an ethical code must be incarnated in some personality before it can become religiously vital. Ethical standards and religious values do not exist in and of themselves. They are functions of the social relationships. It is therefore a fact of cardinal importance that Christianity had in the person of its founder an object of loyalty who represented so beautifully the loftiest potentialities of mankind.

There is of course a sharp distinction between the Jesus of history and the Christ of faith. The latter is a social construct which is enriched by the devotion of nineteen centuries of faithful followers. Around it cluster tender memories and sacred associations. It is something very different from the actual man who lived and taught in Palestine at the beginning of the era. But its value is no less on that account, and always through the pages of the Gospel records there shines forth a figure which is luminous in its own right and sharply enough defined to correct the deviating attributes with which different groups of followers tend to invest him.

5. THE WAY OF SALVATION

a. THE CROSS

The historic doctrine of salvation, as popularly interpreted, is that Jesus through his sacrificial death upon the cross appeased the wrath of a just God because of man's sin. He thus redeemed men from the curse laid upon them through Adam's fall and won the power to save those who believed in him.

If we turn to the Gospel sources, we find that Jesus did have much to say regarding the death to which he was looking forward, but his actual sayings seem quite at variance with the doctrine of the vicarious atonement. The cross, in his teaching, seems rather to represent a summons to the sacrificial way of life. No one, he said, could be a follower of his who did not take up his cross and follow him.

How this clear teaching of Jesus was transformed into the doctrine of the vicarious atonement may be partly explained in terms of the frailty of human nature. It becomes just another escape device by which those who call themselves Christians are enabled to obtain peace of mind without paying the full price.

We may note in passing that one of the weaknesses of present-day liberal Christianity lies in its tendency to make the way of salvation too easy. The Roman Catholic Church has its celibate priesthood and its monastic orders, the Holiness sects summon men to a life of dramatic devotion, but the liberal churches seem to have little to offer to those whose need is to take religion in earnest and to do something heroic about it.

The demand for expiation is a deep-seated one. Among mental patients it may take the form of self-punishment, self-torture, and sometimes of the taking of one's own life in order to atone for past offenses. Present-day writers on mental hygiene have much to say

regarding "neurotic self-punishment." [13] Most of these writers interpret all ascetic practices as escape devices, counterfeit coinage with
which men buy indulgence from a harsh superego in order to cling
to forbidden tendencies which they are unable either to renounce
or to acknowledge.

There are certainly many instances in which such an interpretation
is justified, but it needs to be recognized that the principle involved
in self-punishment may be essentially sound. Even in its less satisfactory manifestations it may be an attempt at self-discipline, an
expression of real abhorrence for certain genuinely undesirable tendencies. In its more constructive forms self-punishment is a drastic
attempt at reorganization; frequently it is an effort by means of some
dramatic sacrificial act to square accounts and to get rid of unacceptable conflicting tendencies. Even in some of the acute disturbances, as
we have seen, the attempt may be more or less successful.

The significance of self-punishment hinges then upon the delicate
question of motive. Is there or is there not a genuine attempt to
square accounts and to get rid of unacceptable components of the
self? Or does the self-punishment represent an attempt to buy peace
of mind without paying the full price?

The motive of expiation is to be seen not only in mental patients
but also in the blood sacrifices of many religions and in many ascetic
practices. Expiatory manifestations may often be explained by the
fact that social organization is commonly based on force and fear.
The representatives of authority rule by arbitrary decree, and the
young child learns that by punishing himself for his misbehaviors he
often escapes the parental rod. In any case there is a widespread tendency to think of God as a ruler who demands absolute obedience and
whose wrath needs often to be appeased.

The significance of the doctrine of the cross as represented in
Christian teaching at its best lies in its requirement of honest and

[13] E.g., Franz Alexander, op. cit., pp. 97 ff.; Karl A. Menninger, Man Against
Himself (New York: Harcourt, Brace & Co., 1938), pp. 87–143; Karen Horney,
op. cit., Chap. 14.

thoroughgoing commitment to the heroic way of life. It lies also in the concept of God which it reflects—a suffering God, a God of love. In the teaching of Jesus all of the law and the prophets was summed up in the principle of love. His death, then, was the crowning act in a life of service to his fellows; it placed the seal of sincerity upon his life and teaching and freed men from the bondage to a God of fear.

b. THE PROCESS OF SALVATION

The Christian Church, wherever its evangelistic task has been emphasized, has taught that the process of salvation involves three steps: repentance, or conviction of sin; reconciliation, or justification by faith; and sanctification, or the transformation of character to accord with the Christian ideal. The insights thus expressed find much support in present-day psychotherapeutic experience.

The proposition that the consciousness of sin or guilt has therapeutic value may not yet be recognized by many of our psychiatrists, and many of the intelligentsia would regard it as rank heresy. There is today a widespread doctrine that worry is the chief cause of mental illness, and the churches often are held responsible for causing unnecessary suffering in such matters as the handling of the sex drive.

According to our findings, however, worry, even to the point of severe mental disorder, is not in itself an evil. It is rather an attempt at reorganization which is analogous to fever or inflammation in the body. In the handling of the sex drive, for example, the real evil would lie in the short-circuiting of a source of power which must be assimilated before the boy can become a man. The real evil is the failure to grow, the failure to attain one's true objectives in life. Worry, then, may represent an awareness that something is wrong and an effort to do something about it. In that case it is an attempt at cure. The man who thinks he has committed the unpardonable sin is likely to get well unless there are complicating factors. The man who does not get well is he who withdraws from real life into the land of fantasy and easy-pleasure-taking or he who maintains his self-respect by blaming others for his difficulties or by resorting to similar escape devices.

The doctrine that the conviction of sin is the first step in the process of salvation seems therefore true to the facts. The recognition of difficulty and the desire to do something about it are preconditions of growth and achievement.

The doctrine of reconciliation also finds its counterpart in present-day psychotherapeutic experience. Consider, for example, Freud's discovery that the essential condition of the healing process in cases of neurotic difficulty was to be found in the "transference" relationship.[14] At first he thought it was something else, which he called "catharsis." But he soon realized that becoming aware of the difficulty is not enough. It was essential that there should be sharing, or socialization. Wider experience in dealing with the mentally ill has brought some modification of his doctrine of transference, but it has served only to increase the recognition of its importance.

The conclusion follows that psychotherapy is dependent upon the principles of confession and forgiveness. Its major task is to get rid of the sense of guilt and estrangement, which is the primary evil in nonorganic illness. Cure, or salvation, is to be found in the re-establishment of right relations with that which is felt as supreme in the interpersonal relationships. Of this the therapist must be accepted as the representative. Restoration to "mental health," the modern term for "salvation," is conditioned therefore not so much upon the resolution of intrapsychic conflict as upon the sense of being received back into the fellowship of the best.

Herein lies the significance of Luther's doctrine of justification by faith. Salvation is not a matter of conformity to a rigid code or standard of conduct; it is a matter of living relationships. It is an internal organization based upon the faith that human destiny is not in the hands of an arbitrary despot who rules by fear and force; neither is it the plaything of blind, impersonal forces. Human life is rather under

[14] Freud, *An Autobiographical Study*, translated by Jas. Strachey (London: Hogarth Press, 1948).

the control of the God of love who looks upon the heart and honors those who are doing the best they can with the resources at their command.

The doctrine of sanctification finds its equivalent in the recognition that the goal of psychotherapy is the achievement of spiritual maturity. The end of mysticism, as Delacroix points out,[15] is not ecstasy but the transformation of the personality. This is true of all vital religious experience. The quickened sense of fellowship with that which is conceived as the best involves the determined effort to bring oneself into conformity with the standards which have value in that fellowship. The experience has ethical implications and registers in the ethical life. It is definitely perfectionistic, but the perfectionism has to do with the goals of life, rather than with the "Thou shalt nots." The great difficulty with most of the Holiness sects lies in a misinterpretation of this principle. They set up a rigid code which must not be transgressed instead of stressing the objectives and the dynamic factors.

C. SOCIAL REDEMPTION

The hope of a new and better social order in which men shall live together in loyalty to each other and to their Father in heaven has characterized Christianity from the beginning. But this hope has been mingled with a considerable degree of pessimism. The early Christians carried over from their Hebrew progenitors the belief that only a remnant could be saved. The new and better social order was to follow a day of judgment in which the good should be separated from the bad. There was a tendency to place the utopia in the future life rather than in the present. Even so, there has been some hope of the future which has made the Church superior to the social order while at the same time it has participated in the social process. In America, where Calvinism has played an important part, the hope of

[15] *Études d'Histoire et de Psychologie du Mysticisme* (Paris: Felix Alcan, 1908), p. 417.

a better social order in the present world has had great influence. Such a hope is central in liberal Christianity.

6. THE CHURCH

This study has shown that the Hebrew-Christian religion is the only one of the great ethical religions which has practiced religious assemblage for the purpose of instruction and common worship. This provision, as we have seen, has had important social consequences. It has created opportunity for rethinking the fundamental religious beliefs in the light of changing conditions. This will go far toward explaining the fact that Christianity, especially in its Protestant form, has been associated with dynamic and changing cultures and with the marvelous development of science and industry which has characterized the modern world.

This inquiry offers the further suggestion that organized religion finds its basis in the social nature of man. The church is in this view no mere body of doctrine or ceremonies but a fellowship, and its central task is the perpetuation and re-creation of religious faith from mood to mood and from generation to generation. The means employed in the accomplishment of this task will be the subject of the next chapter.

RECONSIDERATION

Among our American Protestant churches with all their diversity and with their manifold crudities there is a certain common core of belief. In spite of the constant tendency to by-pass the stern requirements of true religion and to introduce short cuts and protective devices, in spite of the pressure due to special interests and dominant groups, these common beliefs seem to have much to support them in present-day psychiatric experience. They seem also to be justified by their social consequences.

Especially prominent in American Protestantism has been the recognition of the frailty and perversity of human nature; this insight has been combined with a faith in man's divine destiny and an insistence upon the right of the individual to think for himself and follow the dictates of his own conscience. The resulting emphasis upon popular education and free enterprise has had much to do with the development of science and industry in the Western world.

In terms of social consequences, the beliefs of American Protestant churches have much to validate them. At the same time, however, the very achievements with which Protestantism has been associated have unlocked a Pandora's box of uncontrollable furies. These furies have been driving home to us, in the blasts of bombs and the roar of airplanes, the insufficiency of our individualistic emphasis and the need of a comprehensive loyalty if our civilization is not to perish from the earth.

XIII. *The Perpetuation and Re-Creation of Religious Faith*

T HIS inquiry has furnished evidence of the creative possibilities of crisis periods. It has shown that they have profound significance and that the task of organized religion is the transmutation of the strong emotion and clarified vision of these periods into action and structure and their transmission from mood to mood and from generation to generation.

This means that religion must organize or perish. It must have leaders, symbols, practices, creeds by which faith can be kept alive and vigorous. The divergent tendencies found among American churches have already been considered, but the subject demands further attention. This chapter will therefore undertake a detailed consideration of the common procedures and practices of organized religion and of the conditions making for institutional ill health and those making for institutional effectiveness.

1. THE MEANS OF GRACE

a. SOLITARY PRAYER

Most of the world religions place great emphasis upon private devotions, far greater than does American Christianity. The Moslem is required to say his prayers five times each day. Wherever he may be, when the hour comes he must kneel down and repeat in Arabic certain prescribed prayers. Hindus and Buddhists likewise go through

212

certain ritual performances and repeat certain formulas, sometimes in a language they do not understand.

Similar practices have been found also in the Hebrew-Christian religion. The Hebrew prophets had much to say about the spreading forth of the hands and the making of many prayers. Jesus of Nazareth had to warn his followers against stereotyped prayer. The practice of repeating certain Latin prayers and counting them on the rosary was one of the abuses against which the Reformers rebelled. Back of such practices is the assumption that prayers of this type are pleasing to God, or that they are in the nature of magic formulas which have the power to accomplish certain desired results.

But such abuses in no way lessen the importance of solitary prayer. Jesus in warning his disciples against mechanical prayer instructed them to enter into their closets and pray to their Father who seeth in secret. Modern thinkers like Hocking and Whitehead see in solitude the essence of religion.[1] William James regarded solitary prayer as religion in action. "Prayer," he says, "is no vain exercise of words, no mere repetition of certain sacred formulae, but the very movement itself of the soul, putting itself in a personal relation of contact with the mysterious power from which it draws its life—it may be even before it has a name by which to call it." [2]

Why solitary prayer is important seems clear in the light of our hypothesis that man is a social being and that personality is the internalization of the organized attitudes of the group. Since conscience is the inner forum in which one discusses proposed and performed acts, prayer represents talking over one's problems with God, viewing them through His eyes. As Coe puts it, the presupposition of the whole procedure is that God's way of looking at the matters in question is the true and important one. Around his idea of God the interests of the worshiper are now freshly organized. Prayer is a way of

---

[1] W. E. Hocking, The Meaning of God in Human Experience (New Haven: Yale University Press, 1912), pp. 402 ff.; A. N. Whitehead, Religion in the Making (New York: The Macmillan Company, 1926), p. 47.

[2] Varieties of Religious Experience, p. 464.

getting oneself together, of mobilizing one's dispersed capacities, of begetting the confidence that tends toward victory over difficulties.[3]

Prayer may begin with an expression of desire, but at its best it ends in the organization of one's own desires into a system of desires recognized as superior and then made one's own.[4]

It is clear therefore that organized religion has reason to foster solitary prayer and not to leave it to the ebb and flow of mood and circumstance. Among such efforts in this country one thinks of the "morning watch" of the pre-War Student Volunteers, the Bible reading of the older Christian Endeavor societies, the "quiet time" of the Oxford groupers, and the manuals of daily devotion now being issued by many of our churches.

b. COMMON WORSHIP

Common worship, as we have seen, is distinctive of the Hebrew-Christian religion in contradistinction to other world religions. In this fact we have found the explanation of its relatively dynamic character. A careful study of the types of common worship is therefore important. We may distinguish three—the emotional, the ritualistic, and the instructional.

i. Emotional

Religious meetings characterized by contagious enthusiasm are found most frequently in the early stages of a religious movement, when under the stress of some shared strain and of some enkindling vision people are thinking and feeling together about the things that matter most. Under such conditions the individual is likely to feel himself one with a something Greater than himself, and we have meetings of the type described by Mr. T. in Chapter V.

The early Methodist meetings evidently were of somewhat the same nature. We know that the Wesleys made great use of singing.

[3] *Psychology of Religion* (Chicago: University of Chicago Press, 1916), pp. 311 ff.
[4] *Ibid.*, p. 318.

Charles Wesley wrote hundreds of hymns, and John Wesley himself was a hymn writer and edited a hymnbook. These Methodist hymns were of a more dignified type than those which Mr. T. heard in the House of Prayer, but in America Methodism developed its own type of singing. The abnormal manifestations so common in the early camp meetings may be explained in part by the power of group singing to lift the individual out of himself and induce in him the sense of mystical identification.

The Methodist Church has striven faithfully to keep this original enthusiasm alive. So have the Holiness sects. Group singing, personal testimonies, dramatic performances of various sorts are much in evidence. But no matter how hard they try, it is soon found that the religious experience they value is following some standardized pattern and is being induced by devices that are often meretricious.

Here, for example, are some excerpts from the printed program of the national convention of the Tomlinson Church of God which was held in Cleveland, Tennessee, in 1938. It is somewhat in the nature of a caricature, but this crude attempt to regiment the Holy Spirit is illustrative of the devices to which some of these groups resort:

SATURDAY, SEPTEMBER 10

8:00 P.M. Big concert prayer for all men and especially for our own members to be more spiritual. Make this a mighty prayer. All stand.

8:15 P.M. South Carolina program. "We can, will and must do the work marked out by the 1928 Big Business Program—'Every County in My State, '38.' " E. A. McDonald and his fiery helpers.

NOTE: When this discourse starts have all the South Carolina ministers grouped around close to the speaker. Finish the program by singing a fiery South Carolina song—string band and piano music accompaniment. As the song is announced let all the South Carolina saints from all over the tabernacle rush to the platform and help. Come with a blaze of the Church of God pentecostal fire. Crowd right into the group

with mighty zeal and victorious enthusiasm like you mean
to take your state for Christ and the Church of God.

9:15 P.M. As the above program closes, the Bahama Brass Band break
in with quick fiery music while the Church of God fire
sparkles and flashes. Congregation stand and give vent to
their happy feelings in shouts, dances, run, leaps or whatever
each feels to do for the glory of God and to praise him.
Shout for joy. God is worthy to be praised with music,
shouts, hands up, hand clasps and handkerchief waves. Let
God be glorified by his people.

9:30 P.M. Fiery exhortation and altar call by Mrs. Lois McGuire of
Tennessee.

9:45 P.M. Florida String Band furnish music and singing for the big
altar service. Fiery workers rush right into the altar and
work. Go right into the congregation and bring in the lost,
or those who need to be sanctified and filled with the Holy
Ghost. Get excited for fear some of your friends or anybody
may fall into hell.

11   P.M. Adjournment.

It is of course obvious that those who made out this program had
before them an idealized picture of some meetings in the past in
which there may have been some genuine spontaneity.

Crowd phenomena seem best explained in terms of the social
basis of human nature. We have found the basis of the human
personality in the internalization of the group organization by means
of language. It is dependent upon common response to symbols. The
personality is thus seen as a set of social responses which have become organized and habitualized. Furthermore, the social response
which is the basis of the personality is a response not just to others
in general but to those whom we love and admire and whose authority we accept.

The crowd exhibits a different kind of social force. A crowd is a
group of people thinking and feeling together with reference to a
common idea. If the feeling is at all strong, the previous organization which is dependent upon the verbal symbol is likely to be
swept away. The response to the organized best is likely to give way

before the impact of the present living mass. The mob is likely to do what the individuals who compose it would not do in their sober moments.

The mere mass of the crowd carries with it a certain authority whenever it is responding to a common idea and is swayed by a common emotion. And the sense of identification with a crowd is likely to carry with it a definite exhilaration. Few individuals do not feel a sense of exaltation as members of a great cheering crowd at a football game; few do not thrill at the sight of their country's might on military parade. When, as in the case of Mr. T., the power of the crowd reinforces the accepted loyalties and the individual feels himself in the presence of the living God, the impact of the experience is enormously greater. And that of course was precisely the conviction of the followers of John Wesley and George Fox. It was also the conviction of the early Christians.

The manifestations characteristic of the emotional type of religious meeting are to be explained in terms of the assumption that what does not seem to come from ourselves or from any known agency must be attributed to the Spirit of God. Hence the peculiar value placed upon dancing, jumping, jerking, falling on the floor, speaking in a strange jargon. Such behavior is interpreted as evidence of superhuman influence. In the case of the early Christians speaking with tongues was such a manifestation. The present-day Pentecostals place a special value upon phenomena which they believe to be the same. The important consideration is that, once such behavior is singled out as of special value, the skilled evangelist can reproduce it through the power of suggestion and manipulation of the crowd. The dramatic conversion experience and the speaking with tongues then became stereotyped patterns induced by artificial techniques.

ii. *Ritualistic*

Some form of ritualism, or ceremonialism, is unavoidable in all organized religion. Custom and habit are essential to personal and social organization. We have already seen that those who strive most earnestly to avoid them merely make conventions of their efforts at simplicity. The Quaker meeting follows a set pattern. The Quaker dress becomes a mark of separateness. The Quaker leader, who speaks only as the Spirit prompts him, is likely to find that the Spirit is making use of a peculiarly limited set of stock phrases and that the message is confined to a strangely narrow set of ideas. Even religious experience itself may become fixed in formal patterns. Convention and ritual must therefore be. The question is: What forms will best serve the purposes of true religion?

Among American Protestant churches the Protestant Episcopal communion is distinguished by the attention it gives to ritual. For most Episcopalians not the sermon but the service of worship is the important thing. In that service there is much congregational partici- pation, not merely in song but in prayer and response. There are also frequent changes in posture. And no little appeal is made to the eye. The minister and the choir wear vestments. Much attention is given to the altar and the chancel. The service is carefully standardized, with prescribed readings for the different days of the Church year and certain forms that are said constantly. Great stress is laid upon the sacraments. The ritualistic tendency is often carried to the point that prayers and responses are said with such rapidity that it is difficult to follow them.

The Roman Catholic Church is very heavily burdened with ritual- ism. All sorts of forms and ceremonies are prescribed. There is much pageantry. A large part of the service is conducted in Latin, indicating that the chief emphasis is upon emotional effect, not intellectual instruction. Closer examination of the ritual shows that it is an elaborate gesture language [5] in which everything that is done has some deep meaning. The use of Latin serves to heighten the sense of mystery and to enhance the significance of the sign language.

Coe stresses the relationship of ritualism to sacerdotalism. Ritual- ism is nearly always associated with a type of organization based upon authority.[6] It means priesthoods, traditions, sacred formulas,

[5] Delacroix, La Religion et la Foi (Paris: Felix Alcan, 1932), p. 59.
[6] Op. cit., pp. 125 ff.

sacred scriptures, and authoritative teaching. God makes Himself known not to the members of the group but through some special revelation in the past. Of this revelation the priests are the custodians. As such they are sacred persons. Ritual tends to bring attention back repeatedly to the same point, thus controlling by means of constant reference to that which is authoritatively fixed. It does not, therefore, promote reflection and deliberation but tends to preserve the status quo. For this reason ritualistic religion is especially adapted to national and imperialistic organizations.

Ritualistic services acquire great emotional value for persons who have been raised in the Episcopal and Roman Catholic churches. Tender memories become associated with them and the beauty of music and pageantry make the usual Protestant service seem to them by comparison very drab and dull.

Considerable thought has been given in psychoanalytic circles to the significance of religious ritual. Freud in 1907 pointed out similarities between religious ceremonialism and the behavior of certain neurotic persons.[7] Reik[8] and Alexander[9] have given further attention to the problem. Neurotics go through all sorts of ritualistic performances. There may be excessive scrupulousness in washing the hands, in arranging the bedclothes. There may be a compulsion to touch certain objects and perform apparently meaningless acts.

Study of such cases indicates that these performances are due to an attempt to strike a balance between instinctual urges and the claims of conscience. Neurotic compulsions are thus attempts to buy indulgence for forbidden desires which the patient is unwilling to give up. Freud concludes that religious ritual has a similar explanation and that religion is the universal obsessional neurosis of humanity.[10] Unquestionably there is an element of truth in this view, but it fails to recognize that the common tendency to mistake the

[7] Sigmund Freud, "Zwangshandlungen und Religionsuebungen," Zeitschrift zur Religionspsychologie, Bd. I, Heft 1, 1907.

[8] Theodor Reik, Ritual (New York: W. W. Norton & Co., 1931).

[9] Franz Alexander, Psychoanalysis of the Total Personality, 1930.

[10] Sigmund Freud, The Future of an Illusion (London: Horace Liveright, 1928), p. 76.

symbol for the reality it represents does not lessen the need for symbols. Neither does the tendency to substitute minor for major virtues lessen the value of the virtues.

iii. Instructional

American Protestant churches in general have been characterized by their emphasis upon the sermon. In the Anglican and Roman Catholic churches the service of worship is primary, but the Presbyterian or the Methodist goes usually to hear the preacher, hoping for some message which will give him comfort and strength in the trials and difficulties of life and new insight into its problems. At the Sunday morning service, which is the focal point of his church's program, the sermon usually takes up half the time and even more. It is generally rather dry and commonplace, but Protestant worship services are nevertheless geared to the idea that the function of public worship is instructional and inspirational.

Such an emphasis means that religious faith is no mere acceptance of tradition but belief in and devotion to an ideal.[11] The worshiper is encouraged to reflect, to think for himself, and even to question existing standards. The church has been kept alive to new developments in religious thinking. A place has been kept open for the prophet when he comes. The interest in higher education has been undergirded.

On the other hand, all too often the services have become dull. The attitude has developed that one goes to church for what one can get rather than to express one's loyalty and enter into the fellowship of the best. And the encouragement to freedom of thought has frequently resulted in cutting loose from the free church itself.

C. HOLY DAYS AND HOLY PLACES

The Sabbath, like the church, is an institution which seems to be distinctive of the Hebrew-Christian religion. The Babylonians had a monthly holy day from which the word "Sabbath" is derived, but

[11] Coe, op. cit., pp. 134–35.

there was no seventh day of the week devoted to religious observ-ances.[12] In other religions there are days of cessation from work. But in no religion except perhaps the Buddhist, has one day of the week been so definitely set aside for rest and worship as in the orthodox Hebrew and Christian groups. The Mohammedans observe Friday, but they are not required to cease from work except during the hour of prayer.[13] Among the Jews the observance of the Sabbath has been associated with the requirement of instruction in the law.

In America the keeping of the Sabbath has been much stressed. New England still has its blue laws to remind us of the day when the children of godly families were not permitted to whistle on Sundays or to read any books except those that passed as religious. Those days are gone, but in our Southern states Sunday is rather faithfully observed, and in the country at large that day is not as other days. Some Christian sects have made an issue of keeping the "seventh-day Sabbath."

We have also our sacred festivals at Easter, at Christmas, at Thanksgiving, and on Memorial Day, observed by abstention from work but not always reserved for their original purpose.

Holy places are not so much in evidence in the Christian religion as they are in other religions. America, at least, has little in the way of special shrines and pilgrimages. We do have our sanctuaries. Many church buildings, however, have only one or two rooms, which must be used for other purposes besides worship. There are objections to this on the ground of profanation, and it is true that a religious atmosphere—that is, a body of fixed associations—is more easily maintained where it is possible to reserve a place for worship alone.

d. THE SACRAMENTS

Religious symbols are of three types, according to Dr. Dunbar,[14] those which are arbitrary and accidental, such as mathematical signs,

[12] T. G. Pinches, in the Hastings Encyclopaedia of Religion and Ethics.
[13] G. Margoliouth, in the Hastings Encyclopaedia of Religion and Ethics.
[14] H. Flanders Dunbar, Symbolism in Medieval Thought and Its Consumma-tion in the Divine Comedy (New Haven: Yale University Press, 1929), p. 478.

those which are descriptive, and those which have a basis in an association that is neither arbitrary and extrinsic nor sensually intrinsic, but intrinsic and reaching toward the supersensible. For example, the sight of a river may suggest comparison of it with a silvery ribbon flung across the green tapestry of the countryside; or it may invoke the thought of man's life flowing like a river from its source to its known yet unknown end. The first is comparison; the second is interpretation. There is in the second an intrinsic likeness which suggests a true and deeper meaning. Religious symbolism tends to be of the latter type. Such symbolism was especially characteristic of the Christianity of the Middle Ages, which held to the passionate belief in the continuity of essence through ever-changing form and sought for symbols through which its insights might be expressed.[15]

The Roman Catholic Church is today the chief custodian of these medieval insight symbols, outstanding examples of which are to be found in the sacraments.

The term "sacrament" is used in the Christian Church to denote symbolic acts intended to represent an inward grace. Of these the Roman Catholics recognize seven—the Eucharist, baptism, confirmation, ordination, penance, marriage, and extreme unction. Most Protestant churches recognize only two, baptism and the Lord's Supper. A few sects add another, the washing of the feet.

The two rites which are thus observed by both Protestants and Catholics are distinctive of the Christian religion. According to the New Testament account, they came from the Church's Founder and have been handed down from earliest times.

The *Eucharist*, according to the Gospel sources, was instituted by Jesus as a memorial to himself. It is a symbol of fellowship, the fellowship of the best, of which all standards and values are merely functions, according to our theory. The choice of the bread and wine was determined by the facts that they were at that time staple articles of food among the common people of Palestine and that among different races and at different times eating together has been

[15] *Ibid.*, p. 23.

a token of friendship. According to the words of the institution, as given by Paul, the shared food was used by Jesus to denote his giving of himself for the sake of his people and their dependence upon him. It was to be a perpetual memorial to him and has so been observed throughout the centuries. To its original value as insight symbolism at its best there has been added a great accretion of sacred associations. Among Protestant churches this sacrament is observed very simply. In the Catholic Church it has been invested with a great wealth of medieval symbolism.

The rite of baptism is intended to represent cleansing and regeneration. Here also we have an insight symbol of deep significance. It is one which Jung calls an "archetype." [16] That is, it occurs in dreams, in the profound psychoses, and in the religion and mythology of all times and races, denoting nearly always the idea of rebirth.

The original significance, however, has been considerably altered. The practice has arisen of administering this rite to young children, in the belief that it was necessary to salvation—that it was not merely the outward symbol of an inward grace but had some magical efficacy. Most Protestant churches practice infant baptism, interpreting it as an expression on the part of the parents of their purpose to bring the child up "in the nurture and admonition of the Lord" and on the part of the church fellowship of their interest in the child.

That elements of magic still cling to this sacrament even in Protestantism is indicated by the emotional intensity with which some church bodies still emphasize their particular form of baptism. Such insistence is generally to be explained by the supposition that the rite would lose its efficacy if it were not performed exactly right.

The other sacraments recognized by the Catholic Church have to do with the crises of life—marriage, birth of children, coming of age, commitment to the Christian life, penitence, and death. There are

[16] Carl Gustaf Jung, Two Essays on Analytical Psychology (New York: Dodd, Mead & Co., 1928), pp. 67 ff. See also Jung's Psychology of the Unconscious (New York: Dodd, Mead & Co., 1925) and his Integration of the Personality (New York: Farrar & Rinehart, 1939).

ceremonies in the Protestant churches which, although not called sacraments, pertain to these same crisis experiences. They are found also in other religions. Of special interest from the standpoint of this study is the marriage ceremony. According to Malinowski,[17] there is no known society which does not have some kind of ceremonial sanction for marriage. This ceremonial establishes a relationship between two individuals which is derived not from mere instinct but from social pressure.

Until this creative act has been performed, until the marriage has been concluded according to the cultural requirements, a man and a woman can mate and cohabit as long and as often as they like, but their relationship will remain something different from a socially sanctioned marriage. In every known society a man and a woman who attempt to behave as if they were married without the appropriate social sanction are made to suffer more or less severe penalties. And once marriage has been socially sanctioned, a number of duties and obligations are imposed and backed up by legal and religious requirements. The relationship thus established is not easily dissolved.

The universality of social sanction for marriage and the religious form which it commonly assumes may be explained in terms of the social basis of the personality. The powerful sex drive, which in animals is controlled physiologically by its confinement to certain rutting seasons,[18] is in man controlled by the internalization of the social organization in the form of conscience. Any indulgence of this drive, as Rank points out,[19] tends to be felt as something forbidden, even among children brought up according to the most "enlightened" standards.

Rank's explanation is an intriguing one. The child, he says, feels sexuality first of all to be an inner claim of the species hostile to individuality. It is therefore to him something dangerous, not because

---

[17] Bronislaw Malinowski, *Sex and Repression in Savage Society* (New York: Harcourt, Brace & Co., 1927), p. 202.

[18] *Ibid.*, pp. 197 ff.

[19] Otto Rank, *Modern Education* (New York: Alfred A. Knopf, Inc., 1932), pp. 42 ff.

it is too individual, too personal, to be incorporated into the "community ideology," but just the reverse: because in essence sexuality is a collective phenomenon which the individual at all stages of civilization wants to individualize, that is, to control. This view, Rank says, explains all sexual conflicts in the individual from masturbation to the most varied perversions and perversities. Above all it explains the tendency to keep secret everything sexual, which is due to the desire to individualize as much as possible the collective elements in sexuality. The resulting sense of guilt is likely to continue until a solution comes through the experience of love. In love there is a tendency to idealize and hence to deify the other person. When the forbidden and dangerous cravings are accepted and sanctioned by the idealized person, when the collective sexuality is identified with and approved by a beloved representative of the collective, the conflict is ended.[20]

There may be some difficulties in Rank's explanation of the sense of guilt. He does not seem to take sufficient account of the fundamentally social nature of the personality. According to our view, it is the internalization not so much of the "community ideology"—a phase which suggests an intellectualist emphasis—as of the organized values and attitudes of the community. The essence of the sense of guilt is to be found in the sense of inner disharmony due to the presence of dynamic tendencies which can neither be controlled nor acknowledged for fear of condemnation. By the same token the essence of the healing process lies in the socializing of some "unspeakable worry." Rank's suggestion regarding the power of love to relieve the sense of guilt is therefore illuminating but not in itself sufficient.

According to Hocking,[21] the idealizing tendency, which Rank recognizes as of the essence of love, represents the fact that the lover seeks that which is beyond the finite love object, and no love

[20] Rank, *Will Therapy* (New York: Alfred A. Knopf, Inc., 1936), pp. 100 ff.
[21] W. E. Hocking, *Human Nature and Its Re-making* (New Haven: Yale University Press, 1918), Chap. 42.

relationship is complete until the lovers have made a place for the eternal fellowship of which their own relationship is an expression. Herein we may find the explanation of the ceremonial sanction required in marriage among men of all times and all races.

In the Christian religion there is considerable difference between the Roman Catholic conception of marriage and that of the Protestant churches. For the Catholic the celibate life is the holy life, and marriage is looked upon as a concession to human frailty. The sacrament of matrimony is a blessing pronounced by the priest upon a relationship which permits the more or less free indulgence of sex desire. The Protestant view finds its ideal of holiness in the Christian home and in a degree of self-control which shall reserve sexual intercourse to such conditions as shall give it sacramental value.

There is in general an important difference between the Catholic and Protestant conceptions of a sacrament. This may be seen in the rites associated with death. A Catholic chaplain connected with a hospital considers it a matter of the utmost importance that he be called whenever a patient is placed on the danger list. No matter what the hour of day or night he comes at once and performs the sacrament of *extreme unction*. It makes no difference whether the patient is conscious or not; the sacrament is believed to convey grace and to be important to the future well-being of the patient.

A Protestant chaplain also expects to be called when one of his patients is placed on the danger list, but he is likely to ask whether the patient is conscious and whether any members of the family are present. If the patient is not conscious and if no friends are present he probably will feel that there is no further help he can give. And he is not likely to insist upon being called at all if the turn for the worse comes at two o'clock in the morning. Unlike the Catholic chaplain, he is not sure that he has any contribution to make when the end is already at hand. So also in the burial service: The Catholic ritual is concerned with the soul of the departed, the Protestant with the needs of the bereaved.[22]

[22] It may be pointed out that the Catholic view often affords the priest greater

A similar difference is to be observed in the ordination of priests and of ministers. Catholic rites are believed to convey a power and authority which only the ordained can exercise. The priest himself becomes a sacred person, a symbol of the divine, and is entrusted with the responsibility of imparting divine grace through the instrumentality of the sacraments. Protestant ordination is also a solemn ritual, but it is conceived rather as a consecration on the part of the new minister to the cause which the church represents and as a recognition by the church of the minister's qualifications. In most Protestant churches only the ordained can administer the sacraments or perform wedding ceremonies, but the minister is not thought of as invested with any power beyond that to which his character and training entitle him.

The Catholic view of the sacraments is formulated in the doctrine that they work ex opere operato. That is, their efficacy is not dependent upon the faith, merits, or worthiness of the priest who administers them, or even upon the conscious participation of the recipient. It does not depend upon anything human but solely upon the will of God expressed in Christ's institution and promise.[23] The sacrament, according to the Catholic view, is an outward act performed by a divinely appointed priest which imparts a mystic grace not obtainable in any other way. This doctrine, strictly held, makes room for a magical element which in popular forms becomes quite pronounced.[24]

---

power to give help and comfort. The fact that he and his people believe that the sacrament has power to accomplish something gives him a place at the bedside of the desperately ill that the Protestant does not have. It is also to be noted that a supposedly unconscious patient is often not unaware of what is going on.

[23] D. J. Kennedy in the Catholic Encyclopedia. Some qualification may be needed in the matter of the attitude of the recipient. The Catholic theologians say that there must be no impediment, but that if the conditions are fulfilled and there is the intention of submitting to the operation of the sacrament, the wandering of attention will not prevent the receiving of the divine grace. In infant baptism the grace is imparted wholly without the participation of the recipient.

[24] According to Delacroix, the essence of magic is to be found in realistic symbolization which believes that a ceremony produces exactly what it represents and that a rite is automatically a vehicle of religious power. Magic is thus associated with religion but is by no means identified with religion. (Op. cit., pp. 24 ff.

e. ASCETICISM

William James, in the famous chapter on "Habit" in his *Psychology*, suggests that it is well to keep the faculty of effort alive by a little gratuitous exercise every day. Being systematically ascetic in little unnecessary points, doing things for no other reason than that one would rather not do them, is like insurance which a man pays on his house and grounds. When the hour of dire need comes it may find him not unnerved and untrained to stand the test.[25]

This admonition is little observed today among our liberal Protestant churches. On the other hand, in the priesthood and in the monastic orders of the Roman Catholic Church and in the Holiness sects of the Protestant Church, asceticism is much in evidence.

In the Middle Ages asceticism in the Catholic monasteries went frequently to the point of self-torture. An extreme example is Heinrich Suso's chastisement of his body over a period of more than twenty years.[26] During that time he wore hair shirts and leather undergarments studded with tacks; he carried on his back a cross studded with pointed nails; he abstained from bathing and washing; he held himself in solitary confinement and underwent other forms of self-punishment which seem ghastly to us but in his day were considered most praiseworthy. He represented a pattern of piety which in that time was widely prevalent. Today such asceticism is no longer practiced, but life in the Catholic orders is one of rigid simplicity and discipline; it involves regular hours, much hard work, and prolonged periods of prayer and fasting.

Among the Holiness cults also we find great austerity. The Methodists in their earlier years forbade dancing, card playing, theatergoing, gay attire, and light and frivolous conduct. Their modern

[25] William James, *Principles of Psychology*, 2 vols. (New York: Henry Holt & Co., 1896), I, Chap. 4, 126.

[26] *Life of the Blessed Henry Suso by Himself*, translated by Thomas Francis Knox (London: Methuen & Co., 1913), pp. 45–64. An excellent digest of this account is given in William James' *Varieties of Religious Experience*, together with an illuminating discussion of ascetic practices, pp. 296–310.

counterparts insist on modesty in dress and an abstention from worldly amusements, and they tithe very faithfully.

The explanation of such asceticism is to be found far less in the effort at self-discipline which Professor James has commended than in its relationship to mystical experience, which according to our view is the fountainhead of religion. The monastic orders and the Holiness sects are alike in taking religion very much in earnest, and they have discovered that ascetic practices bring the sense of peace and union with God. These practices therefore have been made an integral part of the technique for inducing the mystical experiences. Among the holy men of other religions [27] similar practices are found. Their value lies first of all in the simple and well-recognized principle that we tend to become most interested in those things for which we put forth the greatest effort and make the greatest sacrifices. They may also serve to focus attention to the point where something in the nature of trance or autohypnosis is induced.

The possible origin of such an ascetic practice as fasting is suggested by the case of a stuporous patient who recovered after a period of three months in which he had to be forcibly fed. Although by birth and training a Baptist, he became remarkably interested in all that had to do with fasting. He read all the Catholic literature he could get his hands on and began to observe certain fast days. Questioning revealed the fact that the experience through which he had just passed had induced in him the sense of being one with God. Painful though it had been he felt it as an experience of supreme importance and he recognized that the abstention from food had had something to do with it. Hence his interest in fasting.

The prevalence of fasting in primitive religions may well have had

[27] Max Weber, *Religionssoziologie*, 3 vols. (Tuebingen, J. C. B. Mohr, 1923), II, 167–70.

For further consideration of the motivation of asceticism and its relation to mysticism see James H. Leuba, *Psychology of Religious Mysticism* (New York: Harcourt, Brace & Co., 1925), pp. 156 ff.; also Henri Delacroix, *Études d'Histoire et de Psychologie du Mysticisme* (Paris: Felix Alcan, 1908), pp. 382–87.

a similar origin. Given a few experiences of this type, the practice may pass over into a convention.

Of the ancient practice of human and animal sacrifice we occasionally encounter instances among acutely disturbed mental patients which again suggest its possible origin among primitive peoples.

There is also a significant survival in the Christian doctrine of the vicarious atonement, as it is popularly interpreted. According to that doctrine, Jesus gave his life, the innocent for the guilty, the just for the unjust, in order to satisfy the requirements of justice and appease the wrath of a righteous God against sinful man. This doctrine is symbolized in the sacrament of the Lord's Supper, in which, according to the words of the institution, the bread represents the body of the Lord and the wine his blood. Christianity has taught that through his sacrifice of himself the necessity of animal sacrifice has been eliminated. References to him as "the Lamb of God" and to the "power of his blood" appear in a considerable number of hymns and gospel songs which are still in common use.

2. TENDENCIES MAKING FOR INSTITUTIONAL ILL HEALTH

At every stage of its development a religious institution is beset with dangers. Among them are the following:

a. ECCENTRICITY

The zeal of the early stages is likely to be narrow and intolerant and in many respects mistaken. Very commonly it proceeds from the assumption that the divine manifests itself in the unusual, that the prompting which seems to come from without is of divine or at least superhuman origin. Such an assumption may lead to serious difficulties. We have seen that it figures in the experiences of the mentally ill.

An experience interpreted as contact with the superhuman carries a tremendous impact. In mental patients we see its destructive power. It is destructive because it brings with it a sense of fear and condemnation and because it is borne alone. When the experience is shared the effects are less likely to be destructive or to involve confusion and derangement in thinking. Even though the beliefs seem queer, we do not lock up those who hold them. More than that, there is often a new access of power, with new flashes of insight. Nevertheless, the presupposition that an idea carries authority merely because of the way it comes is a false premise which may lead to difficulty in groups as well as in individuals.

The history of the Christian Church shows many instances in which groups have been led through such a presupposition to embark upon some very peculiar undertakings. The early Christians gave up their work in order to make ready for the second coming of the Lord, and time and again in the centuries that followed others have obeyed some special revelation that the Parousia was indeed at hand. Even within relatively recent times this has happened, as in the cases of the Millerites of the 1840's and the Russellites (now called Jehovah's Witnesses) of the present era. Another fairly recent adventure is that of the followers of a Free Baptist minister named Sandford who established a communistic settlement at Shiloh, Maine, and chartered three ships in which they set forth to scour the seven seas in order to prepare the world for the Day of the Lord.

Even when no such unusual adventures are undertaken, those who place untested reliance upon special revelations are likely to make for themselves a diminutive world, one that is only a little larger than the private world of the mental patient.

b. COMPLACENCY AND SECULARIZATION

With the passing of the years, as we have seen, the ecstatic sect tends to become less unlike other religious bodies. What takes place is something of a leveling process. The forward-looking, prophetic movements are leveled down and conventionalized. The eccentric and regressive ones are leveled up and become respectable. We have explained this process by three considerations: In the first place, emotion tends to wane even in the original believers. In the second place, the social and economic status is likely to be raised, owing to the fact that the ascetic attitude increases productivity and decreases expenditure. In the third place, the original believers are replaced by their children, and the children commonly accept the faith of their parents without having shared their experience. There is always a tendency on the part of the children to introduce short cuts and protective devices, to discharge the requirements of religious loyalty without paying the price of complete commitment.

The sect thus becomes a church, but in the process the original zeal is lost. The sacraments become means of grace rather than symbols of inner experience. The creeds become standards of doctrine rather than confessions of faith. There is increasing complacency and indifference. Religion becomes more and more secularized, more and more a matter of form and duty.

c. DIVISIVENESS

It has been apparent from this study that sects are of two types. They may represent the creative beginnings of organized religion. They may also represent the end stages. They may be groups made up of persons who under the strain of economic distress have been thinking and feeling together about the things that matter most and have found what they feel to be a new and vitalizing experience. On the other hand, there are groups so resistant to change that they refuse to acquiesce in the requirements of growth and progress. Such groups may split off from the main body because the main body stops lining out the Psalms or because it introduces instrumental music or because it ordains ministers who accept the theory of evolution and are agnostic regarding the Virgin Birth.[28] Protestantism, says Professor Holt, is ragged behind and ragged in front.

Resistance to change is most in evidence among rural people and

---

[28] In a recent survey I found one small Southern body that had split over the issue of neckties, a group of perhaps fifteen hundred insisting that true religion forbade them. Two small Churches of Christ had split on the issue of communion cups: A traveling evangelist had discovered that they were using two cups, one for each deacon. This, he said, was unscriptural. The Lord had only used one. There are now four churches where only two had been before, and the "one-cuppers" are arrayed against the "two-cuppers."

among immigrants. This may be explained, as indicated in our Springville study, by the relative strength of the home and neighborhood ties and the relative insulation from the main currents of cultural change. The conservatism of the immigrant groups is accounted for by the struggle to maintain the native culture against the impact of a surrounding alien culture. These factors are dealt with elsewhere.

What interests us especially in this connection is the frequency with which church divisions are due to unrecognized personal ambitions and hostilities among the leaders. The issues of doctrine and principle in many cases are merely pretexts and rationalizations of motives which are not acknowledged. Such divisive tendencies are particularly likely to occur in groups which seek to maintain loyalty not through love and reason but through force and fear and arbitrary authority. Children who grow up under such conditions may feel strong resentment which not infrequently takes the form of open rebellion and the disowning of the loyalty.

More commonly, however, there is an admixture of love which leads the individual to accept the faith of his father. The repressed hostility may then be ready to seize upon some trivial issue in order to express itself. The Covenanters who in 1832 made an issue of voting were undoubtedly genuinely concerned over the alteration of an old custom. Probably they were also resentful of leaders who had perhaps assumed too much authority and had thus awakened hostile feelings arising out of their own stern upbringing. It seems likewise a reasonable conjecture that the stern discipline of the Mennonite bodies and their emphasis upon obedience has had not a little to do with the many divisions into which they have been split.

3. Conditions Making for Institutional Health

Our findings indicate that in the history of religious institutions there is a recurrent process. A new group emerges from the main body of the Christian fellowship. It arises out of deep emotional experiences and strongly held convictions. As time goes on the emotions evaporate and the distinctive features begin to disappear. If the new group has been prophetic and intelligent, there will be a certain leveling down. If it has been bigoted and regressive, there will be a certain leveling up. All such groups tend to become conventional and respectable. The divergent body then takes its place once more in the main body of Christian believers, only to be replaced by some new divergent body under a new emotional impulse and a new set of convictions.

This process is complicated by the fact that in addition to the emerging sects there are also die-hard sects which persist by reason of their strong resistance to change. Religious institutions thus have their periods of youth, maturity, and old age, each with its attendant dangers. In the period of youth there may be enthusiastic eccentricity; in maturity, complacency and traditionalism and scholasticism. When old age comes on, thoughts turn toward the past and there is an unwillingness to be disturbed by the changing currents of contemporary life and thought.

The question arises: How can the church escape the evils of decrepitude and maintain its vigor and effectiveness across the span of the centuries? How can it best accomplish its task of perpetuating the Christian fellowship and of transmitting from generation to generation the successive moral achievements and the growing insights of that fellowship? In order to answer this question we must first determine what we mean by the "church." Are we concerned with the church as a particular institution; or are we interested in the larger fellowship of the Christian religion?

a. THE LARGER PERSPECTIVE

The answer of the Roman Catholic Church of course has been unequivocal. It is interested in its own perpetuation. It says that it is the one true church, the one body of Christ. It refuses steadfastly to recognize any other Christian bodies. For centuries it has had the problem of the emerging sects to deal with. It has had its groups of religious devotees who took their religion very earnestly and has been remarkably successful in controlling them. It has done this by recognizing them and segregating them in monastic orders, where in accordance with its established traditions they are dedicated to the celibate life.

These monastic orders, according to Troeltsch,[29] were the sanctuaries in which the early Christian ideal took refuge, and within the Catholic Church they were a vitalizing power. Where new groups could not be controlled, the Catholic policy has been to brand them as heretics and to suppress them. In this way the Catholic Church has succeeded in building up a powerful institution and in maintaining its effectiveness; but even its most devoted supporters would hardly claim that it has done much to encourage fresh thinking on the part of its people or that it has given much support to the forces which make for change and progress.

The answer of Protestant Christianity has not always been clear. It has insisted on the right of the individual and of the group to think independently, but it has been greatly troubled by the resulting divisions in the Christian Church. The extreme expression of the Protestant idea is to be found in the United States of America. Here the ideal of a free church in a free state has resulted in an astonishing multiplication of churches and sects. This has meant much duplication and much waste, but the results seem to be good. It has been possible here for people of different races, each with their own culture and their own religion, to live side by side, stimulating each other, influencing each other, and gradually drawing closer together. It has been possible here with unusual ease for new faiths to emerge, make their contribution, and then coalesce with the main stream.

The Protestants sometimes in their thinking approach the Catholic position and concern themselves very much with the fate of their particular church, but the logical consequence of the Protestant view is that what happens to a particular institution is not important, provided the Christian spirit and the Christian heritage are kept alive and vigorous. It may be claimed for American democracy that

[29] *The Social Teachings of the Christian Churches*, 2 vols. (New York: The Macmillan Company, 1931), I, 162.

one of its most brilliant achievements lies in the free play which it has given to the process of growth and renewal in organized religion. The system has been wasteful, but out of it should come in the end a higher synthesis.

Our question will therefore have reference to organized religion in its larger aspects.

b. CLEAR THINKING

First of all, if the American plan is to function successfully, there is need for clear thinking and practical wisdom in interchurch relationships. These are at present not always found. I have, for example, a photograph which I took forty years ago of four little churches in a row in a village of five hundred people. In each of these churches there was preaching once a month. The village was without a resident minister. It was a typical situation. The only thing unusual about it was the fact that the churches were side by side so that it was possible to get a picture of them all.

Between these churches there was little difference so far as any vital issues were concerned. They were all old-line Protestant churches of the English and Scotch tradition. They sang the same type of gospel songs. They used much the same form of worship. They listened to much the same orthodox message. Yet there they were, competing with one another, and not always in a friendly spirit.

According to a standing joke which was told to me by an official in one of these churches, on one memorable occasion the congregation in one of these little churches sang, "Will there be any stars in my crown?" and an adjoining church sang in antiphony, "No, not one," whereupon a third church joined in, "That will be glory for me." When I suggested that perhaps sometime they could get together and have a good strong church with a resident minister, my companion looked at me with horror. "Not so long as I have any breath in my body" was his reply.

Twenty-seven years later I revisited this little Tennessee village and got another picture of the same four churches, still operating on the same plan. I talked once more with the same official, listened once more to the same standing joke about the stars in the crown, and once more raised the question about the possibility of church union. This time he was not shocked. He thought it might really be a good idea. Perhaps this is evidence that we are making progress. Perhaps in the course of another thirty years churches that are really alike will get together and put an end to the present wasteful duplication of effort.

C. THE CHURCH AS A FELLOWSHIP

Clear thinking requires the recognition of the fact that the church is above all else a fellowship. It began with the followers of a great teacher, a luminous personality in whose life and tragic death they saw the supreme manifestations of the divine and to whom they gave unreserved allegiance as their Lord and their Savior. With the passing of the years the original faith became greatly altered. Magical accretions grew up around it. Scholastic speculations obscured its deeper meaning. At the same time the original loyalty was enriched through the devotion of countless thousands of believers whose memories became associated with the institutions and symbols of the Christian Church. Amid all the diversities this common loyalty has remained, and in the records of the life and teachings of Jesus Christian churches have found the norm by which their ideals have been shaped and to which they return from their various wanderings.

From the viewpoint of our working hypothesis, the teachings of Christianity are functions of the interpersonal relationships represented by the Christian fellowship. The early disciples accepted the teachings of Jesus because they accepted him and believed in him. And through the ages new believers have been won not so much by being convinced intellectually as through the personal influence of an apostolic succession of believers. It follows that the Christian religion is not to be regarded as an authoritative revelation once for all delivered to the saints. It is rather a living fellowship with a certain body of beliefs in which there is room for growth and for discovery.

This does not mean that beliefs are not important. The periods of the church's greatest growth and influence will be those in which it believes most profoundly in its message. A study made some years ago showed that, as measured by attendance, the church's influence is greatest in those regions of the United States where people still believe in the inerrancy of the Scriptures and the deity of Christ. Influences fell off as popular religious belief became liberalized, and even in the liberalized regions the conservative groups were holding their people far better than the liberal groups.[30]

Undoubtedly the principle still holds. Nebulous beliefs do not make for religious vitality. Nevertheless, a period of groping uncertainty may in the long run be wholesome. The institution which is not to grow old cannot derive its authority from the past alone but must be able to adapt itself to changing conditions and growing knowledge.

The recognition that the church is first of all a fellowship makes clear the significance of the type of religious assemblage distinctive of Christianity and of the Hebrew religion out of which it grew. The group meeting has not merely provided for the rethinking of the central beliefs in the light of changing conditions; it has also provided a means of emotional reinforcement in the heart of the individual; and it has created or deepened within him the feeling of oneness not only with the group but with Something above and beyond the group. The radio service can never take the place of the church.

The recognition of the primacy of fellowship may help us in dealing with the delicate problems of social action and social stratification. This is a chief tool in the hands of the psychotherapist. Any chance he has to help his patient is dependent upon maintaining friendly relations with him. The moment he begins to argue with him, he has become no longer a friend but an antagonist and his influence is gone. So also with the pastor. Crusading or arguing over matters on which there may be an honest difference of opinion is

[30] Boisen, "Factors in the Decline of the Country Church," *American Journal of Sociology*, September, 1916.

likely to destroy the power to help and influence. It may be the part not of cowardice but of therapeutic wisdom to withhold strong expressions of opinion. What is needed is to raise the situation to the level of the higher loyalty in order that the members of the group may be able to see things for themselves.

In the matter of social stratification it must be recognized that cultural differences are hard to reconcile. The dignified service which appeals to the better educated is distasteful to many of the rank and file, and positions of leadership are not lightly to be given to those who are lacking in training and ability. A local church which is composed largely of educated people would not be true to its task if it did not do everything in its power to bridge the gaps between the different social classes, but it can hardly expect a group of Pentecostals to get much of a thrill out of the type of service it conducts on Sunday mornings; neither would it be easy for such a church to accept for itself the swinging music and the ecstatic preaching in which the Pentecostals delight. Perhaps some compromise might be worked out, but the solution would seem to lie in the Protestant principle of unity amid diversity.

d. ADAPTATION TO CHANGING CONDITIONS

Adaptation to changing conditions has been one of the outstanding features of the Christian religion. It goes far toward explaining the fact that Christianity, especially in its Protestant forms, has been associated with dynamic cultures. Provision for adaptation has included religious assemblage, not merely for common worship and the performance of stated rites and ceremonies, but also for instruction. It has laid great stress upon the sermon, something which is educational in its purpose. It has included a church school, which provides not only for the training of the young but also for discussion and conference on the part of older persons.

The part which American churches have had in the program of general education is also significant. It means that they have faith in education and encourage their people to think for themselves. It means also a considerable degree of open-mindedness toward new developments in the field of science. There are of course many exceptions, but the forward look seems characteristic of Protestant America. Such an attitude must always characterize an enduring and vital church.

e. FREEDOM FROM ENTANGLING ALLIANCES

A survey of the world religions shows clearly the danger which besets religion whenever it becomes identified with some special dominant class. India and China furnish striking examples of the extent to which religion may be used as a means of upholding the established order and in other ways furthering the interests of a special class.

In the development of the Christian religion, recognition by Constantine was no unmixed blessing. It brought with it entangling alliances and resulted in abuses and compromises from which the Eastern Church never fully recovered. The emphasis was placed more and more upon ritual and symbol. The deference to the past became so great that little independent thinking was done, and so long as the association of church and state continued the church was required to uphold the established order. In the west the fall of Rome jarred the church loose from its complacency, but it soon made entangling alliances with the feudalistic rulers, which blinded it to many social evils and made it as an organization overwhelmingly conservative. Under Protestantism also state support has tended to tie the church's hands and make it an upholder of things as they are.

In America, with the disestablishment of the church, this evil was done away with, but the fact that the churches found themselves projected into a fierce struggle for existence has forced them in many cases to take account of the attitude of certain large givers. Thus in North Dakota at the time of the struggle between the Non-Partisan League and its opponents it was found that the country ministers were for the most part outspoken supporters of the Non-Partisan League in its radical experiments while the town ministers were equally outspoken in their opposition. The reason? Partly that the minister of a town church supported by merchants and capitalists would immediately lose his job if he ventured to express any favorable views regarding the socialistic experiment, partly that his associations would unconsciously influence his own attitudes.

It seems fairly clear also that the work of the churches has never been more effctive than in those periods when they were undergoing adversity. One reason for this is the freedom from entangling alliances which then obtains. Release from the restraints of the traditionalism which a ruling class is likely to impose makes possible fresh and creative thinking.

f. OPPORTUNITY FOR SACRIFICIAL SERVICE

One of the weaknesses of present-day liberal churches is that they make the Christian way of life too easy. The Roman Catholics have their convents and monasteries, and those who would live the holy life must renounce the world and commit themselves to lives of celibacy and poverty. The essence of the old Protestant revivalism was a commanding summons to a complete commitment. The present-day Holiness churches present the same challenge. There are many persons who require just such an opportunity for a complete break with the past and a dramatic acceptance of a new role. About all that the liberal churches have to offer, in the case of those who are qualified, is enlistment as a minister of religion or as a foreign missionary or entering the ranks of the conscientious objectors.

It is not clear what can be done to correct this weakness. Perhaps the war and its aftermath will in time provide the answer.

g. A MESSAGE OF SALVATION

The rapid growth of the Holiness sects which we found in our study of Blankton calls attention to the fact that liberal Protestant churches today have little to offer to the soul that is sick. This fact needs to be underscored, for sick souls are all around us. Of course the message of the Holiness sects seems to be something in the nature of a patent nostrum. It is treatment without diagnosis, a ready-made formula applied to all alike. But at least it is treatment, whereas the liberal churches too often give neither treatment nor diagnosis. A new type of evangelism is needed, one that is based upon a true understanding of human nature and of the laws of the spiritual life, one that summons men to face their personal problems while there is yet time and to come to terms with their better selves.

The story of Joe Campbell, given in Chapter V, is a case in point. It will be recalled that he was a very sick man. He was alcoholic and epileptic and the doctors gave him no hope. But Joe was converted in a little Holiness mission and he went back to his old home town to show the folks what the Lord had done for him. Joe was no great preacher, but he was dead in earnest. He felt that the Lord had come into his life, and he knew that there were many people in that town who remembered him as he had been before with his sullen, forbidding expression and his many brawls and sprees. These people saw before them now a strong, kindly man with radiance in his face. Here was a dramatic change which spoke louder than his words. And the words he used were those of the common people. He dealt with their problems, from their point of view. Therefore they believed in him. They heard him gladly. He also won the respect of some of the finest spirits in that town, including the univeristy's great president, who became his friend and adviser. Thus he was able to start a vigorous religious movement.

The question which suggests itself is: What is the liberal Christian church doing for and with the Joe Campbells?

In seeking an answer it is well to bear in mind that a little more than a century ago, when the Middle West was being settled, the major Protestant churches sent out their missionaries. Among them the Presbyterian Church had everything in its favor. It had had an important part in the winning of the War of the Revolution. It had a thoroughly trained body of missionary preachers. And most of the people who settled the Middle West were of Presbyterian background. But the West was not won by the Presbyterians. It was won by the Methodists, because they had a message of salvation for the Joe Campbells and found a way of putting them to work when they were saved.

h. ADEQUATE LEADERSHIP

The great majority of American Christians do not think of their minister as having any special power by virtue of his office. He differs from the layman only in the fact that he devotes all his time to religious work and that he has either received training or been adjudged qualified by virtue of some special call or religious experience.

More than a hundred years ago there arose a heated controversy among American Protestants over the training of their ministers. the insistence of the frontier churches upon the ordination of men who were not professionally trained may be regarded as in large measure a healthy rebellion against the type of training which prevailed in that day. That training consisted chiefly in the study of Greek, Latin, and Hebrew, of the ancient Scriptures, and of what theologians had to say about religion. It was a type of training calculated to make religion sterile. The fact that the West was won by those churches which made use of ministers who were not professionally trained does not mean that professional training is unimportant, but rather that there was something lacking in the training then being given.

Theological education has made advances since that time, and yet the situation does not seem greatly changed. We have been passing through a period in which the basis of religious authority is being shifted from a sacred book cantaining a revelation given once for all in the past to organized and tested experience of the living present. In this period there has been on the part of our professional students of religion a surprising lag in the matter of methodology. As has already been pointed out (pp. 188 ff.), the methods of that co-operative inquiry to which we give the name of "science" have not been employed, except sporadically, in the study of the field which is peculiarly their own. Religious experience has to wait until it gets on

library shelves before it becomes a subject of theological investigation. This lag is made the more striking by the fact that those
scientists who deal with human nature—psychologists, sociologists,
anthropologists, psychiatrists—have not carried their inquiry to the
level of the religious. The result is that we are unable to speak with
any degree of authority regarding the spiritual life and the laws
which control it. The liberal minister of today thus finds himself in
an apologetic position, explaining the ancient tenets in terms of
modern thought with a sense of insecurity regarding some of the
basic beliefs of religion.

It remains to be seen what will happen when the servants of the
church begin to apply the methods of co-operative inquiry to the
problems of living men, seeking not only to help but also to understand. It seems not too much to hope that as they learn to ask the
significant questions and to verify and reverify the answers there
may come a surer understanding of the end and meaning of life and
the way to individual and social salvation.

RECONSIDERATION

The outstanding feature in the means by which American Protestantism has sought to keep its faith alive is its reliance upon religious assemblage for the purpose of instruction. In most Protestant
churches the sermon is stressed more than the service of worship and
there is considerable poverty in symbolism and music. Right thinking is thus made paramount and the individual is expected to think
for himself. Magical practices, while by no means absent, are unimportant as compared with those practices in other religions and in
Roman Catholicism. The sacraments in most American churches
are chiefly of symbolic significance and the ministers are not thought
of as sacred persons. No authority is ascribed to them merely by virtue of their office but only that which is due because of training and
character and spiritual insight.

One result of this plan is a considerable degree of confusion. There
is a bewildering array of churches and sects. Lack of clear thinking

and the presence of biasing interests have created numerous problems and difficulties. Many church organizations are kept alive merely by virtue of a tragic loyalty which loses sight of the major objectives in its devotion to a lesser good. This tendency is abetted by the presence of repressed hostilities and the desire for status and self-expression on the part of leaders.

American Protestantism must be judged, however, in its totality. What is important is not the survival and well-being of this or that organization but the survival and development of Christian civilization and the realization of its dream of a social order based upon the principle of good will among men. With all its weaknesses and wastefulness the American system does stimulate creativity, and it gives the new faiths which spring out of personal and social crisis a chance to prove their worth and make their contribution to the social structure. It is, moreover, a system which makes possible the maximum of flexibility and adaptation to changing conditions. Its effectiveness depends upon adequate leadership, upon straight thinking and clear vision, and upon a quickened sense of oneness with a Greater-than-self in bringing in the world that ought to be.

XIV. The Present Crisis and Future
of Christian Civilization

W HAT can we predict regarding the outcome of the momentous crisis through which we have been passing and regarding the future of Western civilization? What is the likelihood that we will recognize and in some measure correct the deep-seated evils of which war has been merely a symptom? What hope is there of a compelling vision which will grip the hearts and consciences of men, of a vitalizing faith which will unite them in the struggle for the world that ought to be? Has this inquiry supplied us with any criteria by which we can forecast that which is yet to be?

It may seem presumptuous to attempt to look into the future, and yet prediction is of the very essence of the scientific enterprise. The fact that the subject matter of this study is enormously complicated and the future full of uncertainties does not relieve us from the duty of attempting to apply the principles we have discovered to a consideration of the consequences which are likely to follow from the conditions confronting us.

1. Religion as a Permanent Component in Social Organization

There will always be some form of religion in any enduring social organization. This conclusion follows from our finding that man is basically social and that religion has to do with the organization of the social relationships and their associated values. We have found religious experience to be man's acute awareness of his relationships to that which is supreme in his system of loyalties. It is the sense of fellowship raised to the level of what for the individual is universal and abiding. The capacity for religious experience is therefore present in all men, and it operates whether they are aware of it or not. Religion is thus a permanent component in the organization of the personality and also of society. This conclusion is supported by the fact that there is no known race of men which does not have some form of religion,[1] and by the further fact that religious experience tends to appear spontaneously in time of stress and crisis.

Some of the recent adventures in social collectivism may seem to be exceptions to this general rule. In Fascism, National Socialism, and Communism there has been little semblance of interest in religion. In fact, there has been often an anti-religious bias. Russian Communists certainly would be horrified at the mere suggestion that there was anything of the religious in their philosophy of life.

So far as Fascism and National Socialism are concerned, there seems to be no reason to look upon them as anything beyond the upsurge of national feeling in the face of impending danger from outside. Their message was for Italians and Germans and for them alone. Their appeal was to pride of race and the response they won was conditioned by the ambition or by the despair and anger of their respective peoples. The sense of solidarity which they induced was based upon narrowly nationalistic motives. The Nazi and Fascist leaders concerned themselves very little with religion beyond their attempt to control the church and bend religion to their own purpose. In their motives and philosophy of life there was very little of the altruism and of the broad perspective which true religion demands. Their religion was comparable to the paranoid formation of a mental patient.

Russian communism, however, has belonged in a different category. Russia also has been threatened by external danger. Ever since she started her experiment, she has been surrounded by enemies. That fact explains the rigid dictatorship, the limitation of free speech,

[1] George Foote Moore, *The Birth and Growth of Religion* (New York: Charles Scribner's Sons, 1924), pp. 1 ff.

and the harsh measures which have been so severely criticized here in America. But that experiment was begun under a wave of idealism. Its outlook was internationalist. Like the democratic movement in the late eighteenth century it was going to save the world. It sought to establish a new order of society in which the motive of service would replace that of profit and the welfare of the workers would have precedence over the special privileges of the aristocratic leisure class. In their struggle the Communists clashed with the Russian church and they came to regard it, not without reason, as an agency of the established order and an instrument of oppression. They therefore accepted the dictum of Karl Marx that religion is the opiate of the people.

There is here no exception to the general rule that men are fundamentally social and that an enduring social order must be founded upon some organization of the loyalties and of their associated values which appeals to the deeper emotions of its people. Whether they recognize it or not, the Russian Communists, insofar as they are loyal to their cause, are actuated by a spirit that is fundamentally religious. For them also heroes and symbols and practices are likely to arise which serve to perpetuate and re-create their faith.

All these recent adventures in collectivism have been associated with militarism, and most of the evils to which we object may be explained in terms of the war situation. Furthermore, the chief difference between the German people and ourselves to be found in the fact that in Germany for several generations the army was dominant. The German civilian culture has been much like our own, but the army is a continuing body with organized beliefs and attitudes so different from those of democracy and Christianity as to represent a different culture. This military culture has indeed its religious aspects—its own hierarchy of loyalties, its own symbols, its own system of values, all centering in the requirement of patriotism and finding expression in salutations to the flag and to officers and in adherence to accepted beliefs. Here is a religion of limited horizons, a religion of form and ceremony, but nonetheless a religion. In

America the military has never been in control for any extended period, but if at any time it should establish control over education and scientific enterprise there might be little to choose between ourselves and our late enemies.

2. CRISIS AND REORGANIZATION

We have arrived at the conclusion that crisis experiences tend to make or break. They bring forth change either for better or for worse. They may be associated with religious quickening. They force men to think and feel intensely regarding the things that matter most. They may thus bring about constructive changes both in personal life and in social organization. But they are also periods of danger. The reactions may be of the malignant type. There may be bitterness and hostility, concealment and self-deception and blaming of others. There may be discouragement and withdrawal and easy pleasure-taking and consequent disorganization. Of especial interest is our discovery that periods of economic distress and suffering have in certain notable instances been followed by important religious movements but that this has seldom been true of war, even though war is social crisis of the first magnitude.

The explanation we have found is that in time of economic distress the reaction is likely to be of the benign type. Large numbers of people react in accordance with the Christian principles in which they were reared. Instead of blaming others they take stock of their own shortcomings; they think and feel together intensely regarding the ultimate realities of life, and religion comes alive for them. In time of war, on the other hand, the prevailing reaction is of the malignant type. The organized attitudes of the army displace the teachings of the Christian Church, and the dominant emotions are hatred and hostility. The deepened sense of fellowship which war engenders is confined to ourselves and our allies. Serious thinking is distorted by powerful emotions. There is a marked tendency to think in terms of black and white, to magnify the motes in the eyes of the enemy and ignore the beams in our own. Hatred bars the door to the God of love and truth. For this reason the social crisis which war represents may increase the spirit of patriotism, but it does not give rise to that of high religion.

We have seen furthermore that war is not necessarily dissociated from religious quickening. In the case of the Hebrew prophetic religion a defeated and humiliated people blamed themselves rather than their enemies and looked for the evils in their own back yards. These searchings of heart resulted in the spiritualization of the old nationalistic hope and in the deep insight of Second Isaiah and its incarnation in the life and teaching of Jesus of Nazareth.

War is then an acute social crisis of the type which tends either to make or break, and on the analogy of what happens in the acute personal crisis experiences we may recognize three possible outcomes as determined by the reaction patterns which dominate:

First, there may be no reorganization. The hatred, the suspicions, the predatory interests, the racial prejudices, the narrow nationalisms, of which war is merely a symptom, may remain uncorrected and unalleviated. In that case there will be further wars and progressive disintegration and destruction. Religions will appear spontaneously under the stress of human suffering, many of them quite primitive in type, none of them having the power to win an inclusive loyalty or to bring into being a better order of society.[2]

Second, there may be a social organization based upon the military dominance of those interests which have been responsible for the war. The Germans and the Japanese and now the Russians and the Chinese will serve as scapegoats and the real evils will remain uncor-

---

[2] According to Toynbee *The Study of History*, abridged edition (London: Oxford University Press, 1947), it is among the oppressed and underprivileged in some "time of troubles" that the great religions have arisen. In any disintegrating society, he says, we find always three sharply divided classes. There are dominant minorities working out philosophies and seeking to produce universal states; there are internal proletariats discovering higher religions which aim to embody themselves in universal churches; there are external proletariats mustering war bands which find vent in heroic exploits. The suggestion follows that the hope of alleviating the evils responsible for recurrent warfare may lie chiefly in some new religious quickening among the defeated and the suffering linked with sympathetic undersanding and far-seeing intelligence on the part of the dominant.

rected. The resulting organization will then be of the type which in an individual is called "paranoid." The integrity of the organization will thus be maintained by repressive concealment devices, and organized religion, probably of a ritualistic type, will be used by the dominant group to maintain the *status quo*, as in India, in China, in medieval Europe.

Third, we may be able to deal with the situation constructively and begin the herculean task of correcting the real evils. How we deal with our enemies is likely to prove the acid test of our fitness for this task. It is likely to be the measure of the success which we achieve. The outcome will be dependent upon and will result in the increasingly broad perspective and inclusive loyalty of true religion.

There is also a fourth possibility—extinction. In the atomic age that possibility has become appallingly real.

3. THE WORLD IN THE MAKING

A third principle discovered in this inquiry is that religious beliefs will be closely related to the character of the new world which is now in the process of becoming. The character of these beliefs will be both a consequence and a causative factor in the shaping of a new social order. The changes themselves will have a determining influence upon religious belief and practice, and the religious beliefs will in some measure affect the changes.

We have seen this principle exemplified in the development of science and industry and business enterprise. This development was made possible by Protestant Christianity, which owed its rise in turn to the growing strength of the trader class and to the inquiring and independent spirit of the educated classes. Any consideration of the future must therefore take into account the changes in social and economic conditions and also the changes in religious belief.

a. THE BREAKDOWN OF INDIVIDUALISM

Probably the most striking feature in the present world situation is the breakdown of the excessive individualism which Protestant

Christianity has fostered. For the past three hundred years throughout Western culture emphasis has been placed upon the welfare of the individual. The right of private judgment, private initiative, and private property has been in the forefront. It has been assumed that the free play of individual self-interest would bring about the welfare of all. Industry, honesty, frugality, self-reliance, and self-control have been stressed, virtues which strengthen the individual for the competitive game and provide some measure of protection for the interests of society. The result has been a culture tremendously stimulating to man's creative capacities in scientific discovery, in industrial development, and in commercial enterprise.

But individualistic democracy has been characterized by great evils. The law of the jungle has prevailed. Individual has been arrayed against individual, group against group, nation against nation. Even in organized religion, Protestantism has split into innumerable sects, each competing with the other, often forgetful of the ends for which the church exists. This cutthroat competition found its culmination in world wars in which the leading Protestant nations were on opposing sides. Here is a clear demonstration of the fallacies of our competitive culture and the need of some new organizing principle. The emphasis upon the rights of the individual, to be socially valid, must be supplemented by a corresponding emphasis upon the individual's responsibility for the common good.

Many obstacles stand in the way of any recognition of these facts. After World War II the victors began quarreling among themselves. Even with the ominous hydrogen bomb to reckon with, we see our own nation putting its trust in bigger bombs and more effective propaganda. Meanwhile Russia and America have become increasingly hostile toward each other. There is grave danger that the evils responsible for the war may be magnified rather than corrected. If this happens, the world is likely to become an armed camp. There will be warring imperialisms, nations armed to the teeth, military chieftains in the saddle, the right of private judgment and free speech curtailed, private initiative reduced, and private ownership and management giving way to depersonalized corporations and cartels seeking to control the resources of the earth for their own profit. And totalitarianism will result inevitably from the facts that under the pressure of war men are willing to surrender their freedom in return for protection, that war requires centralized control, and that the military mind relies upon force.

What would happen to religion under such conditions may be inferred from what happened in Germany when the Nazis came into power. The role of the church would be limited. The spirit of nationalism would be dominant and might even take on a religious coloring. Any teaching that ran counter to the interests of nationalism would be suppressed with a rigor which might exceed that shown toward murderers.[3] True religion, in other words, would be driven underground. Patriotism would be exalted and with it the virtues of courage and unquestioning obedience to established authority.

The achievement of a social order which shall obviate such evils is no mere utopian dream but an imperative necessity if our civilization is not to perish. We must either go forward or revert to a new dark age. There is now imminent danger to all that we hold most dear. To avoid that danger we must be able to make an accurate diagnosis and then correct the evils which are responsible for the recurring warfare.

We may begin by recognizing that the totalitarians are partly right. They are correct in their criticism of democratic individualism. The welfare of all must be placed above the rights of the individual. The difficulty with their position is that they have not gone far enough. They have failed to recognize that the rights of nations must likewise be subordinated to the common welfare.

[3] In World War I there were in the United States of America 506 trials by courtmartial of conscientious objectors. Of this number 503 were convicted. Of those convicted 17 were sentenced to death, 142 to life imprisonment, 5 to 50 or more years, and 92 to from 15 to 45 years. Of course the severer sentences were not carried out, but they are clear evidence of a ferocity which exceeded that shown toward any class of criminals. Our record in World War II was much better but the feeling was still very strong. Cf. Norman Thomas, *The Conscientious Objector in America* (New York: Huebsch, 1923).

This does not mean that the ideals of democracy are mistaken. Our findings indicate that these ideals are based upon a true understanding of human nature. Without minimizing the hatred, the jealousy, the greed, and all the other evils to which humanity is heir, we have found that men are basically social. The distinctive feature of human social organization lies in the fact that it is based not upon blind instinct or outward compulsion but upon the internalization within the individual of the group ideals and attitudes. Democracy is thus the type of social organization which seeks to develop this human capacity for doing the right thing not through external pressure but through inner self-direction. Our findings indicate furthermore, that the individual is unable to live apart from his group, and there seems to be an inner law which forbids him to be satisfied with any social identification which is less than the best he knows.

This means that Protestantism and the democratic culture with which it is associated have merely been inadequate. Democracy has been correct in its assumption that government should rest on the consent of the governed and that necessary social changes should be brought about not by force and not by the manipulating of the sources of information but by the enlightenment of the individual conscience through education, freedom of inquiry, freedom of speech, popular vote, and representative deliberation. What democracy has not seen is the necessity of social planning and co-operation. It has stressed rights rather than duties, privileges rather than responsibilities, and its concept of equality has not taken sufficient account of actual differences of ability and character.

It is not the task of this chapter to suggest the particular measures which need to be taken but rather to clarify the principles involved and their relationship to the future of our civilization. It needs to be repeated and underlined that crisis experiences like the one we are now facing are comparable to an acute psychosis in an individual and that failure to recognize and correct the real evils leads to disaster.

Among sociologists any suggestion that human society as a whole behaves much like an organism meets with chilly disapproval. It may nevertheless be permissible to say that our working hypothesis and the findings which support it all point to the view that as a cell is to the body, so the individual human being may be to something greater. A faith based upon but going beyond the proven facts may then be justified in believing that this larger Being, of which we are a part, is in some way identified with God. All mankind would thus be a functional entity, an entity which perhaps includes the entire evolutionary process as represented on this tiny planet of ours.

According to such a view evolution is in a state of flux. The present situation might be compared to a seed or an egg which is in process of germination. After lying dormant for millions and millions of years, the stored-up resources of the earth are now being drawn upon with accelerating rapidity. This rapid exploitation is a matter of only a hundred years. A few generations more and some of the more important resources will be exhausted. One does not have to be an Adventist to believe that tremendous changes are near at hand. Certainly great calamities are clearly threatened. The divine Spirit which has been seeking expression in human society is now perhaps in grave danger. In any case there comes a ringing summons to all good men of whatever faith to respond to the present need, bringing the same courage and devotion which men have always shown to the tribal gods of war into the service of the universal God of love and truth.

b. THE NEW BASIS OF AUTHORITY IN RELIGION

In the matter of religious belief a revolutionary change is now going on. It is likely to become increasingly important. The reference here is to the change in the basis of authority in religion which comes with the growing influence of science. In place of reliance upon the authority of a sacred book, religious faith is likely to take more and more account of the tested experience of the present. While there is in this matter, even in liberal Protestantism, a surprising lag, it is a development which is sure to take place and one which will have far-reaching consequences. When students of religion begin to make use of the methods of co-operative inquiry in the study of religious experience and when students of human nature begin to carry their inquiries to the level of the religious, there should be increasing knowledge of the forces and laws involved in the spiritual life and an increasing body of tested experience upon which the religious faith of thinking men may be based.

Such a development should help to correct the excessive individualism with which Protestantism is now afflicted. Where the Protestant Reformers stressed the right of the individual to interpret for himself an authoritative sacred book, the religious faith of the future should rely more and more upon the results of co-operative inquiry and upon the contribution of the expert. Thus there will be more basis for agreement among men of different religious backgrounds, more chance to correct the biases now separating well-meaning men. There should also be decreasing influence on the part of those religions which rely upon magic and require unquestioning faith on the part of their adherents.

4. THE OUTLOOK FOR CHRISTIANITY

This inquiry enables us to hazard some guesses regarding the future of Christianity.

A survey of the world religions shows that Christianity is today dominant in two important particulars. First of all, it has the largest number of adherents. There are today some 450,000,000 Christians as against 220,000,000 Hindus, 200,000,000 Moslems, perhaps 150,000,000 Buddhists, and some 350,000,000 Chinese with their blending of Confucianism, Taoism, and Buddhism. More important is the fact that Christianity is the professed religion of the dominant peoples of the world and that it is associated with the highest development of science and industry. According to the biological test, Christianity rates high. It has done much to enable its adherents to survive in the struggle for existence and to achieve a rich and varied life. If therefore the present world crisis does not result in our destroying one another, Christianity should be in an ascendant position.

A further consideration is Christianity's proven adaptability. As we have seen, it has survived several drastic changes in the social and economic order. Beginning as the religious faith of a subject people in the Roman Empire in the days of its greatest strength, it became in time the official religion of that empire. After the fall of Rome it became in the West the ally of feudalism in the task of governing its semibarbarous peoples and conserving the heritage of ancient wisdom. In this capacity it established something in the nature of a theocracy in which the feudal states became the vassals of the Pope. Following the Reformation, Protestantism provided the spiritual undergirding of capitalistic democracy.

This power of adaptation, which stands in sharp contrast to the static character of the other world religions and their respective cultures, is due in large part to an institution which has been peculiar to the Hebrew-Christian religion: The provision for religious assemblage represented in the church and in its progenitor the synagogue has fostered the sense of solidarity and enabled its adherents to rethink their fundamental beliefs in the light of changing conditions.

On the basis of its past record and existing institutions there seems to be no reason why Christianity in some of its forms should not be able to adapt itself to any new social order which may arise.

But how about some new and superior religion? Did not the Founder of Christianity himself have something to say regarding the folly of "putting new wine into old wineskins and patching an old garment with new cloth"? The same great Teacher also compared the task of the teacher of religion to that of a householder bringing forth out of his treasure things new and old. There is true insight in both these sayings, but our findings indicate that the latter is the more pertinent.

Whatever the advantage of an entirely new start, religion must always bring together the old and the new. It would be very difficult to find any great religious teacher and leader who thought of himself as the exponent of something wholly new. Certainly Jesus did not. It is true that he proclaimed a new gospel. He contrasted his teaching with that of the scribes and the Pharisees and boldly set it over against that of the olden time. But he also thought of himself as the interpreter of the great Hebrew prophets and insisted that he came not to destroy the law and the prophets but to fulfill. The same with Buddha and Confucius and Mohammed; and Luther and Fox and Wesley.

Religion calls for the far look, and that look extends both into the past and into the future. Religion never springs full-fledged into the world. Like language, like culture, it is the result of ages of development. It draws ever upon the great sources of strength and insight which come from out of the past and carry forward into the good which ought to be. The task of the great prophets is always to tap anew the sources of power and return anew to the central insights and motivations of true religion.

And in the Hebrew-Christian religion there is surely much of enduring value. The Hebrew prophets still tower like lofty mountain peaks among the religious leaders of the past, and the figure of Jesus still shines forth strong and luminous and beautiful, an embodiment of the finest aspirations of the human race and an object of loyalty worthy of the undying devotion of men of all ages and races. There would be nothing to gain and everything to lose in giving up the rich heritage which the Christian religion represents.

5. What American Christianity Can Contribute

The objective set before us in the present crisis is, then, in the words of Professor Holt, the achievement of a new order of society which shall represent the social solidarity of free men held together by faith and love.[4]

This inquiry indicates that in the struggle to achieve such a new

[4] *This Nation Under God* (Chicago: Willett, Clark & Co., 1929), p. 127.

order of society America and Protestant Christianity with which it has been associated have had three important advantages,

In the first place, there is relative freedom from the hatreds and the exploitive imperialism in which the European and Asiatic peoples are enmeshed. Our hands are indeed far from clean. Our record in the treatment of the Negroes is disgraceful. The attitude we have shown toward them, if extended toward the other colored races of the world, would be fatal to any hope of betterment. Our industrial system is weighted down with unsolved problems. But it still remains true that our role in the present world situation has been that of international policeman. Our main interest has been to see that justice is done and order established. The slogan of World War I still holds. Our task is to see that the world is made safe for democracy.

In the second place, American Protestantism is the foremost representative of the form of Christianity which has gone farthest in meeting the changing conditions of the new age. According to our findings the United States of America is the outgrowth of the Protestant spirit in all its strength and all its weaknesses. Selfishness, individualism, bigotry, sectarianism are all too much in evidence; yet we do see a remarkable development of faith in popular education, the right of free inquiry and free speech, and the encouragement of private initiative. What is most to the point, under our plan of religious freedom and the separation of church and state we see men of many races and faiths living together in some measure of peace, stimulating one another, contributing to one another, and gradually drawing closer together. We have thus in America a more or less successful demonstration of the type of relationship which ought to prevail throughout the world among men of different races and faiths.

In the development of such a relationship on a world scale the practical spirit which American Christianity has shown might be very helpful. Its interest in the problem of social betterment, the interest which it has taken in the foreign missionary enterprise, will, if conditions permit, find a great new field. Foreign missions will then enter upon a new day, and the effort to convert men of other faiths to the acceptance of our symbols and of our way of life will give place to an effort at mutual understanding and helpfulness in the pursuit of a common goal.

Index

Abnormal phenomena
  among early Christians, 89
  in early Methodism, 123
  fallacious assumptions regarding, 82, 90–91
  in Holiness sects, 78–82
Abolition movement
  changing attitudes of Methodism, 121
  solidification of Southern attitude, 126, 173
Adjustment, types of personality
  complacent, 24–26
  defeated, 29–30
  difficult, 28–29
  distressed, 30–31
  faithful, 22–24
  pagan, 26–27
  reorganized, 31–32
Adventist sects, 153, 156
Alexander, Franz, 195
Altman, Leon L., 102
American Christianity
  Colonial immigration policy, 140–41
  common characteristics of Protestant churches, 143–44
  freedom given to creative, 139–40, 143
  future of, 256–58
  lines of advance, 174–75
  types of churches, 144–76
Ames, Edward Scribner, 197
Anxiety
  as benign reaction, 40, 47ff.
  extreme forms of, 54ff.
Appel, John W., 96

Asceticism
  as compromise, 205
  as discipline, 206, 227–28
  as factor in mystical experience, 229
  in Holiness sects, 16, 77
Asiatic religions as supporters of status quo, 134–36, 161–62
Assemblage, religious, distinctive of Hebrew-Christian religion, 39, 136, 169, 210
Assemblies of God, 73, 153
Associate Presbyterian (Seceders), 10, 151
Atonement, doctrine of, 205
Atrocities, in time of war, 102–3
Attention, narrowing of
  in acute schizophrenic reactions, 66–67
  in creative thinking, 3, 67
  in mystical experiences, 116–18
Autohypnosis, 57, 116

Baptism, sacrament of, 223
Baptism of the Spirit
  evidences of, 78–82
  "out-pouring" of, 74
  as required by Pentecostal sects, 72
Baptist Church, 150
Beard, Charles A. and Mary, 126
Belief, religious
  biasing factors, 114–15
  common core of Protestant, 192–211
  criteria of validity, 185–90
  vs. delusion, 88
  innovation in, 111–13, 176–88
  orthodox vs. liberal, 163–64

261